# The New Agenda for International Relations

*From Polarization to Globalization in World Politics?*

# The New Agenda for International Relations

## *From Polarization to Globalization in World Politics?*

*Edited by*
Stephanie Lawson

Polity

Copyright © this collection Polity Press 2002
First published in 2002 by Polity Press in association with Blackwell Publishers Ltd

*Editorial office*:
Polity Press
65 Bridge Street
Cambridge CB2 1UR, UK

*Marketing and production*:
Blackwell Publishers Ltd
108 Cowley Road
Oxford OX4 1JF, UK

*Published in the USA by*
Blackwell Publishers Inc.
350 Main Street
Malden, MA 02148, USA

ISBN 0-7456-2860-5
ISBN 0-7456-2861-3 (pbk)

A catalogue record for this book is available from the British Library and has been applied for from the Library of Congress.

Typeset in 10/12 pt on Sabon
by Kolam Information Services Pvt., Ltd., Pondicherry, India
Printed in Great Britain by T.J. International, Padstow, Cornwall

This book is printed on acid-free paper.

# Contents

# Contributors

**Chris Brown** is Professor of International Relations at the London School of Economics. Before that he spent two decades at the University of Kent (as Lecturer and Senior Lecturer) before taking up a Chair in Politics at Southampton University in 1994. He was also Chair of the British International Studies Association in 1997–8. His books include *International Relations Theory: New Normative Approaches* (1992), *Understanding International Relations* (1997; 2001), and some two dozen papers on international political theory over the last ten years. He is currently writing a monograph on *Cultural Diversity and International Political Theory* and co-editing a collection of *Texts in International Political Theory* with Terry Nardin and N. J. Rengger.

**Richard Devetak** is Lecturer in International Relations at Monash University in Australia. He received his PhD from Keele University and has previously lectured at Manchester and Warwick universities in the UK. He has published book chapters and articles on international relations theory, including chapters in Scott Burchill and Andrew Linklater et al., *Theories of International Relations* (second edition, forthcoming), and is currently working on a book entitled *A Genealogy of the International: The 'Sorry Comforters' and the Origins of International Relations*.

**Jack Donnelly** is the Andrew W. Mellon Professor at the Graduate School of International Studies at the University of Denver. He has also taught at Tulane University, College of the Holy Cross and the University of North Carolina at Chapel Hill. His works include *The Concept of Human Rights* (1985), *Universal Human Rights in Theory and Practice* (1989) and *International Human Rights*, 2nd edn (1998). His chapter draws substantially on his book, *Realism and International Relations: A Critical Engagement* (2000).

**Lorraine Elliott** is Fellow in the Department of International Relations at the Australian National University, prior to which she held a senior lecturership in the Department of Political Science at the ANU. Her major areas of research and publishing are in global environmental politics and environmental security, with a subsidiary interest in critical security studies and in civil society and social justice issues in international relations. She is currently working on a study of regional environmental governance in South-East Asia. Her recent publications include *The Global Politics of the Environment* (1998). In 1997, Dr Elliott received the Australasian Political Studies Association's Crisp Medal for originality and contribution to the discipline.

**K. M. Fierke** is a Lecturer at the Queen's University of Belfast. She received her PhD from the University of Minnesota (USA) in 1995. She has worked as a research fellow at the Amsterdam School for Social Science Research and has held a Prize Research Fellowship at Nuffield College, Oxford University. She works in the general area of post-Cold War security relations and her most recent book is *Changing Games, Changing Strategies: Critical Investigations in Security* (1998).

**Fred Halliday** has held a Chair in International Relations at the LSE since 1985. From 1974 to 1982 he was a Fellow of the Transnational Institute, Amsterdam and Washington. His recent books include *Rethinking International Relations* (1994), *Islam and the Myth of Confrontation* (1996), *Revolution and World Politics: The Rise and Fall of the Sixth Great Power* (1999) and *The World at 2000* (2000).

**Richard Higgott** is Director of the ESRC Centre for the Study of Globalization and Regionalization and Professor of International Political Economy at the University of Warwick. Previous appointments include chairs in government at the University of Manchester and public policy at the Australian National University, where he was also Director of the Graduate Programme in Foreign Affairs and Trade. He is the author of numerous books, book chapters and articles. His latest book, *Non-State Actors and Authority in the Global System* (with Andreas Bieler and Geoffrey Underhill), will be published by Routledge shortly. He is also the editor of *The Pacific Review*. Current research focuses on the relationship between globalization and regionalization with special reference to 'post-financial crisis' international economic policy co-ordination.

**Stephanie Lawson** is Professor of International Relations at the University of East Anglia. She received her PhD from the University of New England in Australia. She has previously worked as a Fellow in the Department of International Relations at the Australian National University. From 1994 to 1998, she was also the editor of the *Australian Journal of International Affairs*. She is the author of many book chapters and articles dealing with issues in the Asia-Pacific region. For her first book, *The Failure of Democratic Politics in Fiji* (1991), she was awarded the Crisp Medal by the Australasian Political

Studies Association. Her recent publications include: *The New Agenda for Global Security: Cooperating for Peace and Beyond* (1995) (edited) and *Tradition Versus Democracy in the South Pacific* (1996). Her present research interests focus on international issues concerning culture, nationalism and democracy.

**James N. Rosenau** is University Professor of International Affairs at the George Washington University. This is a distinguished rank reserved for the few scholar-teachers whose recognition in the academic community transcends the usual disciplinary boundaries. His research has focused on the dynamics of change in world politics and the overlap of domestic and foreign affairs, resulting in more than thirty-five books and 150 articles. His most recent publications include *Along the Domestic–Foreign Frontier: Exploring Governance in a Turbulent World* (1997), *Thinking Theory Thoroughly: Coherent Approaches to an Incoherent World* (1995), *Global Voices* (1993), *Governance without Government* (1991) and *Turbulence in World Politics: A Theory of Change and Continuity* (1990).

**Jill Steans** is Lecturer in International Relations Theory in the Department of Political Science and International Studies, University of Birmingham. Her research interests are in gender and IR theory and international political economy. Her recent publications include *Gender and International Relations* (1998), (with Lloyd Pettiford) *International Relations: Perspectives and Themes* (2001) and *Globalization and Women's Human Rights* (2002).

**Caroline Thomas** is Professor in the Department of Politics at the University of Southampton. She has a long-standing interest in North/South issues and has published widely on Third World security issues and over the last few years, on the impact of globalization on the South. Her recent works include *Global Governance, Development and Human Security* (2000); Annie Taylor and Thomas (eds), *Global Trade and Global Social Issues* (1999); Thomas and Peter Wilkin (eds), *Globalisation and the South* (1998); Thomas and Wilkin (eds), *Globalization, Human Security and the African Experience* (1999). Her current research is on the global politics of inequality and health, with reference to HIV/AIDS, Africa and drugs.

# Preface

Students of international relations (IR) differ among themselves on just about every aspect of their subject – from the very name of the discipline to its proper subject matter and scope. But few would deny that there have been significant periods or eras which themselves have shaped not only the structure of world politics but also the way in which it has been studied. The geopolitical and ideological contours of the Cold War period impacted on almost every aspect of world politics for around forty-five years. And it was virtually impossible for IR students working in this period, whether in a theoretical or a policy-oriented vein – or a combination of both – to avoid at least implicit reference to the way in which world politics was structured around Cold War considerations.

If the year 1989 marked the beginning of the end of a long period of certainty in world politics, the same applies to the discipline devoted to its study. What had been the primary point of reference for the discipline of IR for over four decades simply dissolved. But, far from leaving scholars at a loss, the passing of the Cold War seems to have re-energized the discipline and given it not simply a new sense of purpose and direction, but many new directions. Exactly where these may be taking us is another matter altogether, and exploring such questions is an important task for the collection as a whole.

One direction that cannot be denied – for better or for worse – is the extent to which IR scholars have ventured into any number of different areas of inquiry which have not been considered as traditional concerns of the discipline. This means, among other things, that IR has also opened up considerably to a range of insights from other disciplinary perspectives. Indeed, the post-Cold War period to date has seen IR scholars venturing into every other social science discipline, and beyond. The same can of course be said of fields such as comparative politics, political theory, anthropology, cultural studies, sociology and so on. Thus scholars in other social science disciplines or sub-disciplines have increasingly adopted a more 'international' or 'global' perspective in their work.

The various novel directions of the discipline in the post-Cold War era, in terms of both subject matter and scholarly approaches, together constitute a large part of 'the new agenda' for international relations, and the contributions to this collection reflect the variety of issues and perspectives that have become part and parcel of this agenda in recent years. Beyond the attention to issues and perspectives, however, is the question of structure in contemporary world politics. As suggested above, the Cold War was the major factor shaping both the structure and dynamics of world politics and the way in which international relations scholars generally approached their work over a period of some forty-five years.

If there is a single term which encapsulated the Cold War's geopolitical structure, it is probably 'polarization'. However, polarization should also be understood in terms of ideas and ideologies. So, just as the collapse of the Soviet Union in the period following the fall of the Berlin Wall signalled the end of strategic polarization, for some it also marked the apparent end of a particular form of polarized debate about political, social and economic ideas. This is what clearly inspired the 'end of history' thesis, outbursts of liberal triumphalism, and the heralding of a new world order.

So what, if anything, is filling the structural vacuum left by the Cold War? One obvious candidate is the phenomenon of globalization. This, of course, is one of the most hotly contested concepts of the post-Cold War era and its meaning, utility and application are scarcely settled questions. Moreover, it can be argued that there are new forms of polarization in world politics. The question mark at the end of the subtitle, then, indicates the highly contested nature of the assumptions embodied in it. A question mark could well have been placed after each of the main sections of the book as well. For, although the contributors explore ideas about a new agenda along with a number of new issues and new perspectives, there is also an emphasis on continuities.

The chapters comprising this volume were first presented and discussed at a conference held at the University of East Anglia in September 1999 entitled 'The New Agenda for International Relations: Ten Years after the Wall'. Although not exactly on the date that the Berlin Wall actually fell, the conference was none the less designed to mark the end of the first decade 'after the Fall' – an event that has certainly come to symbolize the end of the Cold War and the beginning of a new era in world politics.

Sponsorship for the conference was received from two principal sources: the Warwick/ESRC Centre for the Study of Globalisation and Regionalisation and the Carnegie Council on Ethics and International Affairs (New York). It goes without saying that I am very grateful to both these bodies for making the conference possible. In planning and organizing the conference, many people also gave valuable assistance and advice. Of my colleagues at the School of Economic and Social Studies at UEA, I'd especially like to thank Hazel Taylor, Peter Handley and Nino Palumbo. For acting as additional chairs and discussants, and therefore contributing directly to the very lively and fruitful discussions throughout the conference, I should also thank Nick Rengger, Nigel Dower, Rorden Wilkinson, David Seddon and Mike Bowker. The latter deserves additional thanks for his invaluable support and advice during the entire planning period. Finally a special thanks to my daughter Katharine who volunteered her time to help ensure that the conference desk ran smoothly and efficiently throughout.

SL

# Part I

# The New Agenda

# 1

# Introduction
## *A New Agenda for International Relations?*

### Stephanie Lawson

## Introduction

There have been several defining moments over the course of the last hundred years that have been described as signalling a new age in world politics as well as stimulating new ways of looking at the phenomena involved. The most recent, and the one that continues to define the present period, was the fall of the Berlin Wall in November 1989, although by then the Cold War that it symbolized had already come to an effective end as a result of the momentous changes that had taken place in Gorbachev's Soviet Union since the mid-1980s. If the fall of the Wall, together with the events that followed with the unravelling of the Soviet empire, symbolized the end of one era and the beginning of another in world politics, it also prompted some serious rethinking about the nature, purpose, methods, scope and subject matter of the discipline that studies world politics, traditionally known as international relations (IR).[1] With the collapse of polarization between the two superpowers and the threat of all-out nuclear warfare in rapid retreat, other significant concerns for world politics gained prominence. And it was not long before scholars and other observers of world affairs were talking about a 'new agenda' for the discipline of IR in a 'post-Cold War era'.[2]

An early version of the new agenda that was put forward in 1991 identified a number of global policy concerns including the environment, drug trafficking, AIDS, terrorism, religious fundamentalism, migration and human rights. At a broader, systemic level, the phenomenon of globalization, and what seemed to be opposite tendencies towards fragmentation, were identified as being among the most significant 'macro' issues.[3] All these, together with the very idea of *global* policy, have become prominent topics in the study of world politics, along with new conceptions of such crucial concerns as security which has expanded from a narrow military definition to encompass many of these new agenda issues. But these developments raise new problems and challenges for students of world politics in terms of how we now define our subject areas either within the broad field of IR or within specialist areas such as environmental politics or security studies. With respect to the latter, as Karin Fierke points out in chapter 8, if 'security' can now mean anything and everything, then it effectively means nothing at all.

This raises the question whether the broadening of the agenda to include an almost boundless array of problems and issues constitutes a problem for the integrity of the discipline itself. This is an especially interesting question in an era of globalization which is widely seen as leading to the almost complete 'unbounding' of the globe. If IR itself is to become unbounded, and to take on board the study of practically everything, then what, in the end, will constitute the core of the discipline and make it distinct from other disciplines? Or does it matter whether the discipline as such dissolves? Is IR becoming an 'interdiscipline' (rather than simply more interdisciplinary in its approach)? And, if so, would it be appropriate simply to abandon the whole idea of IR as a discipline in its own right and reassemble courses of study under something called 'International Studies'? Breaking down the barriers between disciplines may well be a good thing in many respects. After all, how can one possibly contribute effectively to contemporary debates about, say, the role of culture in world politics without having a good understanding of highly influential anthropological approaches to the concept? On the other hand, where does the 'unbounding' of the discipline end, if not in the study of everything?

'Everything', as astronomer John D. Barrow notes, is a very big subject. None the less, he goes on to point out that contemporary trends in the study of the physical sciences also suggest that the quest for a 'theory of everything' is more popular than ever, having entered the mainstream of theoretical physics after a period in which it was sought only by a 'few maverick thinkers and unconstrained speculators' (including Einstein).[4] The more conservative and parsimonious of IR theorists would join in repudiating the utility of any such undertaking. The idea that one can see or grasp 'the whole' and thus be in a position to theorize rationally about it is anathema to conservative social and political thought. And theoretical parsimony has, according to its proponents, been a prime virtue of realist IR thought in both its traditional and its neo-realist forms. Kenneth Walz, for example, defends his version of neo-realism as a theory limited to explaining a certain slice of political activity – not the entire spectrum of social and political concerns – on the grounds that a theory has to be about *something*, not everything.[5]

These are some of the concerns that have been expressed generally about IR in the last decade or so. But they have not all been raised simply as a result of the end of the Cold War. To assume so would be to underestimate the extent to which the discipline had already been undergoing substantial transformation – or had at least had its foundations severely shaken in the previous decade. Kal Holsti, writing in 1987, argued that international theory was in a 'state of disarray' as a result of challenges over the previous ten years or so which had broken down a 'three-centuries-long intellectual consensus' about inter-national politics. In place of a fundamental consensus on the subjects of inquiry and theorizing, new conceptions and images of the world, and how it works, had arisen, most criticizing the realist, or classical, tradition.[6] This fundamental consensus had evolved around three core assumptions: first, that the proper domain of study comprised the causes of war and the condi-tions for peace, security and order; second, that the focus of study must be on the essential units of analysis in the international system, namely nation-states, and their diplomatic/military behaviour; and, third, that states operated in a system characterized by anarchy, understood as the absence of any overarching authority in the international sphere.[7]

The Cold War period certainly produced a great deal of theory reflecting this consensus, which also strongly supported realist approaches. But, as is evident from Holsti's remarks, the consensus was already under challenge well before the events of 1989. Even so, there is no doubt that the end of the Cold War provided a significant impetus for the various directions that IR had started to take, which included a reassessment of existing conceptual and methodological issues and an interest in alternative approaches. For many of the practical issues on the emerging agenda, a theoretical focus concerned almost exclu-sively with the play of power politics, which had indeed dominated throughout the Cold War period, seemed simply inappropriate or even irrelevant. Along-side more conventional approaches such as realism (and neo-realism) and liberal internationalism, the contemporary period has seen a burgeoning of other perspectives, including constructivism, postmodernism, feminism and critical theory, none of which now resides simply at the margins. Moreover, as Jack Donnelly emphasizes in chapter 11, we can also see much more potential for a dynamic engagement between these newer approaches and realism in its various forms.

At another level both the practical issues on the new agenda, as well as the perspectives and approaches that have been applied to their study (including the move away from realism), have combined to produce a much stronger focus on normative international theory. In an earlier work, Chris Brown notes that this refers to a body of work which addresses directly 'the moral dimension of international relations and the wider questions of meaning and interpretation generated by the discipline'. In its most basic form, he says, 'it addresses the ethical nature of the relations between communities [and] states'.[8] As we shall see, normative theory underlies virtually all the issues dealt with in this collection. This is especially so with respect to the phenomenon of globalization and its impact on the nature of political community as well as forms of polarization other than those which were conventionally understood to characterize world politics in the Cold War period.

In thinking more generally about a new agenda for the discipline of IR in a new era of world politics – however we might characterize it – it is instructive to review briefly the development of the discipline along with developments in world politics from the earlier part of the twentieth century. By doing this, we can see both continuities as well as new departures more clearly.

## IR in the twentieth century

As mentioned at the beginning, several defining moments over the course of the twentieth century seemed to mark the beginning of a new age in world politics as well as new ways of looking at problems and possibilities. To be more specific, there have been three such moments. The first two followed the end of the World Wars in the first half of the twentieth century, and were therefore born out of an experience of violence on a massive scale. In both cases, the world seemed ready for remaking.

The discipline of IR as a field of study in its own right, separate from law and history, was itself founded as a direct response to the horrific and unprecedented experiences of World War I. This was marked by the establishment in 1919 of the Woodrow Wilson Chair of International Politics at University College Wales, Aberystwyth. The main focus for the new discipline was, not surprisingly, on the causes of war and the conditions for peace. The discipline's main initial intellectual impetus in the years after World War I drew on idealism; on a belief that the world could – and therefore should – be made a better and safer place for all of humankind. The optimistic idea of inevitable progress in the development of human society as a whole attracted many supporters then. But progress still had to be nudged along with the assistance of purposive human agency. One of the principal ideas of the time was that a new and peaceful world order required an overarching international organization that could mediate relations between the essential components of an anarchical international system – sovereign states – and thereby ensure a viable form of collective security. And so the League of Nations was created.

By the late 1930s, as Europe again descended into mayhem, the idealist approach to world politics with its strong normative basis seemed almost completely discredited. In the wake of this second catastrophic World War, and then with a Cold War between two major powers setting in immediately, a new approach to theory and practice was called for. The discipline therefore took the turn towards realism – a mode of analysis that promised to tell it how it really is. The core assumptions of this school, in its classic form of thought, were a rather pessimistic view of human nature and the inevitability, not of progress towards an ideal or at least better state of existence, but of the unremitting struggle for power.

Realist theories, moreover, gave explicit support to the view that issues of morality can have no place in the international sphere. The premise was that because a structure of sovereign authority is necessary to sustain moral rules and practices, and because such a structure is present only *within* states, it follows that there can be no true morality in the anarchical realm of the international sphere which is constituted by the spaces *between* states. In other words, the international sphere was nothing short of a moral vacuum. In addition, realists have generally supported the view that moral values and beliefs – which give rise to moral rules and practices – can only arise *within* a community and are more or less specific to that community. Here, the 'community' has usually been equated with a 'nation' which is in turn conflated with 'the state'. In short, realist theory has tended towards the position that moral values are relative – and state-bound. In the post-Cold War era, this kind of position on normative issues has also attracted support from communitarian theory in so far as it has been applied to the international sphere.[9]

For many proponents of realism during the Cold War era, to imagine that an international organization could overcome the essential condition of anarchy and form an international community capable of implementing, collectively, an idealist agenda for world order was regarded as pure folly. None the less, another attempt to achieve a measure of international co-operation in the pursuit of collective security was made with the founding of the United Nations. And a commitment to the highest form of idealism was enshrined in the Universal Declaration of Human Rights adopted by the General Assembly in 1948.

In the meantime, however, the contours of the international order were being moulded around a clear bipolar pattern of superpower rivalry and many IR scholars obviously applied themselves to the analysis of this most dangerous manifestation of confrontation. After Hiroshima, this pattern of world order was held together partly by fear as the nuclear arms race commenced. The development of ever more sophisticated weapons of mass destruction delivered not simply a balance of power but a balance of terror which could, if upset, lead to mutually assured destruction – a scenario appropriately labelled with the acronym MAD.

Other important developments in the post-war period included the formal demise of the colonial empires. With this, the principle of self-determination gained increasing prominence as well as practical expression, although independence for many countries in the Third World periphery was heavily compromised by a number of factors, not least of which were the dynamics of Cold War bipolarity. Moreover, for many people at the periphery, the war was far from 'cold'. While the core powers refrained from direct physical confrontation with each other, the violence of the Cold War was played out in proxy wars among their clients.

The polarized structure of superpower relations in the Cold War period is often understood simply in military or strategic terms. But of course there was much more to it than that. A principal characteristic of the period was the bipolarity of ideologies – of normative visions of how the world should be – that were represented by each of the power blocs. The states comprising the

Western power bloc championed the ideas and values underpinning capitalism and liberal democracy. The USSR and its ensemble of supporting states, on the other hand, justified their repressive methods of government as necessary for the realization of the common good through the establishment of communist society. So much is fairly commonplace.

It has also been said that as long as the communist bloc held together and sustained its challenge to the democratic West the space was created for authoritarian governments in the Third World to flourish.[10] This may be true as far as it goes, but it is also the case that the US and its allies lent considerable support and encouragement to right-wing authoritarian regimes and movements around the world. In fact most right-wing regimes were – merely by virtue of their anti-communism – embraced as part of the 'free world'. These included such notorious dictatorships as those of Marcos in the Philippines and Pinochet in Chile. It is little wonder that the messages about what constituted 'democracy' and acceptable human rights practices were somewhat mixed. And it is even less remarkable that the US – and many of its allies – have so often been charged with hypocrisy in foreign affairs. This also reinforced the realist notion that moral posturing in the international sphere is, in the final analysis, merely a reflection of specific self-interest masquerading as humanitarianism.

These issues aside, a remarkable feature of the Cold War period is that despite the emphatic left–right bipolarity of ideologies everyone actually agreed, in normative terms, that 'democracy' as such was a good thing and that there should be more of it. Moreover, virtually every government in the world *claimed* to be a democracy and each one certainly claimed to be concerned for the human rights of its citizens. The same generally applies today. As the rhetorical contest gained momentum in the early Cold War period, the philosopher W. B. Gallie put forward his now famous notion that democracy is an 'essentially contested concept'.[11] By this he meant that because democracy was almost universally regarded as something good and desirable it was something that everyone therefore wanted to claim as their own.[12] But beyond this Gallie also implied that rival uses of the term by people in deeply opposed camps must all be regarded as legitimate – and for this reason Gallie has been understood (rightly or wrongly) as endorsing a relativist or at least sceptical perspective.

The main point to be noted here is that the rival uses of the term 'democracy' during the Cold War period revolved largely around ideological questions of how the good life promised by democracy was to be best achieved – through the freedom and political equality of a liberal democratic and capitalist regime, or through the more extensive socio-economic equality and freedom from exploitation promised by communism. Normative arguments about the *cultural* basis of one version or another, if they were used at all, were usually secondary. As we shall see, however, arguments about the role of culture are now central to a wide range of key normative issues in world politics from discourses of women's human rights to the politics of paranoia evident in many of the debates surrounding the relationship between 'Islam' and the 'West'.

The decisive answer to the ideological debate that dominated the Cold War era, for most people, seems to have been delivered in 1989. And this brings me back to my point of departure.

## The New World Order at the end of history

As the forces which eventually led to the fall of the Berlin Wall gathered momentum, a hitherto obscure State Department official in Washington published a now well-known article, 'The End of History'.[13] What Francis Fukuyama meant by the 'end of history' was that with the collapse of communism there remained no other viable models of economics or politics to challenge the dominance of either capitalism as an economic system, or democracy as a form of rule in its specifically liberal form. He argued that no other system could deliver the proverbial goods and that the massive political and economic changes under way in Europe at the time served to prove the point. So the polarization of ideologies and world-views that had been at the heart of the tensions and conflicts of much of the last half-century effectively collapsed. Capitalism and liberal democracy now seemed unchallengeable.

With the end of the Cold War, many no doubt thought the end of serious warfare had been reached as well. And given that most of the violent struggles in the Third World had been attributed to superpower manipulations it would have seemed quite reasonable to assume that a significant cause of violence in the periphery had also been removed. As is quite evident, however, the vacuum left by the collapse of bipolarity both in military and ideological terms has not been filled everywhere by peace and tranquillity. Warfare has continued to flourish in many parts of the Third World as well as the former Second World as civil wars or wars of state formation have continued to claim hundreds of thousands of lives. The twentieth century closed with few signs that violent conflict, as the pursuit of politics by other means, was about to pass into history. Indeed, much of the violence, especially in places like the Balkans, has been perpetrated in the name of history. It is also evident that the phenomenon of globalization has scarcely been effective in ameliorating the range of political ills that seem to have been generated by various forms of particularism and/or other kinds of polarization.[14]

A significant part of the new agenda for IR devoted to studying these conflicts has therefore been very much preoccupied with the original concerns of the discipline – namely, the causes of war and the conditions for peace. But whereas earlier students of IR focused on inter-state wars contemporary warfare has usually been within states and much research has therefore concentrated on so-called 'internal conflicts'. The international dimensions of these conflicts, however, are numerous and it makes no sense – if it ever did – to treat them as simply 'domestic' affairs. This has led to an increasing recognition of the political porousness of the boundaries of sovereign states in the post-Cold War period. In practical terms, this has been evident across a range of issues from environmental concerns to humanitarian intervention. This new thinking, moreover, was strongly encouraged in the early post-Cold War period by the then Secretary-General of the United Nations, Boutros Boutros-Ghali, in his *Agenda for Peace*. Although he reiterated the importance of the fundamental sovereignty and integrity of states as the basis for common international progress, he none the less stressed that the sovereignty principle (the theory of which, in any case, had never matched the reality)[15] needed to be critically reassessed and balanced by equally important ethical considerations relating to what goes on inside state borders. The legitimate agenda for global security in the post-Cold War period was therefore to include a commitment to human rights and good governance within states.[16] However, as Chris Brown makes clear in chapter 9, the circumstances under which intervention is legitimate today remain anything but clear.

Despite these developments and departures, entrenched perceptions and habits of thought in the study of world politics die hard. James Rosenau argues that the research agenda for IR has been so deeply rooted in a habit of thinking which assumed that the state is the 'terminal entity' for loyalties, policy decisions and moral authority that the discipline faces the danger of lagging far behind in an era in which the international–domestic boundary has been rendered obsolete; an era that is more appropriately defined by the interaction between globalization and localization.[17] This has implications for the way in which practical issues are treated. Lorraine Elliott, for example, identifies the main challenges confronting the environmentalist agenda as residing in the intensification of globalization and its political and normative consequences. She also points out that the reformism inherent in today's dominant neo-liberal orthodoxy, as it relates to the global politics of the environment, means that many efforts have been aimed at making the existing order work more smoothly rather than challenging its very basis. The value of international institutions based on the sovereign state – among other things – therefore remains unquestioned, and indeed unquestionable, by an approach which 'takes the world as it finds it'.

Of course states will remain. Neither Rosenau nor other contributors to this collection such as Jack Donnelly, who are otherwise critical of the way in which states have been given such primacy in traditional approaches to IR, deny the fact that states will be around as formal legal entities for some time to come. Moreover, as many of the internal conflicts in the post-Cold War period demonstrate, control of a sovereign state is still a prize to kill and to die for. But inter-state warfare is by no means obsolete either, as the invasion of Kuwait by Iraq in the early post-war period illustrated. And here it was the violation of the sacred principle of state sovereignty that was considered grounds for a just war.

At another level, the subsequent expulsion of Iraq from Kuwait by an alliance of forces under a UN Security Council mandate regenerated the general mood of euphoria that had followed the collapse of the Berlin Wall. In fact it seemed to offer firm evidence that, in the absence of polarization in world politics and the shift to a globalist mode of thinking, the collective security function of the UN could at last be fulfilled. This led to a revival of idealist aspirations reflected in visions of a 'New World Order' based on effective international law and backed up by the sanction of the UN's new-found solidarity.

All this certainly seemed to reinforce the beliefs of those who saw a democratic and capitalist 'West' led by the US triumphing over its Cold War adversary, and then successfully leading the charge against a new devil in the form of Saddam Hussein, as signalling a genuine idealist prospect. In short, it accorded with a mood of liberal triumphalism prevalent among a considerable number of media commentators, politicians, bureaucrats, military personnel and academics, and no doubt among a significant portion of the general public at large. Moreover, it resonated very clearly with Fukuyama's 'end of history' thesis.

With respect to the end of the Cold War itself, some more critical commentators have noted that the 'endist' interpretation of the events in eastern Europe was 'closely related to, perhaps part and parcel of, a singularly unattractive mixture of moral narcissism and cultural triumphalism in the west'. This was because it was not merely that 'the West' had won in some strategic or material sense – it had won because 'Western *values*' had won.[18] In short, the moral high ground had been captured at the end of the Cold War, consolidated by the Gulf War, and was thereafter set to be held indefinitely by the leaders of the New World Order.[19]

But the return of this particular variety of idealism was soon to be challenged by another very powerful and persuasive way of looking at the post-Cold War order – one which foresaw some much gloomier prospects of disorder emerging from so-called primordial sources of conflict. The critics of endism and liberal triumphalism, many of whom were intellectually oriented around a critical left perspective, were now joined by a conservative and far from idealistic Harvard professor whose prognostications centred on a 'clash of civilizations'.

## Culture and the new normative agenda

The essential burden of Samuel Huntington's 'clash of civilizations' thesis is well known and I will set it out here only in its barest details. The main arguments are based on the assumption that ideological and/or economic factors will no longer serve as fundamental sources of conflict in the post-Cold War era. Rather, the principal source of conflict will be cultural – as reflected in the great civilizational divisions of humankind. For Huntington, a civilization comprises 'the highest cultural grouping and the broadest level of cultural identity people have short of that which distinguishes humans from other species'.[20] He identifies eight mega-entities that qualify as civilizations. These are Confucian, Japanese, Islamic, Slavic-Orthodox, Latin American, 'possibly' African and, last but certainly not least, the West. The main premise for a conflictual scenario is stated in fairly simple terms: 'In the post-Cold War world flags count and so do other symbols of cultural identity...because culture counts, and cultural identity is what is most meaningful to most people.'[21]

There are numerous problems with these broad claims, a number of which are addressed in this collection. But a major point worth emphasizing here is that Huntington's thesis, although non-statist in its formulation, reinforces traditional perceptions of the structure of world politics as predominantly conflictual. Moreover, it promotes the notion that intercivilizational – or intercultural – relations are themselves primarily relations of conflict.[22] This can be attributed, at least in part, to the way in which 'culture' has been conceptualized throughout much of the twentieth century. Because of the centrality of this concept to how normative issues are framed and treated, whether it is explicit or implicit, it is a subject worth exploring in a little detail here.

From an early anthropological understanding of culture, there developed the idea that the world was made up of human communities each in possession of its own 'culture'. From there, the culture concept came to signify a complete self-contained entity – a totality. Moreover, the concept was applied to the demonstration of *difference* between these entities, and this became more important than any demonstration of similarity. And while difference as such need not provide grounds for conflict the causes of many conflicts, especially in the post-Cold War period, have invariably been framed in terms of cultural (or ethnic) difference between groups. Moreover, cultural difference has been invoked frequently in debates about human rights and the legitimacy or appropriateness of liberal-democratic institutions in non-Western contexts.

These issues are central to much contemporary normative theory, especially as it revolves around the themes of cosmopolitanism and communitarianism, or universalism and particularism. Because it is generally assumed that moral values are derived directly from a community's 'culture', and that cultures are in some significant sense 'unique', it has also been assumed that each community is in possession of its own unique moral framework or universe. From a particularist perspective, this leads to the view that the only valid standards available for judging moral behaviour are to be found *within* the group, and not beyond it in some abstract universal or global sphere. It is further assumed that the correct normative position to adopt in relation to these 'cultures' is that each and every one must be regarded as possessing equal intrinsic merit.

Beyond the smaller socio-political units that were the traditional subjects of anthropological research, it also became common to speak of 'cultures' as coinciding with the boundaries of states, and so there is 'Chinese culture', 'Italian culture', 'Brazilian culture' and so on. There has been a strong tendency, from studies in 'national character' to 'political culture' as well as in traditional approaches to international relations, to treat these as homogeneous entities as well. I noted earlier that classical realism confined morality to the domestic sphere by virtue of the state's exclusive sovereign properties in contrast with the anarchical realm of the international. The geopolitical containment of 'culture' within states, deploying a very thinly stretched anthropological conception, has further reinforced this tendency to treat moral issues as belonging solely within the domestic sphere of states' concerns.

Huntington's thesis, however, in keeping with the mood of much post-Cold War thinking, transcends the state. But he obviously stops well short of anything resembling a globalist approach. His extends to a civilizational realm which contains broad, but none the less 'essential', elements of particularism. Here he is picking up on some quite commonly assumed entities – 'Islamic culture' or 'Confucian culture' or 'Asian culture' or 'Western culture'. These are scarcely novel or unfamiliar categories and each is often treated as some kind of totality in everyday parlance. Yet none of these entities will bear the weight of even the most cursory examination for 'cultural' cohesion.

A point that is especially worth emphasizing here is the way in which Huntington has presented a simplistic formulation of 'the West' versus 'the Rest'.[23] He is hardly alone in doing this. In dividing the world into these two great blocs, he is, after all, simply adopting categories that have become part and parcel of everyday thinking and usage, as I've already suggested. Almost everybody talks about 'the West' or at least uses the term without giving much thought to what it is, what it does, who it includes and who it excludes, and so on. In deploying an undifferentiated concept of 'the West' in opposition to a 'non-West' category, Huntington also reinforces some very long-standing Orientalist images. This has contributed very substantially to the more recent phenomenon of Occidentalism – the totalizing and essentializing of 'the West' in discourses such as the 'Asian values' debate, or in certain varieties of 'Islamism'. The result has been the imagining of another great division in world politics. And, although some might suggest that 'culture' has replaced 'ideology' in this exercise, it would be foolish to assume that culture has nothing to do with ideology. As I have argued elsewhere, contemporary debates about the role of culture in world politics remain deeply embedded in issues of ideology and power, especially where culture is linked to the political and economic interests of state and regional elites.[24]

Fred Halliday's observations on the 'carnival of the grand generalization' ushered in by the end of the Cold War capture very well the character of the discourses revolving around the 'cultural turn', not only in IR, but in other social sciences as well. One way to defeat some of the myths, of course, is simply to look at the historical or empirical record, and Halliday does so in exposing the extent to which 'Islam versus the West', as a deep-rooted, historically constituted antagonism, simply does not stand up to scrutiny. There is in fact a much more extensive record of violent conflict *within* the West and *within* the Islamic world than between them. Jill Steans is similarly critical of aspects of the cultural turn, especially where some important feminist concerns have been bracketed off as 'private' and/or 'cultural' matters, and therefore excluded from the realm of legitimate public political issues. The recognition of women's rights as human rights requires breaking the bounds of the particular, as well as the private, and recognizing the possibilities and opportunities provided by a trans-contextual approach in which 'cultures' are not seen as static isolates.

These broad cultural issues on the new agenda underscore a number of others that have come into sharper focus since the end of the Cold War, especially those concerned with sovereignty, security and justice which form the focus for many of the individual contributions to this volume.

## Sovereignty, security and justice in the post-Cold War world

The passing of the old bipolar world order and the unbounding of the globe in many and various ways may seem to have put paid to any notion of polarization at all. But what we usually understand as the polarization characteristic of the Cold War era has not necessarily passed into history. As we have seen, some now favour the notion of a polarized 'West versus the Rest' scenario – at least as a way of conceptualizing a new/old world order. Another way of dividing or polarizing the world that bears some features of the West/Rest dichotomy is the developmental North/South or First World/Third World divide (with much of the former Second World now joining the latter category). As Caroline Thomas demonstrates, however, the emphasis on inter-state and regional polarization – on which these categories are based – has obscured the extent to which there has been a significant intensification and reconfiguration of *intra-state* polarization based on material inequalities. Thus there is a First World within the Third World and a Third World within the First. Thomas also picks up on a number of themes that run through several other contributions to this collection. And, like Elliott, she notes the strength of reformist approaches, which are pursued at the neglect of more thoroughgoing *transformist* positions which so far remain at the periphery of the agenda.

Further serious problems with the neo-liberal agenda, including the extent to which globalization has exacerbated inequality both between and within states, are discussed in detail by Richard Higgott. A related problem is that economic liberalization is often seen as an end in itself, with scant attention to its effects on existing norms and values within societies. What is needed, above all, he suggests, is a normative agenda for international political economy that is critically attuned to the fact that politics and society cannot be governed by market assumptions alone – as well as to the fact that, despite the triumph of capitalism, two billion people live on less than $2.00 a day with about the same number having little or no access to clean drinking water. Here, incidentally, a shift in thinking about security in military terms to a more holistic conception of human security and survival seems eminently appropriate.

While the contributions of both Higgott and Thomas point to the limited ability of economic theory to grapple with the social and political consequences of globalization, Elliott identifies the limitations of a liberal politics of the environment and discusses some of the new critical approaches that promise to challenge the prevailing neo-liberal orthodoxy. One of the consequences of this orthodoxy is that the 'global' becomes synonymous with institutional practices in which the 'local' is often marginalized or ignored. A major theme of a more critical global politics of the environment is the role and significance of civil society. Elliott discusses these issues not simply in terms of debates about democratic pluralism and institutional efficiency but as a response to the environmental (and other) inadequacies of statist forms of international governance and an inequitable world economic order.

If national sovereignty is no longer as stable a concept or principle as it seemed to be in the Cold War period, then the meaning of 'national security' has necessarily become uncertain as well. Karin Fierke, in assessing the new security agenda and the way in which 'security' itself has been undergoing a process of reconceptualization, also draws attention to some of the ambiguities and contradictions surrounding the way in which security is now often understood. Looking at the case of Kosovo, she notes (along with others) the fact that moral concerns over ethnic cleansing were paramount in justifying intervention. Certainly, there was no real sense in which some kind of direct 'national interest' – and therefore national security – was an issue. One should therefore question whether the use of force here fitted the category of 'security' at all, or whether a different concept is required. More generally, with respect to the present era in which polarization seems to have given way to globalization, the consequences of the latter now monopolize much of the agenda for world politics. In this context, she says that security thinking *per se* has shifted accordingly to encompass such issues as financial crises and environmental or ecological disasters as well as massive human rights violations. And this clearly shifts the traditional emphasis of security from a military focus to something which almost defies the very notion of 'a focus' at all.

In terms of the broad normative framework, Chris Brown considers, among other things, the way in which the traditional theory and practice of state sovereignty kept a firm boundary around human rights issues, thereby excluding them from the sphere of the international. The development of the international human rights regime since 1945 saw a steady undermining of the sovereignty doctrine, although actual intervention on human rights grounds was scarcely a regular practice. But now, in the post-Cold War era, intervention on humanitarian grounds has become an almost commonplace occurrence. In his contribution, Richard Devetak argues that, whereas discourses of order consistently prevailed over those of justice during the Cold War, the present period has seen a strengthening articulation of humanitarian principles which, in practical terms, have been linked to assistance, aid, intervention and crimes against humanity. Thus the post-Cold War era has seen a progressive willingness to employ moral discourses grounded in widespread agreement and increasing calls for the 'international community' to respond actively to humanitarian crises – developments which may be construed as signifying a continuing process of enlightenment.

Two further issues concerning international theory are dealt with in the remaining chapters. Jack Donnelly tackles the question of how international theorists devoted to contending approaches can engage productively with each other in the post-Cold War period. Noting first that structural realism's 'disciplinary hegemony' has effectively collapsed under the weight of its inadequacies, in large measure because of its quite barren simplifying assumptions, he goes on to suggest that there are some promising signs of greater openness within the realist fold and that this is evident in some recent work on interactions. But the engagement cannot be a one-way process. He suggests, for example, not only that realists need to engage with institutions, but also that institutionalists might have something to learn from realists. Developments of this kind, rather than those in which contending approaches are seen as marching forth to 'do battle' with each other, are essential for a healthy and productive diversity within the discipline.

No account of IR in the post-Cold War period of intensifying globalization would be complete without a specific account or analysis of IR's central institution: the state. The final chapter therefore looks specifically at this entity in the context of international theory. And since the sovereign state has always been so central to IR it seems appropriate to draw together, by way of a concluding chapter, some of the general themes addressed in this collection as well as in the broader literature as it relates both to this entity and to the sovereign state system which has long underscored the way in which the 'international' in IR has been conceptualized. Given the focus on globalization that runs throughout the collection – and indeed throughout virtually all strands of IR scholarship in the post-Cold War era – particular attention is paid to the impact of globalization on the state. The idea, promoted in many quarters, that the state is under terminal threat from the unrelenting forces of globalization and is unlikely to survive another century is obviously of special concern to a discipline that has been largely built around the edifice of the sovereign state system.

We have entered a new century following a time of significant change in world politics when the apparent certainties of world politics that marked the Cold War period have given way to a much more complex and shifting set of circumstances. But while there is certainly something to the idea that there is now a 'new agenda' for IR this is no reason to believe that the traditional concerns of the discipline with the causes of war and the conditions for peace are no longer central to that agenda. There is every reason to expect that these will continue to occupy IR scholars well into the twenty-first century. How we approach the issues is another question, especially since peace alone (in terms of the absence of war) is a goal that many believe falls well short of what can and should be attained. There has always been a concern to achieve peace with justice in world politics. It is this normatively attuned approach which informs the contemporary agenda addressed in this collection.

## NOTES

The original version of this chapter, entitled 'The New Agenda for International Relations', was presented as an inaugural lecture at the University of East Anglia, 28 September 1999.

1  I use the term 'IR' to denote the name by which the *discipline* of international relations is generally known. To describe what has commonly been called 'international relations' in denoting the general *subject matter* of the discipline I shall generally use the term 'world politics'. This term denotes something much broader than simply the interactions between nation-states. That is why the title of this collection as a whole, while retaining the traditional term 'international relations', to denote the discipline, uses 'world politics' to convey the broader, less exclusive sphere of activity with which the discipline is actually concerned. For further discussion of the same point, see John Bayliss and Steve Smith, 'Introduction', John Bayliss and Steve Smith (eds), *The Globalization of World Politics: An Introduction to International Relations* (Oxford, Oxford University Press, 1997), pp. 2–3.

2  This has been reflected in a large number of books and articles which speak, in one way or another, of a 'new agenda' or 'new conceptions' for either IR or certain subfields such as security, normative theory or peace studies. See for example: Fred Halliday, 'International Relations: Is There a New Agenda?', *Millennium*, 20, 1 (1991), pp. 57–72; Stephanie Lawson (ed.), *The New Agenda for Global Security: Cooperating for Peace and Beyond* (St Leonards, Allen Unwin, 1995); Paul B. Stares (ed.), *The New Security Agenda: A Global Survey* (Tokyo, Japan Centre for International Exchange, 1998); Nigel Dower, *World Ethics: The New Agenda* (Edinburgh, Edinburgh University Press, 1998); Ho-Won Jong (ed.), *The New Agenda for Peace Research* (Aldershot, Ashgate, 1999); Phil Cerny, 'The New Security Dilemma: Divisibility, Defection and Disorder in the Global Era', *Review of International Studies*, 26, 4 (2000), pp. 623–46.

3  Halliday, 'International Relations'.

4  John D. Barrow, *Theories of Everything: The Quest for Ultimate Explanation* (London, Vintage, 1992), p. ix.

5  'Interview with Ken Walz', conducted by Fred Halliday and Justin Rosenberg, *Review of International Studies*, 24, 3 (1998), p. 379.

6  K. J. Holsti, *The Dividing Discipline: Hegemony and Diversity in International Theory* (Boston, Allen Unwin, 1987), pp. 1–2.

7  Ibid., p. 10.

8   Chris Brown, *International Relations Theory: New Normative Approaches* (London, Harvester Wheatsheaf, 1992), p. 3.
9   For further discussion on this see Stephanie Lawson, 'Dogmas of Difference: Culture and Nationalism in Theories of International Politics', *Critical Review of International Social and Political Theory*, 1, 4 (1999).
10   Barry Buzan, 'New Patterns of Security in the Twenty-First Century', *International Affairs*, 67, 3 (1991), p. 439.
11   W. B. Gallie, 'Essentially Contested Concepts', *Proceedings of the Aristotelian Society*, 56 (1956), p. 171.
12   Ibid., p. 184.
13   Francis Fukuyama, 'The End of History?', *National Interest*, 16 (1989), pp. 3–18.
14   It should also be noted that the incidence and intensity of ethno-nationalist conflicts is often seen as a post-Cold War phenomenon. Others argue that the empirical evidence does not support this impressionistic assumption and, indeed, that more conflicts have been resolved, especially by peaceful methods, since the end of the Cold War than in any other comparable period in recent history. See R. William Ayres, 'A World Flying Apart? Violent Nationalist Conflict and the End of the Cold War', *Journal of Peace Research*, 37, 1 (2000), pp. 105–17.
15   See Boutros Boutros-Ghali, *An Agenda for Peace: Preventive Diplomacy, Peacemaking and Peacekeeping*, Report of the Secretary-General pursuant to the statement adopted by the Summit Meeting of the Security Council on 31 January 1992 (New York, United Nations, 1992).
16   Ibid., pp. 9, 47. See also Lawson, *The New Agenda for Global Security*, pp. 4–5.
17   Many recent works in IR, particularly outside the US, have made similar critical observations about the extent to which ingrained habits of thinking, especially in terms of the state, have shaped the discipline. See, for example, Gillian Youngs, *International Relations in a Global Age: A Conceptual Challenge* (Cambridge, Polity, 1999).
18   Colin Crouch and David Marquand, Editorial Commentary, 'The End of "Endism"?', *Political Quarterly*, 62 (1991), p. 2.
19   These developments, incidentally, gave the US, Britain and others in NATO the confidence to mount the attack on Serbia in 1999, even without the approval of the UN Security Council.
20   Samuel P. Huntington, 'The Clash of Civilizations?', *Foreign Affairs*, 72, 3 (1993), pp. 22, 24.
21   Samuel P. Huntington, *The Clash of Civilizations and the Remaking of World Order* (New York, Simon & Schuster, 1996), p. 20.
22   See Jacinta O'Hagan, 'Civilisational Conflict? Looking for Cultural Enemies', *Third World Quarterly*, 16, 1 (1995), p. 19.
23   An alternative formulation which denotes a more explicit developmental understanding is North/South.
24   See Stephanie Lawson, 'Democracy and the Problem of Cultural Relativism: Normative Issues for International Politics', in Hazel Smith (ed.), *Democracy and International Relations: Critical Theories/Problematic Practices* (Basingstoke, Macmillan, 2000), esp. pp. 71–3.

# 2

# Ageing Agendas and Ambiguous Anomalies
## *Tensions and Contradictions of an Emergent Epoch*

## *James N. Rosenau*

> In the next century I believe most states will begin to change from cultlike
> entities charged with emotion into far simpler and more civilized entities,
> into less powerful and more rational administrative units that will repre-
> sent only one of the many complex and multileveled ways in which our
> planetary society is organized.[1]
>
> Václav Havel

## Introduction

There is both alliteration and causation embedded in the title of this chapter. It
bends unduly in the direction of alliteration because, in many cases, the
anomalies that pervade world affairs are ambiguous and the agendas that
guide our inquiries are ageing. It has a causal dimension in the sense that the
anomalies are rendering our agendas obsolete. Put differently, we need to
update our research agendas because the proliferating anomalies are indicative
of a transforming world, a world that can no longer be adequately grasped by
the research priorities that have guided us in the last few decades. To be
sure, some items on the ageing agendas will persist on the new ones. Doubtless
the world will have to continue to be alert to the problems of nuclear proliferation, civil strife, population trends, Russia, global warming, and the growing
gap between the rich and poor. Still, I believe the transformations at work
in the world are so extensive that we can no longer confine our inquiries to
these long-standing staples of our profession. If we do, if our research priorities
are not updated to account for the new agenda items that lie just across the
horizon, we'll be spinning our wheels while the world moves on without our
input.

The updating task is not as easy as it may seem at first glance. The ageing agendas are founded on a deep-seated habit that prevents us from pondering the implications of new empirical data, that does not readily yield to new conceptualizations, and that inhibits us from treating the anomalies as signifying new and persistent patterns. Shackled by this habit – which I shall discuss at length shortly – we are likely to dismiss startling new data as merely more of the same, as easily interpreted by currently available conceptual equipment, rather than as anomalous indicators of emergent and significant trends.

Before examining the conceptual habit that diverts us, let us look first at some data and anomalies that ought to give us pause and that suggest challenges which should find a place high on our reinvigorated research agendas. Consider these three bits of data that I regard as startling:

1   It is estimated that today 1.4 billion email messages cross national boundaries every day. Quite possibly, moreover, these dynamics are poised for another step-level leap forward with the advent of the Internet (which is growing by one million web pages a day) and new computer technologies that include the prospect of a chip *100 billion times faster* than those available today.[2] Future generations might look back to the latter part of the 1990s and the widening scope of the Internet as the historical starting point for a new phase of modern globalization.

2   It has been calculated that Indonesia had only one independent environmental organization twenty years ago, whereas now there are more than 20,000 linked to an environmental network based in Jakarta. Likewise, registered non-profit organizations in the Philippines grew from 18,000 to 58,000 between 1989 and 1996; in Slovakia the figure went from a handful in the 1980s to more than 10,000 today; and in the US 70 per cent of the non-profit organizations – not counting religious groups and private foundations – filing tax returns with the Treasury Department are less than thirty years old and a third are less than fifteen years old.[3]

3   The movement of people – everyone from the tourist to the terrorist and the migrant to the jet-setter – has been so extensive that around 5 per cent of the people alive today are estimated to be living in a country other than the one where they were born.[4] Indeed, every day half a million airline passengers cross national boundaries.[5]

What do we do with data like these? Treat them as simply an extension of past patterns? Or are they so extraordinary that we need to pause and ponder what they signify about the underpinnings of world politics? My response is that they point to the likelihood of political dynamics with which we have little familiarity and, consequently, we may lack the conceptual tools to comprehend their underlying import. Indeed, I would argue that they reflect but a few of the new and powerful patterns around which political systems are going to have to develop new agendas and policies if they are to exercise even a modicum of control over the needs and demands inherent in the emergent patterns. And, if the political world evolves new agendas, surely we need to do the same.

This need seems even more compelling as one ponders the anomalies that pervade the current scene. The anomalies are at a much higher level of abstraction than the foregoing data, and as such they constitute even more of a challenge to our research agendas. Here are five anomalies that I view as inexplicable by our current conceptual equipment:

1   One involves the widespread idea that one of the US's major military adversaries, China, is also among its biggest trading partners. That is surely an ambiguous anomaly in terms of the way we conventionally understand global politics.
2   Another consists of the contradiction between the widespread presumption that states are rational actors and the accepted understanding that at the same time they are internally divided, pursue a multiplicity of inconsistent goals, lack effective means for adapting to rapid change, never have sufficient information, and depend on unwieldy bureaucracies for innovative policies.
3   Furthermore, if states are rational actors, why do the powerful ones provide aid to the poor ones and why do they accord small and weak states the same voting rights as they have in international governmental organizations (IGOs)?
4   And of what use is the rational-actor model when 'highly disparate states of varied capabilities, following unique historical trajectories and responding to immensely variable local circumstances, "decide" all at once (i.e. in a very brief historical period)' to pursue the same policies such as initiating nationwide pension systems or protecting threatened species from extinction?[6]
5   Then there is the 'paradox ... that while the governments of established states ... are suffering this progressive loss of real authority, the queue of societies that want their own state is lengthening'.[7] Put differently, the present era is marked by a simultaneity of 'the crisis of the nation-state and the explosion of nationalisms'.[8]

Implicit in both the foregoing data and the anomalies are at least four interrelated items that I think should be located high on our new research agendas. Unfortunately time and space constraints prevent elaboration of them. Here I can only take note of them by casting them as questions that I find puzzling and that are illustrative of possible foci on our new agendas.[9] The four questions are:

1   What are the implications and consequences of the deterritorialization that accompanies the accelerating collapse of time and space in response to a continuing wave of technological innovations?

2   What are the consequences for culture and identity of the enormous prolifer-
    ation of organizations and the vast movement of people around the world?
3   Is a global elite emerging?
4   As the competence of states wanes, will new spheres of authority (SOAs),
    even new terminal entities, emerge to capture the loyalties and refocus the
    orientations of people?

In addition to these substantive agenda items, there is one methodological
dilemma that will have to be faced, namely, how do we empirically assess
phenomena in a non-linear, ever more complex world pervaded with endless
feedback loops. The long-standing empirical procedure of positing independent, intervening and dependent variables is a linear method and it is no longer
viable because under conditions of complexity and globalization every dependent variable is an independent variable in the next millisecond. Put differently,
the agenda items that lie ahead will focus essentially on non-linear processes
and not linear outcomes. One could avoid this serious methodological challenge by resorting to critical theory and other non-empirical approaches, but
avoidance will not do for those who are empirically oriented. Rather, they may
have to tool up in computer sciences in order to evolve non-linear models with
which to identify the data they need for simulations and data analysis.

## The states-are-for-ever habit

Given startling new data, ambiguous anomalies and hints of new questions to
investigate, it seems clear to me that our research agendas have become
hostage to convention, to habitual modes of inquiry that are increasingly
removed from the dynamics and statics of world affairs at the outset of a
new century. Perhaps the most clear-cut indicator of this discrepancy between
the emergent world and our tools for analysing it are the innumerable research
agendas still rooted deeply in a conception of the world as criss-crossed by
boundaries that divide the international from the domestic and that accord to
nation-states the role of presiding over these boundaries. Such a conception of
world affairs is, I am convinced, profoundly flawed. The institutions, structures and processes that sustain economic, political and social life today are
undergoing extensive transformations that are rendering the international–
domestic dichotomy obsolete and, even worse, severely distorting our grasp
of how the world works. Today what is foreign is also domestic, and what is
domestic is also foreign. The two domains overlap and in some respects they
are even one and the same. They form a new frontier where politics unfolds, a
frontier that is marked by an endless flow of new technologies, by an endless
proliferation of new organizations and by an endless movement of people
across borders, not to mention the endless flow of polluted air and water,
crime, drugs and diseases.[10]

Earlier I suggested that there is a prime habit that inhibits our coming to grips with the pervasive dynamics of transformation. I call it the states-are-forever habit. The widely shared beliefs as to what states represent, what they can accomplish and what they can prevent are virtually innate. Most people simply assume that the terminal entity for loyalties, policy decisions and moral authority is, for better or worse, the state. Those familiar with history know that the state is of relatively recent origin, that for millennia it was preceded by other terminal entities; but even history-minded observers seem unable to envision a future world in which states are not the terminal entity. Indeed, despite myriad evidence that states, even the long-established and coherent ones, are less and less capable of coping with the twin challenges of globalization and localization, the inclination to assume that states are the terminal entities through which authority is exercised and order maintained remains undiminished, unquestioned and unexplored. We are so accustomed to assuming states are the sole terminal collectivity that we lack any inclination to ask whether ongoing changes might be the first traces of emerging terminal entities. There are exceptions (noted briefly below), but for many analysts the diminution of state competencies is neither ambiguous nor anomalous; for them, it is a misreading of the role states play in the course of events, a vast underestimate of their power and influence.

I share the notion that the state's decline is neither ambiguous nor anomalous; but in my view the diminution is a clear-cut central tendency, an accurate portrayal of a major trend line unfolding in the current era. Yes, state institutions still have a modicum of authority, but their capacity to exercise it has lessened considerably. States cannot prevent ideas from moving across their borders. They cannot control the flow of money, jobs and production facilities in and out of their country. They have only minimal control over the flow of people and, to repeat, virtually no control over the flow of drugs or the drift of polluted air and water. Their capacity to promote and maintain cohesion among the groups that comprise their society is at an all-time low as crime, corruption and ethnic sensitivities undermine any larger sense of national community they may have had. Cynicism toward politicians and major institutions is widespread and people increasingly perceive no connection between their own welfare and that of their communities. Selfishness and greed have replaced more encompassing loyalties. Thus many states are unable to enforce laws, prevent widespread corruption, collect taxes or mobilize their armed forces for battle. They cannot collectively bring order to war-torn societies. In short, landscapes have been supplemented and – in many instances – replaced by ethnoscapes, financescapes, ideoscapes, mediascapes, technoscapes and identiscapes.[11]

This listing of the weaknesses of states could be enumerated at length, but it is sufficient for the purpose of emphasizing that the central institution of modern society is no longer suitable as the organizing focus of our research agendas. Rather than divide up the world in terms of clear-cut boundaries that separate the domestic from the international, it needs to be seen as consisting of indeterminate and shifting boundaries that differentiate the local from the global. Put in terms of our research agendas, we need to cease thinking of ourselves as students of international relations and begin to view our inquiries as devoted to the study of global affairs, a reorientation that makes it easier to remove the state from the centre of our concerns and that allows for unfettered probings of the relations that link the local and the global, the regional and the provincial, the social and the political, the private and the public, the multinational corporation and the non-governmental organization (NGO), the US's cultural artefacts and their adaptation into non-American settings, the social movement and its disparate supporters, and a host of other connections that tend to be obscured by the imposition of state-based conceptions. Stated in an even more general way, students of politics need to approach political processes as unfolding in decentralized, often nebulous institutional contexts.

Such an orientation might not be difficult: other disciplines have accomplished it. Anthropologists, for example, 'have now acquired the habit of contrasting the local and the global, and tend to take for granted that the local is to the global more or less as continuity is to change'.[12] Yet, it is a measure of the degree to which specialists in world affairs are entrapped in the states-are-for-ever habit that I immediately need to intrude a caveat and emphasize that I am not anticipating the demise of the state as a political entity. It ought to be unnecessary to make this disclaimer, but states are so deeply ensconced in our paradigms that I feel compelled to stress what I am not saying. The state will surely be around for the foreseeable future and I am not saying otherwise. Rather, I think it is probable, as will be seen, that other SOAs designed to cope with the links and overlaps between localizing and globalizing dynamics will evolve and render the global stage ever more dense. Some SOAs will prove to be rivals of states, while others will become their partners, but in either event SOAs – or whatever they come to be labelled – ought to be moving to the top of our research agendas. They may seem anomalous today, but they strike me as destined to be patterned regularities in our future inquiries.

While the states-are-for-ever habit is widely shared, it is perhaps significant that some thoughtful analysts have broken away from this conventional mode and recently published lengthy, serious, responsible and impressive inquiries that explore ways in which the authority of states may be undergoing relocation. Although coming from different research traditions, for example, three distinguished scholars have reached the shared conclusion that the economic, social and cultural dynamics transforming modernity are also enveloping the political realm and its centrepiece, the state. Castells, Held and his colleagues, and Strange have all authored lengthy and major analyses of currently unfolding trends[13] and each has found that, as Castells puts it,

> the nation-state is increasingly submitted to a more subtle, and more troubling, competition from sources of power that are undefined, and, sometimes, undefin-

able. These are networks of capital, production, communication, crime, international institutions, supranational military apparatuses, non-governmental organizations, transnational religious, and public opinion movements. And below the state, there are communities, tribes, localities, cults, and gangs. So, while nation-states do continue to exist, and they will continue to do so in the foreseeable future, there are, and there will increasingly be, *nodes of a broader network of power*. They will often be confronted by other flows of power in the network, which directly contradict the exercise of their authority.[14]

To repeat, however, these formulations are the exception. They may be a portent of intellectual changes that lie ahead – especially if it is the case, as one observer contends, that younger generations of scholars are both weary and wary of state-based assumptions[15] – but for now the states-are-for-ever habit continues to have a hold on many analysts and virtually all policy-makers. It is a deeply ingrained impulse, a given, a cast of mind, an article of faith so embedded in our organizing premises as to be beyond questioning. And even the weary, while they may be ready to move beyond a state-based conception, offer no alternative formulation that enables them to do so.

## Rebuilding the state in war-torn societies

Lest there be any doubt that I have overstated the strength of the states-are-for-ever habit, one need only note how brilliantly visible and evident it is in efforts to rebuild war-torn societies. Even as practitioners and academics alike ponder the challenge of governance in the context of war-torn societies, they do so by falling back on the well-worn and long-standing presumption that the state is the repository of governance, that it is the only effective institution available for managing the affairs of large aggregates of people and their societies. This presumption is so fully engrained in the culture of modernity that it is not treated as problematic. The idea that a collapsed state might be replaced by widespread disarray is so widely shared that any state teetering on extinction is considered worth propping up rather than permitting the disorder that might result if its various subgroups go their own way. Thus, for example, one of the reasons why the thirty-two-nation coalition that won the Gulf War did not carry the battle to Baghdad was a fear that Iraq would break up, that the Kurds and Shiites would go their own way, and that a level of disorder would then set in that could lead to unforeseen consequences. The certainties that attached to Saddam Hussein remaining in power were viewed as preferable to the uncertainties that might follow from his and his country's political demise or truncation.

Likewise, to cite a more recent example, NATO's aspiration to prevent Serbs from leaving Kosovo and thereby maintaining a semblance of multiculturality would appear to be rooted in treating the preservation of states and their boundaries as a given. Rarely, if ever, do voices get heard that say, in effect, 'OK, the Serbs are fleeing Kosovo and only the Kosovar Albanians remain. So be it. Why try to force the two highly antagonistic groups to live together?'[16] Put very differently, allowing history to follow a fragmenting course is roughly the sociological equivalent of Darwinian processes whereby the fittest survive. The Darwinian analogy would be that some groups will survive by being members of a multicultural state while others will survive by forming their own terminal entity.

The states-are-for-ever habit opposes partition and favours forcing antagonistic groups to remain together on the grounds that a rebuilt society and state will lead to degrees of stability and progress such that the antagonisms and hatreds will give way as conditions improve, as if hatred derives from rational calculations as to what is in the best interest of those who hate. To be sure, if the resources are available, the material destruction accompanying war can be cleared away and roads, bridges, homes and factories rebuilt. But the logic of hatred is not readily amenable to alteration by the advent of new infrastructures. Nor is it necessarily susceptible to reduction by the presence of outsiders who can keep hateful enemies from acting out their animosities. It is as much wishful thinking as sound analysis to presume that a firm, humane and prolonged external intervention can diminish hate.

Another indicator of the strength of the state as a deeply entrenched habit is the aforementioned anomaly wherein many subgroups around the world are pressing for the establishment of states of their own despite the evidence that such entities are increasingly ineffective. It would seem that the diverse pressures for statehood validate the state as the terminal entity. Even as leaders of established states welcome these validations of their basic premises, moreover, so do they often seek to preserve their inter-state system by resisting any pressures that might lead to the evolution of new types of terminal entities. Consequently, when an internal war ravages a society and leads to a collapse of its state, the unquestioned impulse in the halls of government everywhere is to 'rebuild' the state. Fragmentation along ethnic, economic, political and cultural lines is considered such a dire threat to global stability that rebuilding the state is, to repeat, considered preferable to letting the fragmenting dynamics unfold in whatever ways history may dictate. It is as if the poverty, pain and violence that accompany the rebuilding process are but temporary conditions and bound to be less costly than the price of not undertaking the effort to rebuild.

## Framing a new research agenda

Given a readiness to treat the new technologies, the proliferation of organizations and the massive movement of people as reflective of patterns that impel a struggle to free ourselves of the states-are-for-ever habit, how do we proceed beyond the ageing agendas? What terminal entities should be the focal point of our inquiries? I think the answer involves a two-stage process. The first is to view the world as entering a new epoch dominated by the tensions and contradictions generated by the clash of globalizing and localizing dynamics. The second is to follow Havel's lead set forth in the epigraph and focus on the diffusion and relocation of authority to which these tensions have given rise.

Freed from the shackles of state-based models, it seems clear that the emergent epoch is defined by the interaction between globalization and localization, between those dynamics that promote an expansion of activities and attitudes beyond their existing confines and those that generate a contraction of activities and attitudes from their prior limits. In other words, I conceive of globalization not as referring to developments and orientations that are global in scope, but rather as denoting expansivity which may or may not eventuate in global phenomena, as 'processes whereby social relations acquire relatively placeless, distanceless and borderless qualities'.[17] Similarly, localization does not refer to events that culminate in what is conventionally known as the local community; rather, it depicts processes of devolution that may or may not converge on local communities. Thus, for example, a state can be viewed as a local entity when nationalistic forces take it over and press for a cancellation of treaty obligations, just as a city can be treated as globalizing when it paves the way for investors from abroad.

As the world shrinks, as communications technologies render the distant ever more proximate and vice versa, as more and more people move around the world, as money in the trillions is transferred in milliseconds from and to accounts everywhere, as goods and services are increasingly produced far from where they are consumed, as drugs, diseases and weapons move readily from continent to continent, so do the interactions between globalization and localization intensify. And the more they intensify, the more do the interactions subsume the phenomena conventionally known as diplomatic relations, international political economy, Americanization, cultural exchanges, institutional isomorphism, transnational ties, and so on, across all the processes and structures usually grouped under the heading of 'international relations'.

The outlines of a new research agenda can be discerned in the subordination of the diverse subfields of our discipline to the intensified interactions between global and local phenomena. In effect, the agenda is framed by the contradictory interactions that pervade the course of events. Each day brings word of a world inching slowly toward sanity even as it moves toward breakdown. And not only do these integrative and disintegrative events occur simultaneously, but more often than not they are causally related. More than that, the causal links tend to cumulate and generate a momentum such that integrative increments tend to give rise to disintegrative increments, and vice versa. The simultaneity of the good and the bad, the global and the local, the coherent and the incoherent, the centralizing and the decentralizing, the integrating and the fragmenting – to mention only a few of the interactive polarities that dominate world affairs – underlies the emergence of the new epoch in human affairs and the differences in kind that distinguish it.

These polarities amount to an endless series of tensions in which the forces pressing for greater globalization and those inducing greater localization interactively play themselves out. Such dynamics can be discerned in the tensions between core and periphery, between national and transnational systems, between communitarianism and cosmopolitanism, between cultures and subcultures, between states and markets, between decentralization and centralization, between universalism and particularism, between pace and space,[18] between self and other, between the distant and the proximate – to note only the more conspicuous links between opposites that presently underlie the course of events. And each of these tensions is marked by numerous variants; they take different forms in different parts of the world, in different countries, in different markets, in different communities, in different professions and in different cyberspaces, with the result that there is enormous diversity in the way people experience the tensions that beset their lives.

It is important to stress the interactive foundations of these tensions. To disaggregate them for analytic purposes, to confine inquiry only to globalizing dynamics or only to localizing dynamics, is to risk overlooking what makes events unfold as they do. As one observer puts it, 'the distinction between the global and the local is becoming very complex and problematic'.[19]

In order to facilitate a continual focus on this interactive perspective, I use a label that some find awkward but that serves to capture the tensions and polarities that mark the emergent epoch. The label is *fragmegration*, a concept that juxtaposes the processes of fragmentation and integration occurring within and among organizations, communities, countries, regions and transnational systems such that it is virtually impossible not to treat them as interactive and causally linked.[20] To be sure, the label is probably too grating ever to catch on as the prime descriptor of the epoch[21] – to speak of the Westphalian system as having given way to the fragmegrative system runs counter to the need for historic landmarks as a basis for thinking about global structures – but it is none the less the case that fragmegrative processes are so pervasive and generic that the emergent epoch seems likely to acquire a label reflective of them.[22] In the absence of a widely accepted label, however, for the present I argue that we live, not in an age of globalization, but in a fragmegrative age.

Given its many causal factors, each of which reinforces the others, the fragmegrative epoch defies reduction to an overarching theory. There is no easy or overriding answer to the question of what drives the course of events. Power is too disaggregated, and feedback loops are too pervasive, to assert that global affairs are now driven by the United States, or by globalization, or by capitalism, or by whatever grand scheme may seem most compelling. No, what drives the emergent epoch consists of complex dynamics that spring, in turn, from numerous sources and cannot be traced to a singular origin.

It is reasonable to presume that the numerous causal factors and the fragmegrative tensions they generate are no less operative at the level of individuals than they are in the agendas of political systems. That is, the forces of fragmentation are rooted in the psychic comfort people derive from the familiar and close-at-hand values and practices of their neighbourhoods and communities. Contrariwise, the forces of integration stem from the aspiration to share in the distant products of the global economy, to benefit from the efficiencies of regional unity, to avoid the dangers of environmental degradation, and/or to yield to the implications of the pictures taken from outer space that depict the earth as a solitary entity in a huge universe. Stated more generally, and in the succinct words of one astute observer, 'There is a constant struggle between the collectivist and individualist elements within each human.'[23]

## Spheres of authority

The prevalence of fragmegrative tensions at every level of community raises a number of crucial questions that could well serve as the basis for new research agendas: How are both individuals and collectivities going to adapt to the tensions? How can they manage the simultaneous pull toward the local and the global? How well, that is, will societies, groups and individuals be able to keep their essential structures intact and move toward their goals in the face of dynamic changes that are giving birth to a new epoch? In a decentralizing global system undergoing continual processes wherein authority is undermined and relocated, how can publics be mobilized and problems addressed? If territorial landscapes are giving way to ethnoscapes, technoscapes, financescapes, mediascapes, ideoscapes and identiscapes, what is likely to happen to the loyalties, commitments and orientations of individuals and groups? Is it possible, as some contend, that global markets 'increase the incentives and wherewithal for organizing' new social contracts because they liberate 'social, political, and cultural intentions from spatial constraints, and from economic domination'?[24] If the ability of states to control the flow of ideas, money, goods and people across their boundaries has been substantially diminished, are new political structures likely to evolve, or is the world descending into ever greater disarray?

My point of departure in responding to such questions is to focus on the diverse spheres of authority – the SOAs – which are proliferating at an exponential rate. The proliferation is a consequence of the processes whereby the loci of authority are undergoing continuous disaggregation as the clash of global and local dynamics has weakened states and led to the evolution of new and myriad SOAs. Many of the new SOAs are the product of the inordinate complexities inherent in fragmegrative dynamics, while others result from the negotiation of new identities that are filling the social and psychological spaces vacated by weakening states and fragmenting societies, spaces that may have the capacity to siphon off the commitments and orientations that states are no longer able to serve. Some are loosely organized networks in which authority rarely needs to be exercised, while others are hierarchical and tightly structured. Some are transitory, while others are enduring. Some of the SOAs have long histories, but most derive from fragmegrative dynamics and are thus of recent origin.

Many observers are inclined to view the continuous devolution of authority away from states as amounting to the emergence of civil society. But this concept carries so much baggage and is the focus of so many different formulations that I prefer to speak of the world stage as simply becoming ever more dense with collective actors, with SOAs. The population of SOAs includes states as well as a wide range of other types of collectivities, from corporations to professional associations, from neighbourhoods to epistemic communities, from non-governmental organizations to social movements, from professional societies to truth commissions, from Davos elites to trade unions, from subnational governments to transnational advocacy groups, from networks of the like-minded to diaspora, from gated communities to vigilante gangs, from credit-rating agencies to strategic partnerships, from issue regimes to markets, and so on, across a wide range of entities that have little in common other than being repositories of authority that evoke compliance on the part of others.

All the SOAs are founded on rules designed to serve their purposes and retain the involvement and commitment of their members. In effect, the old Westphalian social contracts on which states are founded are being supplemented – and in some instances supplanted – by new social contracts that are based on new and diverse forms of authority. And it is here, in the framing and promotion of new social contracts, that the ageing of agendas and their replacements become extremely relevant: for it is in the interaction of global and local dynamics that the nature and direction of new agendas organized around new social contracts will be shaped and solidified. In the absence of interactions that help form new contracts founded on values that enable collectivities to remain intact and move toward their goals, it is reasonable to anticipate that the world is indeed headed for ever greater disarray – for circumstances in which, in effect, there is no social contract or, put even more negatively, social contracts do evolve but they are founded on the principle that every individual is beholden only to himself or herself.

But what might be the bases of new social contracts? Leaving aside self-beholden contracts and the fact that contracts involving aggregates of people cannot be simply imposed from the top, or at least that they must resonate broadly with the affected publics, on what values should the new contracts rest such that localizing and globalizing forces can be reconciled and the tensions between them ameliorated? Whatever contractual variations may derive from local circumstances, is there a core set of values on which all the contracts can be founded? What, then, might be the essential terms of the new contracts? And, no less important, who shall be the parties to the new contracts?

Clearly full answers to these questions require a lengthy treatise that would far exceed the space available here. Elsewhere I have made a first pass at identifying and elaborating the circumstances under which the new social contracts will evolve, the identity of the signatories to them, and the key terms likely to be found in all the contracts.[25]

## Conclusion

From the perspective of the turn of the century, a focus on the new social contracts generated by fragmegrative dynamics may seem idealistic and un-realistic. My efforts to spell out the new contracts have thus far been short of clauses that allow for the reconciliation of fragmegrative tensions or otherwise assure the effectiveness of SOAs in wielding their authority and achieving compliance. Nor have I managed to specify contractual clauses that allow for the handling of the troubled spots in the world where localizing dynamics are such as to have fostered violence and resistance to new sources of authority. On the contrary, there is no basis for believing that the emergent epoch will not be as marred by difficult and intractable trouble spots as the expiring epoch has been; indeed, such situations may never achieve that level of shared confidence that permits the drawing up of meaningful social contracts. And surely it is also the case that any new contracts will be slow to develop and that the habits necessary to support them may require generations to become fully implanted.

But such qualifications derive from the states-are-for-ever habit and the reasoning that has sustained the ageing agendas. It ignores the transformative dynamics at work in the world and presumes that the future is bound to emulate the past. Thus it is equally reasonable to presume that the uncertain-ties inherent in the multiplicity of fragmegrative tensions are so pervasive that today's ambiguous anomalies may unfold into patterns consistent with the items seemingly destined to comprise the world's agenda in the future. Viewed in this way, it may not be idealistic to conclude that the acceleration of technological innovations, the organizational explosion and the vast move-ments of people render the probability of new institutions expressive of new social contracts evolving no less than the likelihood of the old contracts perpetuating a state-dominated world. Havel's conception of the organization of the future of our planetary society may well prove sound.

## NOTES

1  Vaclav Havel, 'Kosovo and the End of the Nation-State', *The New York Review of Books*, 46 (10 June 1999), pp. 4–6.
2  Office of the Press Secretary, 'Remarks by President Clinton at University of Chicago Convocation Ceremonies', http://www.whitehouse.gov/WH/New/html/19990612.html (12 June 1999), pp. 1–2; John Markoff, 'Tiniest Circuits Hold Prospect of Explosive Computer Speeds', *New York Times*, 16 July 1999, p. A1.
3  David Bornstein, 'A Force Now in the World, Citizens Flex Social Muscle', *New York Times*, 10 July 1999, p. B7.
4  Shashi Tharoor, 'The Future of Civil Conflict', *World Policy Journal*, 16 (1999), p. 7.
5  Office of the Press Secretary, 'Remarks by President Clinton', p. 2.
6  John Boli, 'International Nongovernmental Organizations in World Society: Authority Without Power', paper presented at the Conference on 'International Institutions: Global Processes – Domestic Consequences', Duke University, 9–11 April 1999, pp. 1–2.
7  Susan Strange, *The Retreat of the State: The Diffusion of Power in the World Economy* (Cambridge, Cambridge University Press, 1996), p. 5.
8  Manuel Castells, *The Information Age*, Vol. 2: *The Power of Identity* (Oxford, Blackwell Publishers, 1997), p. 306.
9  Initial efforts to probe the first, second and fourth questions can be found in James N. Rosenau, *Along the Domestic–Foreign Frontier: Exploring Governance in a Turbulent World* (Cambridge, Cambridge University Press, 1997). An attempt to explore the third question through survey research is presently under way.
10  For an elaboration of the frontier concept see Rosenau, *Along the Domestic–Foreign Frontier*, chs 1–3.
11  All but the last of these 'scapes' are discussed in Arjun Appadurai, *Modernity at Large: Cultural Dimensions of Globalization* (Minneapolis, MN, University of Minnesota Press, 1996), pp. 33–7. I am indebted to David Earnest for the addition of 'identiscapes' as a concept designed to capture that dimension of the emergent epoch which embraces the normative content of trans-border affiliations.
12  Ulf Hannerz, *Transnational Connections: Culture, People, Places* (London and New York, Routledge, 1996), p. 19.
13  Castells, *The Information Age*, Vol. 2, ch. 5; David Held, Anthony McGrew, David Goldblatt and Jonathan Perraton, *Global Transformations: Politics, Economics and Culture* (Cambridge, Polity, 1999), pp. 49–52; Strange, *The Retreat of the State, passim*.
14  Castells, *The Information Age*, Vol. 2, p. 304 (italics in the original).
15  'I got the clear impression at the ... conference [on international institutions] that, among the many younger scholars there, the fixation on the state is seen as outmoded and even a little silly. They all assume that there are many sorts of significant actors in the world, and I was struck by how comfortable many people were in talking about the importance of NGOs, the idea of world culture, and so on.' John Boli, personal communication, 30 April 1999.

16  For an exception in this regard, see John J. Mearsheimer and Steven Van Evera, 'Redraw the Map, Stop the Killing', *New York Times*, 19 April 1999, p. A23.

17  Jan Aart Scholte, 'Globalization and Modernity', paper presented at the Annual Meeting of the International Studies Association, San Diego, 15–20 April 1996, p. 15.

18  The reference here is to 'an increasingly pervasive and contentious political struggle between a "discourse of pace" linked, on the one hand, to accelerating transitions, speeding flows, overcoming resistances, eliminating frictions, and engineering the kinematics of globalization, and, on the other hand, a "discourse of place" centered upon solidifying porous borders, bolstering breached containments, arresting eroded identities, and revitalizing faded essences'. Timothy W. Luke and Gearóid Ó Tuathail, 'Global Flowmations, Local Fundamentalism, and Fast Geopolitics: "America" in an Accelerating World Order', in A. Herod, G. Ó. Tuathail and S. M. Roberts (eds), *An Unruly World? Globalization, Governance and Geography* (London and New York, Routledge, 1998), p. 73.

19  Roland Robertson, 'Mapping the Global Condition: Globalization as the Central Concept', in Mike Featherstone (ed.), *Global Culture: Nationalism, Globalization, and Modernity* (London, Sage Publications, 1990), p. 19.

20  This concept was first developed in James N. Rosenau, '"Fragmegrative" Challenges to National Security', in Terry Heyns (ed.), *Understanding US Strategy: A Reader* (Washington, DC, National Defense University, 1983), pp. 65–82. For a more recent and elaborate formulation, see James N. Rosenau, 'New Dimensions of Security: The Interaction of Globalizing and Localizing Dynamics', *Security Dialogue*, 25 (September 1994), pp. 255–82.

21  Other terms suggestive of the contradictory tensions that pull systems toward coherence and collapse are 'chaord', a label that juxtaposes the dynamics of chaos and order, and 'glocalization', which points to the simultaneity of globalizing and localizing dynamics. The former designation is proposed in Dee W. Hock, 'Institutions in the Age of Mindcrafting', a paper presented at the Bionomics Annual Conference (San Francisco, CA: xerox, 22 October 1994), pp. 1–2, while the latter term is elaborately developed in Roland Robertson, 'Glocalization: Time–Space and Homogeneity–Heterogeneity', in Mike Featherstone, Scott Lash and Roland Robertson (eds), *Global Modernities* (Thousand Oaks, CA, Sage, 1995), pp. 25–44. Here the term 'fragmegration' is preferred because it does not imply a territorial scale and broadens the focus to include tensions at work in organizations as well as those that pervade communities.

22  One observer has suggested that the world has entered 'the age of deregulation', but this label lacks any hint of the integrative dynamics at work on the world scene, and it too fails to specify a historic landmark, which may be why one reviewer 'suspects...[the label] will not catch on as the paradigm of the year'. The deregulation label is offered in Richard Haas, *The Reluctant Sheriff: The United States after the Cold War* (New York, Council on Foreign Relations Press, 1997), and the suspicion it will not take hold is expressed in David C. Hendrickson's review of Haas in *Foreign Affairs*, 76 (July/August 1997), p. 155.

23  Harry C. Triandis, *Individualism and Collectivism* (Boulder, CO, Westview Press, 1995), p. xiv.

24   Judith R. Blau, *Social Contracts and Economic Markets* (New York, Plenum Press, 1993), p. 97.

25   James N. Rosenau, 'In Search of Institutions', paper presented at the Conference on International Institutions: Global Processes – Domestic Consequences, sponsored by the Center for International Studies, Duke University, Durham, NC, 9–11 April 1999.

# Part II

# New Issues

# 3

# Transnational Paranoia and International Relations
## *The Case of the 'West versus Islam'*

## *Fred Halliday*

This chapter, along with others in the book, was written prior to the events of September 11th, 2001.

### Introduction: a new great fear

No discussion of international relations since the end of the Cold War can fail to note the supposed onset of civilizational or cultural conflict. If analysis of the post-1989 world has been marked by a carnival of the grand generalization, from the 'new world order' to the 'end of history', the 'new Middle Ages' and the 'clash of civilizations', much of this, in IR literature and public debate alike, has concerned this prevalence of 'culture'. While such conflicts include that of 'Asian' versus 'Western', and 'Western Christian' versus 'Slavic' or 'Orthodox', pride of place amongst the claims made in this category must go to the argument, diffused in both the Muslim and non-Muslim worlds, of an overriding conflict between 'Islam' and 'the West'.[1] The 2000s began with the strategic position of the two former superpowers dominated, or obsessed, by this – the USA in its concern at the moment of transition to 2000 with the terrorism of Islamists, which had led it in 1998 to launch cruise missile attacks against targets in Sudan and Afghanistan, the Russians in military mobilization against Islamist rebels in Chechnya, whose drive for independence was said to challenge the very survival of the Russian state.

In some cases, this clash is said in a general way to have replaced the East–West Cold War as the dominant fissure of international relations. In other cases, a stronger claim is made, namely that in a strategic vacuum left by the end of the Cold War this conflict has been actively promoted by the West to fill the gap left by the disappearance of the communist threat. This argument as to the salience of cultural conflict, however, goes well beyond that of relations between 'Islam' and 'the West'. There have been recurrent claims about the place of cultural conflict in the contemporary international epoch: in Huntington's claim about the primacy of culture and civilizational clash in international relations, in discussion of the particularist, cultural, backlash to globalization, in invocation by cultural studies and IR alike of the return of 'deep structures' of identity and antagonism within Western and non-Western politics.[2] Political theory has increasingly come to be concerned with issues of community, identity and the 'other'. All of this has, of course, played into what is termed the 'cultural turn' in IR.

Three initial observations may be in order about these claims.[3] First, as in other claims about the novelty of the contemporary epoch, an element of proportion, historical and thematic, may be in order. On closer examination, the novelty and, in the overall balance of the new international situation, the significance of this topic may be exaggerated. Secondly, we are certainly seeing something that is stimulated by other dimensions of the new international situation: the decline of communism and the Cold War, on the one hand, and on the other the anxiety about 'globalization' as both economic and cultural force within many Third World countries. This interrelation is in part demonstrated by the fact that claims about the conflict are not specific to one side of the supposed divide: claims about Western hostility to the Muslim world are at least as common in Muslim countries – in press, radio, political speeches and the mosque preachings – as they are in Western media and political statements. Whatever else, this is a shared claim, and alarm, not simply a projection of one side or the other. Thirdly, assessment of this claim involves more than just an adjudication about current issues in international relations, about the relative truth, falsity or plausibility of claims about Islam and the West. It involves theoretical issues: the roles of culture, identity and religion in international relations. It also invites examination of a question in historical sociology, namely the role of confrontation, of the 'other' in the constitution of Western states and foreign policies. Much is made of the role of such antagonistic alterity in political life.

If, as I shall argue, the claim about an 'Islam versus the West' conflict is simplistic, then, given the diffusion of this idea, analysis of it also requires analysis of the role of myth, of conspiracy theory and myth, in the post-1989 world. It may be not so much in Islam–Western relations as in these latter issues, in the constitution of myths about culture and identity, and in their use by political forces for instrumental reasons, that the more substantive significance of the 'Islam versus the West' claim may lie. Discussion of the issue of culture and identity, and of how political forces use these, may also have implications for the normative discussion on universalism and relativism which is so pervasive in contemporary political theory: not all that appears particular, relative, in Walzer's terminology 'thick', may indeed be as specific as its proponents suggest. The example of airlines with 'national' names but universal functions illustrates this. In other words, examination of this issue may indeed tell us something about the post-1989 world, but not what proponents of the myth would themselves claim.

Claims of this kind, in keeping with the grand sweep of post-1989 generalizations, are both comprehensive and elusive. They rest on a basis, some would say shifting sands, of historical, cultural, mediatic and political claims. When evidence fails, a debased form of psychoanalytic speculation, about 'the repressed', 'silence', 'the other', itself neglectful of the disciplines of that science, is invoked. If there is validity in these claims, beyond the fact that they are widely repeated, the threshold of credibility has, none the less, to be raised. In order to get an analytic grip on this claim the argument will be examined here in four broad dimensions: historical, inter-state, cultural, theoretical. The aim is both critically to examine this argument in its own right, and to use such an examination to elicit discussion of other pervasive questions in assessment of the post-1989 world.

## Historical correctives

The first dimension of the claim to be examined is historical, the argument that in some way this conflict between Islam and the West has been a creation, or re-creation, of the post-1989 world. As a political fact, there can be little dispute: the incidence of claims, in the West and in the Muslim world, about this conflict has certainly risen over the past decade. It has become a stock in trade of journalists, political leaders and intellectuals on both sides of the 'cultural divide'.[4] It is, moreover, indisputable that conflicts along a Muslim/non-Muslim divide have also been evident: in the former Yugoslavia, Palestine, Kashmir, Indonesia and Sudan, to name but some. Closer examination of the historical record may, however, show a rather different picture.

First of all, we can examine whether there is some historic basis, a 'substratum', 'fault-line' or 'collective unconscious', on which the contemporary dispute rests. It has become fashionable, in all sorts of contexts, to talk of a 'return of the repressed' and this, rather easy, claim is often made in the context under discussion. To the extent that the argument rests on the return of some historically constituted antagonism, it is, however, doubly questionable. It is factually questionable because the record of relations between Muslim states and western Europe is far from being one of unrelenting hostility. There were recurrent strategic confrontations, most notably in the eighth century, with the Arab incursions into Spain and France, and in the sixteenth and seventeenth centuries, with the Turkish advances towards central Europe. In many other periods no such Islamic aggression against Europe existed. If aggression there was – strategic and commercial – it came from the European states. However, from the late seventeenth century onwards relations between the Ottoman Empire and Western states were conducted on the basis of shifting alliances, as were those of Western states themselves. Istanbul sought allies against

Russia – not least, until its disappearance in the 1790s, with Poland. On occasion Britain, France and other states sided with the Ottomans, on others they opposed them. In the Crimean War (1853–6) Britain allied with Turkey against Russia. In World War I (1914–18) the Turks allied with Germany and Austria against Russia, France and Britain.

The same contingent record applies to a segment of history much invoked to explain contemporary politics, colonial relations: while with French colonialism there was significant confrontation with peoples designated as 'Muslim', that is, in North Africa, the British had no such generic term. Some confrontations between British colonial rule and Muslims took place (in the Indian mutiny of 1857, in the Sudan in 1886) but the main enemies, not least those who were lodged in military and popular imagination, were not Muslim, but other – before World War II, American colonists, Irish Fenians, Zulus, and, after 1945, Malayan Chinese communists, Zionists in Palestine, Greek Cypriots in EOKA, Mau Mau in Kenya, the IRA. Even if one concedes the existence of an 'anti-Muslim' substratum it is far less coherent than much current discussion would suggest.

Moreover, if there is a substratum of conflict in western Europe it is not one constituted primarily by conflict with the colonial world at all, but by the intra-European conflicts themselves. Despite the claims of 'post-colonial' studies, it is this intra-European dimension that has, in large measure, constituted the political, strategic and economic development of modern Europe itself. The claim, derived from its legitimate place in psychology, that identity is defined in part by contrast with the other, is of little relevance in this respect, if by the 'other' is meant the Muslim world.

To this historical challenge must be added a theoretical critique, namely one that questions the contemporary salience of historical and traditional meaning. Here one can apply to the study of prejudice, and to this prejudice in particular, the theoretical debate that has been applied to nationalist ideology. The nationalist assumption is that such prejudice is perennial, the critique is that it is modern. As with national symbolism and identity, so with transnational antagonism, the past cannot explain the present: the present is rather that which determines the uses to which the past is put as it is selected, ransacked, invented for contemporary purposes. The international relations, or popular attitudes, of the post-1989 world cannot be explained by wordy invocations of such conflicts with Muslims as the Battle of Tours (AD 745) or the Siege of Vienna (1683). Everyone who eats a *croissant*, a shape in the form of a Muslim crescent first baked to commemorate the defeat of the Muslims, is not reproducing this antagonism. Invocation of folk memory, popular culture and identity politics needs to be reinforced by demonstration of *how* this particular sentiment was reproduced. In this sense the frequent resort to historical references, as causes, is unfounded. For all the associations of Muslim states with antagonism there are derivations of another kind – alcohol, coffee, sugar and sherbet (all words taken from Arabic), Turkish baths, Persian gardens and arabesques, harems and odalisques. Anti-Muslim prejudice, as much as any other contemporary ideology, has to be explained by modernist analysis, by reference to contemporary causes.[5]

The claim that the conflict with 'Islam' has replaced the Cold War is, however, often substantiated by reference to the rise of radical, Islamist, movements. This is a more specific argument yet it does not, on closer inspection, get things further. This might seem to confirm the post-Cold War 'vacuum' theory but it is questionable on another ground, namely one of chronology: for, *far from being a product of the post-1989 world*, the emergence of militant Islamism, and of conflict between it and secular forces, is, to a considerable extent, a product of the Cold War itself. In the Cold War both sides sought to use 'Islam' for international purposes. In the aftermath of the Bolshevik Revolution, it was Soviet policy to appeal for *jihad* against British imperialism in India: this was Zinoviev's message at the 1920 Congress of the Peoples of the East in Baku.[6] In the post-1945 world it fell to the West to play this card, against secular nationalist and communist forces in a range of Muslim countries: thus in the 1960s Saudi Arabia, Iran and Pakistan were encouraged to promote conservative Islamic forces against Soviet influence in the Middle East. This was to reach its apogee in the 1980s when, following the Soviet invasion of Afghanistan, the US Central Intelligence Agency (CIA) engaged in its largest ever covert operation (costing over $3 bn) in support of the Afghan opposition, the residue of which has now spread, with disruptive effect, through many Arab countries. Whatever else, this history indicates that the politicization of Islamic movements pre-dated 1989, and cannot therefore be seen as caused by a collapse of the Cold War. It also suggests a rather firm corrective to the view, often articulated by Islamic radicals, that the West has been unremittingly hostile to their interests, and pockets.[7]

If Western states played a role in encouraging Islamism, so too did secular regimes in the Middle East themselves. In retrospect it is striking how many of the Islamist forces that came into prominence in the 1990s within Muslim states were promoted, for tactical considerations, by the states themselves, during the Cold War. This was done for one reason above all, namely as a counter to the left and to secular nationalism. In Pakistan, successive military and civilian regimes sought to use Islamist parties against their opponents. In Turkey in the 1970s the military, faced with strong secular opposition, sanctioned increased activity by the Islamist forces. In Algeria, as a result of factionalism within the Front de Libération National (FLN), President Shadhli Benjadid in the 1980s licensed the Front Islamique du Salut (FIS) to develop a political following. In Israel too the state for a time fostered Islamist opposition as a counter to the secular politics of the Palestine Liberation Organization (PLO). The rise of Islamism cannot be reduced to such state sponsoring, from the West or from the indigenous states, but it is a widespread and significant part of the story.

This interconnection of Cold War and Islamic politics at the international level was reinforced during the same period by a series of trends within Muslim countries themselves that were shaped by the Cold War. The rise of Islamist politics, especially from the 1970s onwards, was in large measure a result of the failure of the politics pursued within these states, by states and oppositions alike. In regard to the former, oppositions developed to the secular states, of left *and* right ones that defined their politics in terms of the internationally legitimated and sustained modernization programmes of the Cold War period. This was as true of the pro-Western Shah of Iran as of the authoritarian nationalist military regime in Egypt or the revolutionary FLN in Algeria. In Indonesia the left nationalist regime of Sukarno was drowned in blood in 1965 in a combined Islamist–military counter-revolution. At the same time, the character of opposition shifted, from secular ideologies, nationalist and communist, to a religious politics because of the defeat of the former by internationally sustained regimes: this was the revenge of the 1953 events in Iran – the CIA- and MI6-backed coup which restored the Shah and crushed the National Front and the Tudeh laid the ground for the advance of Khomeini's Islamist politics a decade later. To compound this process, the Islamists themselves took much, in ideology, programme and organizational form, from their secular opponents. While they deployed elements in the Muslim tradition for political ends, they also incorporated ideas – of imperialism, nationalism, economic change, political organization – from communism and secular nationalism.[8] Islamism was, therefore, to a considerable degree a product of the Cold War itself, not of its passing or end.

This interconnection is evident in regard to one further process often associated with the post-1989 world, namely terrorism and the spread of low-intensity, transnational, forms of violence. Here again, there is, on closer examination, no simple break at the end of the 1980s. Terrorism in the form of assassination, an instrument used worldwide by secular and religious groups, had been prevalent in modern politics for a century at least. It is no prerogative of the Muslim or Middle-Eastern world, as the Irish, the Armenians, Russian populists, Serbian nationalists and many factions in India would be the first to point out. Its resurgence in the Islamic world during the late 1960s and 1970s was very much a product of the Cold War – of the frustration of secular, nationalist and radical groups in Palestine, Iran, Turkey and elsewhere and of inter-ethnic conflict in such countries as Lebanon. The transnational Islamist terrorism that emerged in the 1980s was, in this way, a consequence of an earlier, predominantly secular and nationalist, current.

The one place, significantly, where the Cold War did not produce Islamism was, paradoxically, in the most authoritarian, secular, context of all, namely the USSR: neither under the Soviet system itself, nor, with the exceptions of Tajikistan and Chechnya, in the first decade of the post-Soviet period, did significant Islamist forces emerge in the Muslim republics or amongst the 15 million or so Muslims of Russia. Here, where the West and anti-communist states in the Middle East most hoped for, and predicted, an 'Islamic' revival, politics took another form, of corrupt clientelism at the top, and consumerist and democratic discontent below.

## International relations since 1989

Turning to the post-1989 world, there was certainly much to confirm the views of those who believe in a growing clash between the Muslim and Western worlds, be they proponents of cultural confrontation in the West such as Samuel Huntington, or Islamic fundamentalist advocates of such a confrontation in the East. The conflict with Iraq that began with the latter's invasion of Kuwait in 1990, and a series of subsequent terrorist incidents in Europe and the USA, seemed to add support to this view. Politicians in Europe and the USA talked of the confrontation with Islam, while Islamist politicians in the Muslim world itself echoed this view. The firing of US missiles against targets in Sudan and Afghanistan on 21 August 1998, following attacks on US embassies in Africa, was accompanied by much warning of a future drawn-out war: while former President Clinton was at pains in his statement justifying the strikes to say that this was not a war with the Islamic world, Secretary of State Madeleine Albright talked in starker terms. 'This is going to be a long-term battle against terrorists who have declared war on the United States,' she said. For many in the Muslim world the target was the Muslim world, not sites about which the evidence was, in the Sudanese case especially, uncertain.[9] On the Russian side, the matter was much closer: the USSR had fought a costly war in Afghanistan between 1979 and 1989, and was to face renewed challenges from Islamists in the post-1989 period, culminating in two wars in Chechnya (1994–6, 1999–2000).

One does not, however, have to believe in a common Islamic politics, or any shared international organization of the kind associated with international communism from the 1920s to the 1970s, to identify a shared political sense, a discursive community in which Muslims in different countries identify the West, in whole or in part, as their enemy. This perspective combines attacks on Western imperialism in its historic form with a critique of contemporary politics and of globalization. Within this discursive community, and with local variations, at least eight distinct themes recur: the past, and present, of Western domination and intervention (Iran, for example, was invaded twice in the twentieth century by Britain and Russia); partition of Muslim states – Palestine being the classic case, southern Sudan and the safe haven in Iraq being recent examples, Western intervention in East Timor seen as another; indifference to the sufferings of Muslims – Palestine, Bosnia, Eritrea, Kashmir, Sinjiang; cultural corruption, *fisad*; support for Israel; support for dictatorial regimes; double standards in the application of human rights policies, sanctions and UN Security Council condemnations; diffusion of anti-Muslim stereotypes in the Western press and media.[10]

It sounds like an impressive list of denunciations, and it is. Yet it is only part of the picture. Once the conflict, supposedly unique, between 'Islam and the West' is set in comparative perspective, its supposedly religious or cultural character seems less dominant. For many of the issues on which Muslims denounced the West in the 1990s, expressed as they may have been in Islamic terminology, were not specifically Muslim at all. The sense of anger at Western colonial and post-colonial domination was strong in China, India, Africa and Latin America. Much was made of the Islamic tendency to conspiracy theory, but such a mind-set is far more pervasive than that: examination of the political culture of Serbia or China would yield comparable perspectives. Many Chinese, like others, sometimes see themselves not only as victims but as the *prime* targets of US antagonism. The attack on Western human rights policies for being instrumental and hypocritical was also heard as much in China as it was in the Middle East. Nor was all that put itself forward as Muslim to be taken at face value: Saddam Hussein called for *jihad* and issued postage stamps with his own head next to that of Saladin, the defender of Muslim Jerusalem against the Crusaders; but his was, despite Islamic invocations, a thoroughly secular regime, one that had crushed the religious establishment and opposition in his own country. Whatever else the Revolutionary Command Council of the Arab Ba'ath Socialist Party may be entitled to do, it is most certainly not qualified to issue calls to *jihad*. Elsewhere all was not as it appeared. The vogue for 'Islamic Banking' reflected a specific financial interest, not cultural alterity: in the end, the capital is invested in Western markets.

The same critical argument can be turned around, and applied in this case to the policies of Western states. To put the question baldly, but not inappropriately: how far did culture, and more specifically hostility to Islam as a religion, play a part in determining the foreign policies of Western states over the post-1989 decade, or, for that matter, in the policies of multinational corporations? How far indeed was Islam, as a belief system, seen as a threat to Western interests? At the strategic and economic levels, the answer is an overwhelming negative.[11] The threat posed by individual states was a result of specific military policies they pursued, be they of territorial acquisition or of procurement of weapons of mass destruction. As such the response was no different from that seen in regard to non-Muslim states, Russia during the Cold War, North Korea in the 1990s. Indeed Western military policy showed at times considerable support for Muslim states: NATO carried out in effect three wars in the 1990s – Kuwait in 1991, Bosnia in 1995, Kosovo in 1999 – *all three in defence of Muslim peoples*.

Economically, the Muslim world presented no threat at all. The oil of some Gulf states *was* important, but that had nothing to do with religion. Where the cultural and religious issue did become more salient was in regard to immigration, i.e. to the presence *within* western European states of large numbers of people from Muslim countries. Whether this would have been different – if they had been, say, non-Muslim African, Hindu, Bolivian or Chinese – is debatable. But a degree of cultural resistance was expressed here. Its most concrete manifestation was with regard to Turkish entry into the European

Union. Here no single factor was determinant: it would be impossible to separate out the factors making for European hostility – authoritarian state practices, Turkey's comparatively low level of development, its Islamic character. That culture played *some* role would be difficult to deny. Yet, by the end of 1999, Turkey had obtained the right to put forward its candidacy, not by chance, at an EU summit held in another country, Finland, that had experienced Russian hostility.

In clarifying the Islam–West relationship, it is equally important to get away from the image of a single, united or even co-ordinated, Muslim world. The impression of a growing conflict between Western states and the Muslim world misses the fact that, despite the existence of common sentiments and political links, the Muslim world is itself composed of different states: the Islamic Conference Organization has fifty-four members. They may share a common stance on Palestine, or Bosnia, but that is about it. Interests of state, ethnic rivalries and confessional differences, between Sunni and Shiite Muslims, all play their part. In the 1980s and 1990s and amidst the clamour about an Islamic–Western conflict we saw the development of particularly alarming confrontations between Muslim countries. Iran and Iraq fought a war from 1980 to 1988 in which hundreds of thousands were killed. Iran and Afghanistan came near to war in 1998 after the Taliban government in Afghanistan killed nearly a dozen Iranian diplomats and journalists: here the issues included a long-running rivalry within Afghanistan between the militantly Sunni Taliban and the 15–20 per cent of the population who are Shiites, and a growing sense in Iran that the Taliban were instruments of a Pakistani, and Saudi, expansion into central Asia. Iran reacted as a nationalist state, marshalling troops along the frontier. Its spiritual leader, Khamenei, spoke of the need to defend the interests of what Ayatollah Khomeini had termed *millat-i bozorg-i iran*, 'the great nation of Iran'. The Afghans, towards whom most Iranians retain feelings of superiority, were, Khamenei said, *juhul*, a Koranic term meaning literally 'ignorant', but with the implication of being un-Islamic.

Iran talked after the revolution of 1979 of Islamic solidarity, and supported militant groups in other states. Yet in each case where it did so – Lebanon, Iraq, Afghanistan – it encountered local, state and national opposition. Its own foreign policy showed a flexibility that defies any religious community: thus, in the conflict between Shiite Muslim Azerbaijan and Orthodox Christian Armenia, it was Iran which provided financial and diplomatic, as well as possibly military, assistance to the Armenians. In its long smouldering conflict with Pakistan, brought to the fore in 1998 over Afghanistan, Iran always maintained cordial relations with India. Its relationship with Beijing overrode support for any secessionist movements in Sinjiang.[12]

In other respects too the appearance of a united Muslim world does not correspond to reality. Turkey may be perceived in western European, especially EU, terms as a Muslim state but it has enjoyed scant Muslim solidarity over the years. Many Turks feel that they were stabbed in the back by the Arabs in

World War I, and they have received no significant Arab backing over Cyprus.[13] The escalation of relations with Syria in 1998 demonstrated that here too it is interests of state, not religious solidarity, that shape policy. In Turkey itself and in much of the Muslim world there is a growth of conflict between Sunni and Shiite Muslims: Sunni–Shia tension is an axis of the Iran–Afghan conflict; it is evident in communal killings in Pakistan, in the growth of tribal and sectarian politics inside Iraq and in social tensions inside Saudi Arabia and Bahrain. The force with which many in the Arab Sunni world have sympathized with the Taliban against Iran is an index of how deep these tensions run.

Nowhere is this variety of responses more central than in regard to the issue that led to the American missile attacks of 1998, fundamentalism.[14] Fundamentalists in the Islamic world, like their counterparts in the Hindu, Judaic and Christian worlds, denounce foreigners and alien corruption. But their prime target is within their own society, the secular forces in their midst: the battle to which Secretary of State Albright referred is at its core internal to the Muslim world. The main cause of the growth of fundamentalism is dissatisfaction with the post-independence, modernizing, secular state. This is as true of the revolt against the FLN in Algeria as it was of the Islamic revolution in Iran.

## Cultural conflict and inter-state relations

So far the discussion has examined the historical and post-1989 role of 'Islam' in international relations. To locate the argument about this within an IR context, and in particular to relate it to the shifts within IR of recent years, it is not sufficient, however, to show that international relations are not determined by culture.[15] It is necessary to look critically at the vocabulary in which the question is discussed. Here we come to the distortions involved in the very terms used, 'West' and 'Islam'. First of all, there is no one 'West', any more than there is one 'East'. There are different cultures and nations within the West, and different views, from conservative to liberal and socialist, of how the world should be ordered. The history of conflict between East and West has been paralleled, throughout modern history, by conflicts within the West – the great revolutions and social movements, whose agendas continue to this day, by wars, by debates on how to order society. There is no *one* Western position on, say, rights or market–state relations. The history of the Arab world is also marked by such upheavals and debates. Islam, supposedly monolithic and timeless, has been rent by differences of interpretation and, one might suggest, interest. Beyond the five core injunctions of the Islamic faith, the Koran does *not* allow for any one reading especially on social and political issues.[16] These debates within Europe or the Arab world, or Iran, are as important, intellectually and politically, as the conflict between them.

In the Islamic world the main target of fundamentalists is internal. We see this in, for example, Iran: Khomeini's 'cultural revolution' was, like that of Mao in China, supposedly directed against foreign influence but was in fact mainly against literary and ideological currents within Iran that he did not like. The best way to silence internal critics is always to brand them as agents of a foreign power. Writers like Huntington are wrong to draw their conclusions from this delegitimation: the enemy is as much within as without. Neo-traditionalist movements are directed against internal foes – this is true of Hindu revivalism in India, of the religious right in Israel, and of the 80 million Christian fundamentalists in the USA. We must also look at the political and social interests being served by this internal call to order – it is not the culture which explains what is happening.

There are, as we have seen, certain recurrent themes in Islamic discourses: a critique of Western domination and corruption, solidarity with Palestine, a socially conservative position on women, an appeal to a virtuous people, transnationally constituted, and variously described as *mostazafin, umma, mo'minin*.[17] These movements also influence each other. But there are enormous differences, too. Take the example of the caliphate, the *khilafat* – some Islamists advocate this but they would not be advised to propagate it in Mecca or Iran. Khomeini's regime has both *velayat-i faqih*, the authority of the religious 'jurisconsult', and a strong, institutionalized, degree of popular suffrage. Some Algerian fundamentalists say they want *al-mujtama'al-risali*, 'prophetic society', though no one is sure what this means. There are as many political programmes as there are movements – above all because, for all the common influences and culture, they operate in distinct countries, with specific histories and political systems.

Islamic fundamentalists make an argument whose premises are similar to those of Western cultural essentialists: they argue that there is a common programme, indeed that there must be, because all such programmes are derived from the founding texts of Islam. Huntington, for his part, claims that Muslims see the world in terms of two categories, the *dar al-harb*, or house of war, and the *dar al-islam*.[18]

The claim that Islam as a religion is identical with Islam as a political or social system is, however, unsustainable, as examination of the historical, and contemporary, records shows: we must look at what people do, not what they say or believe they are doing.[19] First of all, the history of the Islamic world shows a great variety of political and social forms, as does the contemporary Islamic world.[20] The history of the Muslim empires, from the seventh century onwards, is of the consolidation of states, along tribal, factional and ethnic lines, using religion to justify the legitimacy of these states, to enjoin submission and to exclude others. You can, of course, write a purely religious history of the Muslim world from the *hijra* onwards, but you can also write a secular one: the Abbasid revolution, or the rise and fall of the Fatimids, need not be explained in religious terms, indeed it is hard to do so, except in very general terms of purity and corruption. In the contemporary world the same applies: no paper in any Muslim country divides its news coverage into *dar al-harb* and *dar al-islam*. If Islam explained political and social behaviour you would have a unity of political and social life, which you most certainly do not. The great richness of the Muslim world is its variety.[21]

A theory of international relations based on a clash of civilizations is a bad argument. Culture has, as already noted, rarely been the basis for conflict in the international system and is not so today. Conflict has been more between states of similar cultural orientation: look at China and Japan, Germany and France, Iran and Iraq. Here is the falsity, a pernicious falsity, of Huntington's claim that 'Islam has bloody borders'.[22] This is doubly false in that many of the conflicts in the Muslim world are internal, and because where there has been conflict along cultural lines it is often the non-Muslim protagonists who have the main responsibility – in the Balkans, India, Palestine, Burma.

There is, moreover, a misleading use of history in Huntington's argument. He seems to assume that cultures, civilizations or whatever are given, like blocks of colour on the map. But they are not. They are defined and redefined by each generation, in response to current concerns, and are defined by some people at the expense of others. This applies to the invocation of 'Asian values' in the Far East. The phenomena being invoked as specifically Asian – high savings ratios, family values, deference to government – are contemporary phenomena articulated to meet current needs of those in power. But as Chris Patten, the former governor of Hong Kong, put it, their main use is often for one group of people to tell another group to be silent. In the Islamic world we see that those in power resort to religion to justify their hold on power, or, when people are out of power, to justify their claim to it. Culture is flexible and instrumental. We should look at the structures of power, and wealth, in states, societies and families, and see in whose interests all this invocation of culture and tradition is: a sociology, and history, of culture is preferable to the assertion of timeless identities.

## IR theory and the politics of culture

An informed, and sober, look at the reality *and* diversity of this culture may help to resolve some of the broader confusions that beset much contemporary discussion of international relations. Demonstrating the limits of the 'Islam versus the West' argument is not, therefore, sufficient to locate its place in the analysis of the post-1989 world. Rather, the critique of this idea should serve as a path to identify deeper issues within contemporary international relations which this myth expresses. Here one may identify four of these, four aspects of contemporary politics, and *Zeitgeist*, which underlie a discussion of cultural clash.

First is the question of how far we can talk at all, in broad macro-historical terms, of different civilizations and cultures and their impact on international relations. The division of the world into separate and static cultural spheres is a modern, invented, creation, but no less effective for all that. Of course there are different languages, religions, races and literatures but they change and have always interacted and borrowed from each other. An example is the interaction of Greek political thought with medieval Islam: the early Arab political theorist al-Farabi's (AD 870–950) concept of *al-madina al-fadhila*, the 'just city', is a link between the classical Greek concept, Islamic thinking, and modern concepts of civil society and democracy. We can look at religion: the two central ideas in the current concept of human rights are the moral value of the individual, and the need to limit the power of the state, in extreme cases the right to revolt against the state. Both are present in the religions of the Middle East: Europe took them from Judaism, Christianity and Islam. Another example is mathematics: at the point of the millennial transition, the world was obsessed with the Y2K 'Millennium Bug', the problem of computers adjusting to the year 2000. Central to this problem was the number zero: it is an Indian invention, which reached Europe in the twelfth century. The word 'cipher' is itself derived from the Arabic for zero, *sifr*. What is today presented as a 'Western' politics or mathematics or food is a product of cultural inter-action.

There is, moreover, a questionable normative principle at work here, which I have termed 'the fallacy of origin'. The fact that something originated in one part of the world does not mean it cannot be taken up and applied in others. To take two simple examples: no one complains during the World Cup that football is an English invention or golf Scottish; equally no one objects to the principle of national self-determination and the sovereignty of states. All over the world, whatever the culture, these ideas are accepted. The argument that democracy originated in the West is distinct from the argument that it can only exist in the West. Moreover, so much of what is today presented as against the West is influenced by it: Khomeini's political thought borrowed from Marxism and populism. A careful study of what appear, in the contemporary world, to be 'alternative', 'subaltern', 'authentic' voices reveals far more shared, 'thin', vocabulary and concept, moulded to local use, than at first sight appears.[23]

Secondly, in contradistinction to the argument on cultural blocs and fault-lines, we may be able to give more substance, as regards internal processes and with proper regard to the conflicts of interests involved, to an international sociology of values. We can, with due caution, speak about global values and a global field of discourse, partly as a result of the shared challenges of the modern world (everyone needs an ethics of traffic codes, or banking, or parental responsibility for children), partly as a result of the diffusion of values, through conquest and struggle, across the world. All countries in the world are part of a single world economy, a single information system and, increasingly, a world which professes shared norms: every state that is a member of the UN adheres to the defence of certain values. All states, and peoples, are formally committed to economic prosperity, to peace. We are all within the same system, and so cannot prosper if the rest of the system does not. This approach includes but is broader than the 'international society' (of states) discussed by the 'English School' of international relations. Beyond the 'international society' model, we can identify a world of conflicting interests. The shared discourse is a sign not so much of common interests but of a language within which conflict can be expressed.

Thirdly, we may come to an argument that was recurrent during discussion in the 1990s and which persists beyond, particularly with regard to the Islamic world. This is the supposedly appealing, but actually facile, resort to the 'necessary threat' argument. According to this view, the West lost an enemy in communism, after 1989, and has had to reinvent one in the form of Islam. This has both a specific, historical, version and a broader, transhistorical, socio-psychological, one.

This is not a convincing argument, for several reasons. First of all, the Western world did not invent the communist threat: it was not a case of projection or misperception. It existed, as Lenin, Stalin, Khrushchev, even Brezhnev, would have been the first to state themselves. The USSR did participate in an arms race, and a competition for influence in the Third World, that was not illusory. Moreover, the underlying assumption of this 'necessary threat' argument is that somehow the Western world needs a threat, an external enemy. Of course, external challenge can galvanize states and societies: war and economic competition formed the modern state. But what the West, in the form of the industrialized democracies, wants is basically a world as much like itself as possible, with which it can trade, enjoy peaceful relations and so on. It was Voltaire who in his *Lettres Philosophiques* (no. 6) said that 'in the market place there is no Christian, no Mohammedan, no Jew. The only infidel is the bankrupt.' This is the truth of what Marx and Engels wrote in the *Communist Manifesto*, that capitalism transforms the world in its own image. Within this there are threats, but they are those as much as anything of economic competition: if there is a threat to the West today it comes from the industrialization of East Asia and the shift of power to the Pacific. On this scale, the Middle East is marginal – it is, with Africa, largely outside the economic transformations of recent times. Here the 'Islamic' is not a meaningful category at all. Oil money has masked this marginalization, but in comparative terms the Middle East has missed out on the changes in the world economy over the past three decades except in so far as it has invested, to the tune of $800 billion, in the West. This is what makes talk of an Islamic threat so false. It should also lead one to doubt how far the kinds of solution being proposed by fundamentalists or cultural nationalists in the Middle East really address the problem. They do not, it can be argued, have an answer on this front.

Finally, we return to the issue of myth, of what one may term 'transnational paranoia' itself. Here again we enter a world of the transhistorical and the particular: each country, or political culture, sees its own tendency in this regard as peculiar. One can, for example, contrast literature on Islamic political myths with the literature on the paranoid, the alarmist, the fearful in American politics – the latter also ascribed to deep substratum religious, in this case Puritan, tendencies in American political life.[24] Much writing on the place of conspiracy theory in Middle East politics – an unavoidable fact of life, fuelled by globalization and contemporary change – also abstracts it from its modern, and material, context.[25] A similar resort, to explanation in terms of the 'atavistic', is found in much literature on nationalism – not least that of liberal critics who wish to discredit nationalism by casting it as a hangover from an earlier, irrational, age.

The critical reflex can, however, be applied here: to be comparative, not singular, to be modernist, not transhistorical. The cultures of paranoia have a historical component, and historical causes, but their resurgence in the contemporary post-1989 world reflects contemporary, and transnational, factors. On the one hand, the context in which issues of domestic concern, notably migration, are confused with issues of international politics; on the other, an intellectual climate where wild, even 'global', claims are made without recourse to empirical or historical perspective. In all of this, of course, such arguments are abetted by a carelessly and whimsically formulated 'cultural turn' in social theory, and IR, a tendency that places primacy on hypostasized forms of culture, even as it dispenses with conventional criteria of historical and substantive verification. The New Agenda should not be a licence for a New, and not so New, Confusion.

## NOTES

1  Abdelwahab El-Affendi, 'Islam and the Future of Dissent after the "End of History"', *Futures*, 31 (1999); Bobby Sayyid, *A Fundamental Fear: Ethnocentrism and the Emergence of Islam* (London, Zed, 1997). For a judicious survey see Fawaz Gerges, *America and Political Islam: Clash of Cultures or Clash of Interests?* (Cambridge, Cambridge University Press, 1999).
2  Samuel Huntington, *The Clash of Civilizations and the Remaking of World Order* (New York, Simon & Schuster, 1996). For an extreme European nationalist view, casting the Islamic threat as part of an American assault on Europe, see Alexandre del Valle, *Islamisme et États-Unis. Une alliance contre l'Europe* (Lausanne, Editions L'Âge d'Homme, 1997).
3  Here I summarize arguments made elsewhere, notably in Fred Halliday, *Islam and the Myth of Confrontation* (London, I. B. Tauris, 1996); *Nation and State in the Middle East* (London, al-Saqi, 2000); 'The Politics of "Islam" – A Second Look', *British Journal of Political Studies*, 25 (1995), pp. 399–417; 'Islamophobia Reconsidered', *Ethnic and Racial Studies*, 22, 5 (1999).

4    See Halliday, *Islam and the Myth of Confrontation*, ch. 6.
5    I have gone into this in greater detail in ibid., chs 6 and 7.
6    Hélène Carrère d'Encausse and Stuart Schram, *Marxism and Asia: An Introduction with Readings* (London, Allen Lane, 1969), pp. 170–8.
7    On the CIA support for the Afghan guerrillas see James Scott, *Deciding to Intervene: The Reagan Doctrine and American Foreign Policy* (London, Duke University Press, 1996), and the memoirs of former CIA director Robert Gates, *From the Shadows* (New York, Simon & Schuster, 1996).
8    On the modernity of Islamist ideas, and their debt to secular radical and at times Leninist themes, see Ervand Abrahamian, *Khomeinism* (London, I. B. Tauris, 1993); Sami Zubaida, *Islam, the People and the State* (London, Routledge, 1989); Bassam Tibi, *The Crisis of Modern Islam* (Salt Lake City, University of Utah Press, 1988); Aziz al-Azmeh, *Islam and Modernities* (London, Verso, 1993); Olivier Roy, *The Failure of Political Islam* (London, I. B. Tauris, 1994); Giles Kepel, *The Revenge of God* (Cambridge, Polity, 1994).
9    The US government later conceded that the attack on the Sudanese site was unjustified. See also 'A Year Later, US Officials' Doubts over Sudan Bombing Surface', *International Herald Tribune*, 28 October 1999.
10   For one account of an often diffuse indictment, see Yvonne Yazbech Haddad, 'Islamist Perceptions of US Policy in the Middle East', in David Lesch (ed.), *The Middle East and the United States* (Oxford, Westview Press, 1996). On US cinematic portrayal of Arabs, Charles Glass, 'A Prejudice as American as Apple Pie', *New Statesman*, 20 November 1998.
11   See Gerges, *America and Political Islam*; see note 1 above, for clarification on this.
12   Iranian foreign policy since 1979 has been an interplay of national, revolutionary and religious themes, in which the implicit internationalism of the latter two has been subordinated to interests of state. See Ruhollah Ramazani, *Revolutionary Iran: Challenge and Response in the Middle East*, 2nd edn (London, Johns Hopkins University Press, 1988). On the interplay of religion and state interests see Wilfried Buchta, *Die iranische Schi'a und die internationale Politik* (Hamburg, Deutsches Orient-Institut, 1997).
13   See Nicole and Hugh Pope, *Turkey Unveiled: Atatürk and After* (London, John Murray, 1997), for a lucid discussion that includes the role of Islam, and Islamist parties in Turkey, without reducing all of social and political life to cultural determinants.
14   See references in note 8, also Fred Halliday, 'Religious Fundamentalism in Contemporary Politics', in Patricia Fara et al. (eds), *The Changing World* (Cambridge, Cambridge University Press, 1996).
15   For a trenchant discussion of these themes see Ken Booth, 'Three Tyrannies', in Tim Dunne and Nicholas J. Wheeler (eds), *Human Rights in Global Politics* (Cambridge, Cambridge University Press, 1999). I have discussed the treatment by IR of culture in Michi Ebata and Beverly Neufeld (eds), *Confronting the Political in International Relations* (London, Macmillan, 2000).
16   Nasr Hamid abu Zeid, 'The Modernisation of Islam or the Islamisation of Modernity', in Roel Meijer (ed.), *Cosmopolitanism, Identity and Authenticity in the Middle East* (Richmond, Surrey, Curzon Press, 1999); Women Living under Muslim Laws, *For Ourselves: Women Reading the Qur'an* (Grabels, France,

1997). For an astute work of political theory that none the less allows reified categories of the West and Islam see Roxane Euben, *Enemy in the Mirror: Islamic Fundamentalism and the Limits of Modern Rationalism* (Princeton, NJ, Princeton University Press, 1999).

17  Meaning, respectively, 'oppressed', 'community', 'faithful'.

18  Huntington, *The Clash of Civilizations*, p. 264.

19  This is persuasively argued in Michael Gilsenan's *Recognizing Islam* (London, I. B. Tauris, 1990), a closely observed account of Muslim practices which never relies on holy texts. See also Dale Eickleman and James Piscatori, *Muslim Politics* (Princeton, NJ, Princeton University Press, 1996), and Stephen Humphreys, *Between Memory and Desire: The Middle East in a Troubled Age* (Berkeley, CA, University of California Press, 1999), for two other cogent demystifications of Islamic political or social essence.

20  One example among many is the Muslim attitude to monarchy, something that varied across centuries and countries, and which is as subject to external non-Muslim imitation and example, and to pressures of local interest, as to any doctrinal essence. Aziz al-Azmih, *Muslim Kingship* (London, I. B. Tauris, 1998). The holy texts are of no use here since they can be used to argue for everything.

21  On the variety, and the modern, socio-economic, formation of the Middle East, see Simon Bromley, *Rethinking the Middle East* (Cambridge, Polity, 1994); Roger Owen, *State, Power and the Politics in the Making of the Modern Middle East* (London, Routledge, 1992); Halim Barkat, *The Arab World: Society, Culture and State* (London, University of California Press, 1993).

22  Huntington, *The Clash of Civilizations*, pp. 54–8.

23  Mention has already been made, in note 8, of the modernity of Khomeini. A similar argument could be applied to Gandhi, who borrowed much from Tolstoy. For the transnational influences on another supposedly authentic exemplar of alterity see Wolfgang Deckers, 'Imperialism and Anti-Imperialism in the Thought of Mao Tse-tung', PhD thesis, LSE (1997).

24  Richard Hofstadter, *The Paranoid Style in American Politics and Other Essays* (New York, Knopf, 1965); David Larsen, *The Puritan Ethic in United States Foreign Policy* (London, Van Nostrand, 1966).

25  Richard Pipes, *The Hidden Hand: Middle East Fears of Conspiracy* (London, Macmillan, 1996).

# 4

# Globalization and the Discourse of Women's Human Rights: *Transgressing Boundaries in a Post-Cold War World*

## *Jill Steans*

## Introduction

The late 1980s undoubtedly marked a significant turning point in the study of international relations. The breaching of the Berlin Wall and the mass trespass across a boundary which had been considered inviolable had an immediate impact on a discipline profoundly shaped by the Cold War. The ensuing transgression of boundaries and renegotiation of political space has provoked discontent with the limitations of great power politics analyses and the constraints of realist discourse. In recent years, the discipline of international relations (IR) has been characterized by a multiplicity of new approaches.[1] The opening up of theoretical debates in the past decade or so has also challenged state-centrism in the study of international relations, as evidenced in the large number of recent IR texts with the terms 'global' or 'globalization' in their title.[2]

The end of the Cold War and contemporary globalization have created a favourable climate in which to articulate 'new agendas'. In this context, human rights has moved to the forefront of debate. Of course, discussion about human rights is not new. Interest in human rights within the broad domain of IR pre-dates the collapse of communism and the waning of Soviet influence in world politics.[3] However, historically human rights has been regarded as somewhat peripheral to the agenda of international politics. The international realm has been viewed as the realm of anarchy in which the imperatives of security take precedence over the demands of justice or right. During the Cold War, human rights was employed as an ideological weapon or a tool of foreign policy by the USA against the Soviet Union and its 'satellite' states, and this seemed further to justify their marginalization in the study of IR.

As with all periods of seemingly radical change, one can also identify continuities. Despite the rather sceptical view of the relevance of human rights to IR, the United Nations (UN) actually played an active role in promoting human rights throughout the Cold War period. Indeed, since 1945, the UN has served as a central source of human rights through its conventions on economic, social and cultural rights and civil and political rights. In the context of the ideological strife and political division of the Cold War, the content of human rights was disputed. Nevertheless, there was a large degree of consensus among governments across the world, on the principle at least that certain rights should be protected under international law. Thus, even during the period of Cold War polarization, a set of rights capable of commanding the agreement of people across the globe was established.[4]

Moreover, human rights has been linked to major global issues since at least the 1969 'Proclamation of Tehran'.[5] What is 'new' is the explicit linkage which is being made between human rights and globalization. It has been argued that the language of human rights has moved in to fill the gap left by the demise of grand political narratives in the aftermath of the Cold War.[6] Friedman suggests that the decline of unifying ideologies since the end of the Cold War has led to a search for new ones, because people need to identify with a movement that crosses national boundaries and has some common values.[7] In consequence, human rights must now be seen as one of the most globalized political values of our time.[8]

Since the concept of globalization has no firm disciplinary home, inevitably attempts to think about human rights in a global context have encouraged the transgression of disciplinary boundaries too. Globalization has provided a new context in which to reframe older debates in IR. The globalization of the discourse of human rights is indicative of the degree to which the boundaries of international law have been displaced. Whereas people were once treated as objects of international law, individuals and groups are now recognized as subjects of the law, who hold international rights against their own governments.[9] Sociologists have also turned their attention to the challenges which globalization presents for thinking about the boundaries of society and the values which tie people together.[10] Even the field of cultural anthropology has been stirred by the phenomenon of globalization, as the discourse of human rights has served to re-pose questions of universalism and cultural relativism.[11]

This chapter begins by mapping out the interconnected social, political, economic and normative dimensions of globalization and draws out explicitly the implications for human rights. It then turns specifically to the growing demands for the promotion and protection of women's human rights. In focusing on contemporary globalization and struggles to promote a women's human rights agenda, this chapter illustrates how a concern with prevailing gender relations and the status of women necessarily involves the transgression of conceptual and territorial boundaries and the (re)articulation of political spaces. In conclusion, this chapter reflects on the main implications of gender studies and feminist theorizing for the future development of IR.

## Gender and globalization

Just as globalization has no privileged disciplinary context, there is no single, widely accepted definition of the term.[12] Most commentators agree that the term 'globalization' addresses the increasing transnational dimensions of economic, social and political life impelled by technological change, the globalization of production and the increasingly global scope of communications technologies.[13] Jameson and Miyoshi define globalization as the enlargement of world communications, as well as the horizon of world markets, both of which are held to be far more tangible and immediate than the earlier stages of modernity.[14]

The analysis of globalization and human rights cannot be divorced from issues of power. Marxists have long noted the link between globalization and the expansion of capitalism. Capitalism is seen as the major transformative force shaping the modern world. In this view, the building blocks of a theory of globalization are transnational corporations, the increasing global division of labour, the emergence of global markets, the dominance of a transnational capitalist class in the political sphere and the increasing prevalence of a culture of consumerism.[15] In the industrial societies of the modern world, consumption has long been a key means of creating a dominant culture. Increasingly, societies across the world are based upon consumerist values, where, according to Sklair, no one and nothing seems immune from commodification, commercialization, being bought and sold.[16] In the developing world, the activities of transnational corporations, transnational investment, global restructuring and the creation of global markets are legitimized by dominant discourses of globalization, modernization and progress. In much of the so-called developing world, institutions like the International Monetary Fund (IMF) and World Bank are working to promote the interests of sections of global capital, pushing structural adjustment policies on the reluctant governments of poor people. The ideology of neo-liberalism, which informs the enframing of orthodox development theory, has similarly been described as a globalizing discourse, characterized by the significance attached to private property and market relations, and which generates a culture of possessive individualism.[17]

Marchand argues that in theoretical terms feminist analysis makes a major contribution to our understanding of globalization by investigating its interconnected material, ideological and discursive dimensions and by offering more complex 'sightings' or conceptual renderings of global restructuring.[18] For a long time, there has been a feminist literature which has charted the continual failure of development strategies to improve the material conditions of women's lives.[19] There is now a growing literature which draws attention to the frequently negative impact of economic globalization on women.[20] A central feature of the global economic, social and political order is the naturalization of women's social subordination and the marginalization of women's labour.[21] 'Women's work' is frequently unpaid and so does not appear in *public* statistics, and it has not, historically, been deemed to be part of the activities of states, markets and international institutions which collectively constitute the 'global order'.[22] However, the contribution of women's labour is significant not only in national terms, but increasingly in global terms. In the contemporary global economy, restructuring debt, even the negotiation of trade agreements, can and does have a gender-specific impact.[23]

Although gender relations appear locked into the private or cultural sphere, states and international institutions are involved in the social and political institutionalization of gendered differences by confirming and institutionalizing the arrangements that distinguish the public from the private.[24] States have been active agents structuring the exploitation of women for their own benefit. Women have been manipulated as a socio-economic resource in post-colonial states which are increasingly driven by the imperatives of economic development.[25] A phenomenon of contemporary global political economy has been the 'rolling back' of the state and welfare services. This has impacted on women across the world, because women have taken on a greater burden of care. Along with the emergence of national and global markets and the decline of the subsistence household around the world, there has been a privatization of the intimate sphere – the care of the old and the sick.[26]

The changing global division of labour, and the public and private identities and roles which underpin it, is being shaped and reshaped by globalization.[27] Feminist analyses of globalization introduce questions of subjectivity and identity into an otherwise abstract discussion of the globalization of states and markets. Globalization has certainly opened up opportunities for women, who are entering the paid workforce in increasing numbers. Moreover, globalization exposes more and more of the world's peoples to 'outside' influences, including images and ideas about what it is to be 'male' or 'female' and the possibilities which this opens up or closes off for individuals. Historically, Western liberal feminism has advocated an emancipatory politics whereby women are 'liberated' by escaping from the family and negotiating new identities in the public realm. In the context of 'restructuring' in post-Cold War central and eastern Europe, True has argued that new opportunities have opened up for women to negotiate new identities, and that this might be a source of emancipation.[28]

However, participation in the formal economy either as workers or as consumers and the 'freedom to choose' should not be confused with 'emancipation'. While capitalism might espouse certain liberal, egalitarian values, the changes associated with globalization and restructuring can also work to 'privatize' women's labour and, consequently, result in a loss of power and autonomy.[29] Women are contributing to the global economy in terms of both their unpaid and paid labour, and so shoulder a double or triple burden in terms of overall workload. Moreover, as True herself acknowledges, increases in prostitution, trafficking in women and the objectification of women's bodies in a thriving pornography industry have also accompanied the move to market economies in the former Eastern bloc. Globalization, then, inevitably raises questions about the impact on cultural and social practices, changing gender relations and the construction of gendered identities. However, questions about whether globalization is 'good' or 'bad' for women are not easily answered.

## Globalization, human rights and cultural 'imperialism'

Robertson, who is widely credited with the first use or invention of the term 'globalization', chose to articulate its meaning not only in terms of transnational processes, networks or political and economic structures and social forms, but also in terms of a global vision, ethic and consciousness of the world.[30] Proponents of globalization make a number of related claims. First, globalization is breaking down the boundaries and divisions which have long separated and divided humankind. Second, and consequently, many contemporary problems which beset the human race need to be theorized in a global context. Third, this has significant implications for how we pose normative questions, including those of justice and 'rights'. Just as there are competing conceptions of globalization, there are differing views on whether globalization is a source of emancipation or of transnational domination. The globalization of human rights raises this question directly. Do debates about human rights provide evidence of the emergence of a global society or global moral community? Or is the articulation of a global society or community just another Western project – another manifestation of Western imperialism?

One manifestation of imperialism has been, if not the imposition of Western cultural values, at least a disposition among Westerners to look down on the rest of the world from a position of assumed moral superiority. The 'rightness' or 'oppressiveness' of social and cultural practices have been judged from the point of view of a Western experience, presented as a 'universal' standard. The Kantian conception of human rights rests upon universal rationalist foundations which serve as the basis for generalizable norms and categories of justice.[31] The thrust of the Enlightenment project has been to protest against the needless, senseless suffering inflicted on humans in nature in the name of some greater good or larger community, and on the unnecessary constraints on human freedom and autonomy. For universalists of all kinds, contemporary globalization adds further weight to the claim that there are no good reasons why the boundaries of moral community should be drawn more narrowly than around the whole human race.[32]

Law in the Kantian sense represents an imperfect, or gradual, actualization of the Transcendental Idea. Therefore, in this view, 'the Rights of Man' have no history, or specific cultural context, but rather impose the final goal and direction to History.[33] Throughout the Cold War, human rights served as a powerful rhetorical resource in US foreign policy.[34] Human rights were also used as a yardstick in measuring the degree of development or modernization – respect for human rights was seen both as a constituent element in the overall 'quality of life' issue and as a measure of how far any society has come in realizing a just society.[35] In this view, Fukuyama's 'End of History and the Last Man' can be viewed as a powerful example of post-Cold War Western triumphalism.[36]

The contemporary human rights movements clearly draw on Western concepts of law and legality. Marx critiqued rights discourse as a manifestation of bourgeois individualism, pointing out that law had served as a mode of control, establishing and enforcing property rights and organizing the economic and social relations on the basis of 'free' contracts. In so doing, law had worked to legitimize and perpetuate exploitative social relationships. Contemporary Gramscian analysis of globalization is fiercely critical of prevailing ideas because dominant ideologies are an important element in keeping people subordinate. Capitalist hegemony relies on a balance of consent and coercion, so subordinated groups must be persuaded to support the prevailing order. From this perspective, then, framing problems of inequality, political oppression, poverty and insecurity in terms of human rights obscures the exploitative nature of capitalism. Capitalism is really subversive of human rights, because it generates structural relationships of inequality. Feminists have also criticized rights discourse, claiming that it is rooted in a male point of view which is taken as the standard for universality.

As Legesse suggests, the parallels with imperialism and human rights have been too close for comfort.[37] This raises the question: is the concept of universal human rights appropriate for what is still, after all, a diverse, heterogeneous, multicultural world? Historically, anthropologists have tended to position themselves in critical opposition to universal values and transnational processes such as human rights, believing them to be ethnocentric extensions of absolutism. All power tends to justify itself and the Western discourse of freedom, progress and rights has served to disguise the political, economic and cultural domination of certain social groups in the West, and domination of the West over the rest of the world.[38] Critics of human rights discourse also point to the historically and culturally bounded notion of rights. Relativists claim that international human rights law is fundamentally grounded in individual rights and so inflexible and unable to respond to the diversity of global legal systems, having, for example, a normative blindness to indigenous peoples.[39]

However, this is not an entirely accurate picture of the status of human rights in the world. The notion that the discourse of human rights is merely an extension of masculine, bourgeois or Western values can be challenged on a number of grounds.[40] During the past few decades there has been a gradual but sustained rise in the application of international human rights law, as well as the extension of a wider public discourse on human rights. At a time when human rights violations have become subjected to global scrutiny, cultural relativists have often found themselves compelled to defend certain practices considered cruel and inhumane, and not just from a Western perspective. The recent wave of post-colonial and postmodern critiques of Western discourse and political practice in the context of colonial and imperialist expansion has proved to be a valuable and much needed corrective to universalist claims. In recent controversies over practices like genital mutilation, feminist demands that women must be protected have been juxtaposed against the claims of cultural relativism. At the same time, it is no easy task to distinguish between 'legitimate' expressions of identity, community and culture, which should be celebrated, and the (ab)use of 'culture' and 'tradition' to obscure the misuse of power.

In calling for the recognition, promotion and protection of women's human rights, feminists have challenged what is conventionally thought of as culture or 'private'.[41] Clearly the cultural context is crucial in understanding the specificity of gender relations and cultural practices.[42] However, the cultural relativist position seems to rely upon the notion of culture as unchanging. Culture can be viewed as a set of practices and norms that underpin material structures or as a series of constantly contested and negotiated social practices. In either conceptualization, culture is not seen as essential, authentic or static. Cultural practices change over time, in accordance with the needs, demands and circumstances of peoples at particular times in history.

Similarly, cultures and societies cannot be viewed as bounded, isolated entities.[43] As Erikson claims, the idea that people are neatly divided into bounded nation-states has always been something of a fantasy.[44] While the impact of globalization is uneven and the relationship between global trends and national specificities is never simple, one consequence of globalization is the increasing difficulty of maintaining any social or cultural tradition 'in the traditional way'.[45] Globalization evokes images of hybridity and suggests possible openings for new means and contexts of identity formation – periods of rapid transformation and flux – in which people are forced constantly to remake their identities. Under such conditions, people are more likely to question the prevailing social and political order and the dictates of tradition. Appeals to culture and tradition lose their legitimacy simply because tradition is the way of the past.[46]

If culture is understood as a set of practices and beliefs that are open to change by human beings on the basis of political interventions conforming to the possibilities and needs produced by socio-economic change, then it is possible to link questions of culture and the expansion of human rights discourse directly with processes of globalization. It would be misleading simply to equate globalization with homogenization, or Westernization. It is not the case that in the wake of globalization societies across the world are wholeheartedly embracing Western, liberal values.

In some circumstances, these same forces can provoke a backlash in the form of nationalist or fundamentalist movements which feel threatened by the onslaught of capitalism and the individualistic values which it promotes. At such times the position and role of women assumes a crucial place in dominant discourses of identity and in the drawing of cultural boundaries.[47] When conflicts arise between different legitimate categorizations of social cohesion, the question about which should prevail is inevitably raised and not easily answered.

For this reason, the notion that the realization of women's human rights is the ultimate vindication of the 'end of history' thesis should be treated with some scepticism.[48] However, after successive waves of colonial expansion, 'modernization' and, latterly, globalization, there are no longer 'cultures' for whom the values of the West are totally alien or irrelevant. The debate about women's human rights certainly demands that questions of culture and difference be taken seriously. Indeed, as Kothari argues, the current debate about women's human rights suggests the greatest challenge is to marry respect for identities with the requirements of justice. At the same time, this debate also illustrates how a cultural relativist position is becoming difficult to defend in the face of feminist and human rights activists' demands for global attention to practices such as violence against women.[49]

While there is no Archimedean viewpoint from which to judge the rightness or justness of specific cultural practices, those which seemingly flout human rights must be justified and defended in dialogue with other traditions in the public sphere.[50] In recent times, universalists have been forced to defend their position. Perhaps it is now time to subject the claims made in the name of culture and tradition to critical scrutiny? Is it now incumbent upon relativists to answer the charge that ultimately their position does not take into account the issue of power and, moreover, does not allow for the possibility of change?

## The dynamism of human rights

The view that human rights are a Western invention of no relevance to people in the non-Western world can be disputed on the grounds that human rights discourse is a dynamic and changing one with considerable critical potential. As suggested above, women's human rights discourse has historically been used to articulate the issues that Western middle-class men fear.[51] However, while the concept of rights emerged at a particular historical moment and rights were defined in terms of the needs of a limited section of the population, human rights, like all vibrant visions, are not static, nor the property of any one group. Human rights can be understood as continually transformed as a result of struggles over political, symbolic or economic resources both within a state and in a transnational or global context.[52]

The discourse of rights has been a crucial resource for 'counter-hegemonic' or oppositional groups. In taking up the language of human rights, oppositional groups have transformed the concept to address problems of environmental degradation, threats to human dignity, the right to life, the security of person and, of course, gender inequalities.[53] Rather than simply dismissing rights discourse as ideological mystification, it is important to recognize that the discourse of human rights requires individuals to be treated equally regardless of how they are situated within a set of social relations.[54] As such, Chinkin argues, rights discourse provides a familiar and symbolically powerful vocabulary to challenge political and societal wrongs. In this view human rights is not a possession of the West, but an open text capable of appropriation and redefinition by groups who are players in the global legal arena.[55] Bunch claims that the dynamism of human rights and their ongoing relevance stems from the fact that more people are claiming them and, in so doing, expanding the meaning of rights to incorporate their own hopes and needs.[56]

It was pointed out earlier in this chapter that there has been a gradual expansion of the concept of human rights and an expansion of the domain of human rights legislation. The broadening conception of rights has contributed to the global spread of human rights values as a means of promoting and protecting the interests of a growing constituency of people.[57] In the debate about human rights and dominant Western influences, it is important not to lose sight of the degree to which dominant projects are contested. Critical social movements mobilize resistance to globalization because it is identified with unfettered capitalist accumulation, escalating inequality, exclusion and environmental destruction.[58] Globalization cannot simply be understood in terms of a global, capitalist hegemony, then, but must also include the 'solidarist' trends and forms of international society which may be emerging from the greater prominence of NGOs and critical social movements.[59]

The growth of women's struggles can be seen in part as a challenge to contemporary development and globalization processes. What is being asserted in this struggle is the right to have greater influence and control over the output of markets and even in the informal sector.[60] Recent conventions, which address gender discrimination and the inferior status of women in many parts of the world, have served to mobilize and galvanize women's movements and organizations across the world. The strategy of organizing women around the promotion of human rights has resulted in some notable successes. Throughout the UN Decade for Women (1975–85) the UN adopted strategies to address gender inequality and discrimination centred on improving women's access to and participation in development projects. The gradual 'mainstreaming' of gender in other areas of the UN's work has resulted in the emergence of what Kardam has called an international women's regime, which has brought pressure to bear on states, resulting in a deluge of gender-focused policies over the past three decades.[61] The Beijing Conference placed the issue of women's human rights firmly on the agenda of global politics, both reflecting and further encouraging a more systematic codification of the human rights of women.[62]

The representation of NGOs on government delegations, and the extent of NGO networking which goes on before, during and after UN conferences, have grown massively since the beginning of the UN Decade. International NGOs play a central role in translating international agreements and norms into domestic realities. NGOs establish international networks to promote the Convention on the Elimination of Discrimination Against Women (CEDAW). The International Women's Rights Watch started life in 1985 at the Nairobi Conference. The Institute for Women, Law and Development, the Latin American Committee for the Defence of Women's Rights, the Asia–Pacific Forum of Women, Law and Development and Women in Law and Development in Africa, GABRIELA in the Philippines, Women Living Under Muslim Law in France and the Global Fund for Women in the USA are all examples of non-governmental groups which have become established since 1985. Despite their differences, women have forged international connections, identified common goals and engaged in co-operative projects.[63]

Demands for women's human rights to economic and social security and decent working conditions inevitably spill over into the domain often regarded as cultural or private.[64] One approach to thinking about human rights in a global context has been to look for conceptual similarities in different legal systems and moral traditions.[65] In a number of Islamic countries around the world there is a lively debate between feminist groups who want to fight for rights within a framework of religious injunctions, and those who assert a secular basis for women's human rights. A more productive approach might be to look at how concepts, including the concept of rights, are implanted in contexts from which they did not necessarily originate. Wilson argues that a diversity of normative orders still prevails, but they are no longer predicated upon isolation. The 'universality' of human rights has thus become a question of context, necessitating a situational analysis. It is possible to have contextualization without relativism because we can keep open the possibility that contexts are interlinked.[66] Taking this notion of interconnectedness as a starting point, it is possible to posit the interactions of legal processes operating on different levels, to see how rights-based discourses are produced, translated and materialized in a variety of contexts.[67] Calls for recognition and respect for women's human rights necessarily lead to the redefinition of the traditional scope of human rights law. Chinkin claims that, to be relevant to women, the boundary between state sovereignty and transnational law must be collapsed.[68]

Globalization might not quite be sweeping away all traditional types of social order in unprecedented fashion, as Marx predicted, but it is the case that all societies are now subjected to overlapping local, national and transnational legal codes.[69]

Of course, these 'achievements' have to be seen in the larger context of widespread resistance in some parts of the world to the very concept of 'gender', equality and women's human rights. In practice, states have often refused to ratify CEDAW, entered significant reservations or ratified the convention, but then taken no concrete steps to implement the measures. Women's conventions have been criticized for the weak language in which commitments and state obligations are framed.[70] States retain considerable discretion on what constitutes 'appropriate measures' to eliminate discrimination. In this context, the use of culture and religious codes in defiance of international norms has become a feature of many post-colonial states. Moreover, the conventions still provide few specific rights based upon the life experiences of women. There remains, then, a disparity between regulations and realities.

Nevertheless, collectively these conventions attempt to break down the public/private divide and articulate an international standard for what is meant by equality between men and women which goes beyond formal equality. While understanding of the public/private differs across cultures, the location of women in the private confers power on the male world and supports the global exercise of power by men and the devaluation of women generally.[71] Collectively this body of conventions confirms women's equality in both the public and the private realm.

Earlier in this chapter, it was suggested that globalization addresses the increasing transnational dimensions of economic, social and political life impelled by technological change, the globalization of production *and* the increasingly global scope of communications technologies. The globalization of communications technologies has facilitated the growth of transnational networks among NGOs and social movements. Like other movements, the women's human rights movement has evolved from women organizing on local, national and international levels around issues that affect their daily lives. Gradually, over a period of twenty-five years, women's groups have claimed the political space opened up by the UN Decade and more recent UN conferences and used these opportunities to transform the political agenda. At the same time, across the world societies have become increasingly integrated into global networks, which disseminate information on human rights and, as such, encourage dialogue among women of diverse backgrounds and cultural experiences.[72]

## Conclusion

This chapter took as its point of departure the openness of theoretical debates and the emergence of 'new agendas' in international relations in the post-Cold War period. These developments have provided a more intellectually accommodating ground for the study of gender and feminist scholarship in IR. It is beyond the scope of this chapter to undertake a comprehensive review of how what might broadly be called 'gender studies' in IR, or feminist IR, has developed over the past twelve years or so. However, the dominant theme of the 'first wave' of feminist scholarship has been the need to challenge the mapping of political space in conventional (realist) IR.[73] That is, there is a need to escape from rigid notions of what is inside and outside, international or domestic. Collectively the gender/IR literature has begun to develop new visions of security and community; rethink questions of ethics and human rights; broaden our understanding of violence and conflict; highlight the significance of gendered identities and subjectivities; document the gender dimension of globalization; and, of course, expose the powerful forms of exclusion inherent in 'mainstream' approaches to these areas.

In all of these ways, our understanding of all aspects of international or global relations is being 'engendered'. The end of the Cold War and the current explosion of interest in globalization presents IR with what might be considered both a challenge and an opportunity – the need fundamentally to rethink the constructed nature of boundaries and political spaces. As the above discussion of women's human rights demonstrates, focusing on questions of gender relations and the status of women in a global context goes even further in shaking or transgressing boundaries, pointing to new areas of investigation in the struggle over the appropriate demarcation of public and private and the ways in which issues are politicized and depoliticized as the boundaries of the public/private shift. As such, the study of gender and feminist analysis is central to the post-Cold War IR agenda.

## NOTES

1  For example, postmodernism/post-structuralism, social constructivism, critical theory, green thought and feminism. See Jill Steans and Lloyd Pettiford, *International Relations: Perspectives and Themes* (London, Longman, 2001).

2  See John Baylis and Steve Smith (eds), *The Globalization of World Politics: An Introduction to International Relations* (Oxford, Oxford University Press, 1997); Ian Clarke, *Globalization and International Relations Theory* (Oxford, Oxford University Press, 1999); Ian Clarke, *Globalization and Fragmentation in International Relations* (Oxford, Oxford University Press, 1997); Andrew Hurrell and Ngaire Woods, *Inequality, Globalization and World Politics* (Oxford, Oxford University Press, 1999); Martin Shaw, *Global Society and International Relations* (Cambridge, Polity, 1994); Eleonore Kofman and Gillian Youngs (eds), *Globalization: Theory and Practice* (London, Pinter, 1996); David Held, Anthony McGrew, David Goldblatt and Jonathan Perraton, *Global Transformations* (Cambridge, Polity, 2000); Jan Aart Scholte, *Globalization: A Critical Introduction* (Basingstoke, Macmillan, 2000).

3  See, for example, Hedley Bull, 'Human Rights and World Order', in Ralph Pettman (ed.), *Moral Claims in World Affairs* (London, Croom Helm, 1979); R. J. Vincent,

*Human Rights and International Relations* (Cambridge, Cambridge University Press, 1986); David P. Forsythe, *Human Rights in International Relations* (Cambridge, Cambridge University Press, 2000).
4 Anthony Woodiwiss, *Globalization, Human Rights and Labour Law in Pacific Asia* (Cambridge, Cambridge University Press, 1998), p. 12.
5 Theo Van Boven, 'Human Rights and Development: The UN Experience', in David P. Forsythe (ed.), *Human Rights and Development* (Basingstoke, Macmillan, 1989), p. 121.
6 Richard A. Wilson (ed.), *Human Rights, Culture and Context: Anthropological Perspectives* (London, Pluto Press, 1997), p. 2.
7 Elizabeth Friedman, 'Women's Human Rights: The Emergence of a Movement', in Julie Peters and Andrea Wolper (eds), *Women's Rights, Human Rights: International Feminist Perspectives* (London, Routledge, 1995), p. 19.
8 Wilson, *Human Rights*, p. 1.
9 Rolondo Gaete, *Human Rights and the Limits of Critical Reason* (Aldershot, Dartmouth, 1993).
10 See, for example, Roland Robertson, *Globalization: Social Theory and Global Culture* (London, Sage, 1992).
11 Sally Engle Merry, 'Legal Pluralism and Transnational Culture: The *Kaho'okolokolonui Kanaka Maoli Tribunal Hawaii* 1993', in Wilson, *Human Rights*, p. 28.
12 Roland Robertson is credited with the original invention or use of the term; see Robertson, *Globalization*.
13 Martin O'Brien, Sue Penna and Colin Hay, *Theorizing Modernity: Reflexivity, Environment and Identity in Giddens' Social Theory* (London, Longman, 1999); Fredric Jameson and Masao Miyoshi (eds), *The Cultures of Globalization* (London, Duke University Press, 1998); John B. Thompson, *The Media and Modernity: A Social Theory of the Media* (Cambridge, Polity, 1995).
14 Jameson and Miyoshi, *Cultures of Globalization*, p. 20.
15 Leslie Sklair, 'Social Movements and Global Capitalism', in ibid., p. 30.
16 Ibid., p. 35.
17 Stuart Hall, 'Brave New World', *Socialist Review*, 21, 1 (1991), pp. 57–64.
18 See Marianne H. Marchand, 'The New Challenge: Gender and Development Goes Global', *Connections*, 3 (September 1996), pp. 16–19.
19 See, for example, Irene Tinker, *Persistent Inequalities: Women and World Development* (Oxford, Oxford University Press, 1990).
20 There is an extensive literature. See summaries in Jill Krause, 'The International Dimensions of Gender Inequalities and Feminist Politics: a "New Direction" for International Political Economy?', in John MacMillan and Andrew Linklater (eds), *Boundaries in Question: New Directions for International Relations* (London, Pinter, 1994); Jill Steans, *Gender and International Relations* (Cambridge, Polity, 1998), see esp. ch. 6.
21 Marxists understood that capitalism was characterized by a conventional split between the 'home' and the 'workplace', the 'public' and the 'private', and drew attention to the ways in which women's inequality was predicated upon the public/private division and the relegation of women to the private realm. See Friedrich Engels, *The Origins of the Family, Private Property and the State* (London, Lawrence Wishart, 1972). Marxist feminist theory provides some analytical tools

to make sense of specific forms of gender inequality informed by a broader analysis of the changing global economy. See Kate Young, Carol Wolkawitz and Roslyn McCullagh (eds), *Of Marriage and the Market: the Subordination of Women Internationally and its Lessons*, 2nd edn (London, Routledge & Kegan Paul, 1984).

22  The UN now requires member states to produce statistics which estimate women's contribution to 'national production'. See earlier discussion of the problem of underestimation of women's labour in Lourdes Benería, 'Conceptualizing the Labour Force: the Underestimation of Women's Economic Activities', in Nici Nelson (ed.), *African Women in Development* (London, Frank Cass, 1981).

23  See Diane Elson, *Male Bias in the Development Process* (Manchester, Manchester University Press, 1990).

24  Sandra Whitworth, *Feminist Theory and International Relations* (Basingstoke, Macmillan, 1994).

25  Christine Chinkin, 'Gender, Inequality and International Human Rights Law', in Hurrell and Woods, *Inequality, Globalization and World Politics*, p. 45.

26  Elson, *Male Bias in the Development Process*.

27  Marianne H. Marchand and Anne Sisson Runyan, *Gender and Global Restructuring* (London, Routledge, 1999).

28  True sees the growing market of women's magazines as offering new identities for women and a chance to escape from old lives. True sees the Czech experience as countering the assumption that there is a one-way relationship between global markets and local identities akin to patriarchal imperialism. See Jacqui True, 'Expanding Markets and Marketing Gender: The Integration of the Post-Socialist Czech Republic', *Review of International Political Economy*, 6, 3 (1999), p. 380.

29  True acknowledges the importance of a dual public–private labour market emerging here, with employees paid vastly different wages. There has been an overall decline in labour market participation, in part because of the policy designed to push those who have lost jobs out of the labour force. Women have lost their jobs disproportionately in the transition to a market economy across eastern Europe. In the Czech Republic, gender is the most telling single indicator of income inequality. This is not a legacy of communism, but a consequence of market transition. See ibid., p. 361.

30  Jameson and Miyoshi, *Cultures of Globalization*, p. 92.

31  Charles Taylor, *The Sources of the Self: The Making of the Modern Identity* (Cambridge, Cambridge University Press, 1989).

32  See, for example, Andrew Linklater, *The Transformation of Political Community* (Cambridge, Polity, 1998).

33  Gaete, *Human Rights*, p. 2.

34  Ibid. See also Tony Evans, *US Hegemony and the Project of Universal Human Rights* (Basingstoke, Macmillan, 1996).

35  Gaete, *Human Rights*.

36  Ibid.

37  Antonio Legesse, 'Human Rights in African Political Culture', in Kenneth W. Thompson, *The Moral Imperatives of Human Rights* (Washington, DC, University of America Press, 1980).

38  Gaete, *Human Rights*, p. 2.

39  Wilson, *Human Rights*, p. 19.

40  Gaete's claims that to dismiss human rights as a manifestation of Western imperialism is a betrayal of the process of critical thought the Enlightenment encouraged. See Gaete, *Human Rights*.

41  Maxine D. Molyneux, 'Mobilization without Emancipation? Women's Interests, State and Revolution in Nicaragua', *Feminist Studies*, 11, 2 (1985).

42  True contends that gender must be read contextually, since gender relations and their representation refer always to other social and cultural relations that are embedded in particular histories and geographical places. Gender relations in this region should be understood in terms of global power relations and the struggle among dominant and subordinate, Western and non-Western, masculinities and femininities. True, 'Expanding Markets', p. 360.

43  Thomas Hylland Erikson, 'Multiculturalism, Individualism and Human Rights', in Wilson, *Human Rights*, p. 41.

44  Ibid., p. 41.

45  See Benton, 'Radical Politics: Neither Left nor Right?', in O'Brien et al., *Theorizing Modernity*, p. 54.

46  Anthony Giddens, 'Living in a Post-Traditional Society', in Ulrich Beck, Anthony Giddens and Scott Lash, *Reflexive Modernization* (Cambridge, Polity, 1994), p. 105.

47  See discussion in Jill Krause, 'Gendered Identities in International Relations', in Jill Krause and Neil Renwick (eds), *Identities in International Relations* (Basingstoke, Macmillan, 1996); Steans, *Gender and International Relations*, ch. 3; Marysia Zalewski and Cynthia Enloe, 'Questions About Identity', in Ken Booth and Steve Smith, *International Relations Theory Today* (Cambridge, Polity, 1995).

48  Merry, 'Legal Pluralism and Transnational Culture'.

49  Smithu Kothari, 'The Human Rights Movement in India', in Forsythe, *Human Rights and Development*, p. 97.

50  Ibid., p. 97.

51  Merry, 'Legal Pluralism and Transnational Culture'.

52  Gaete, *Human Rights*, p. 4.

53  Charlotte Bunch, 'Transforming Human Rights from a Feminist Perspective', in Julie Peters and Andrea Wolper (eds), *Women's Rights: International Feminist Perspectives* (New York and London, Routledge, 1995).

54  Wilson, *Human Rights*, p. 14.

55  Chinkin, 'Sender, Inequality and International Human Rights Law'.

56  Bench, 'Transforming Human Rights'.

57  To include social, economic and cultural rights, prohibitions against racial discrimination, the rights to self-determination and the violation of human rights in armed conflict.

58  Non-governmental organizations (NGOs) and social movements have limited access to and influence over the activities of organizations like the World Bank, the IMF or the G7. Nevertheless, while the relative distribution of resources, power and influence lies with global capital, NGOs and social movements play an important role in delegitimizing the authority and claims to impartiality of such organizations and might be instrumental in bringing about change through the mass mobilization of individuals and groups in civil society.

59  Stephen Gill and David Law, *The Global Political Economy: Perspectives, Problems and Policies* (New York and London, Harvester, 1988); Stephen Gill, *Ameri-*

*can Hegemony and the Trilateral Commission* (Cambridge, Cambridge University Press, 1988).

60  Kothari, 'The Human Rights Movement in India'.

61  Kardam quoted in Sonia E. Alvarez, 'Advocating Feminism: the Latin American Feminist NGO Boom', *International Feminist Journal of Politics*, 1, 2 (1999), p. 182.

62  The UN Rights Conventions of 1966, the International Convention on Civil and Political Rights and the International Convention on Economic, Social and Cultural Rights, prohibit discrimination in exercise of rights enumerated in the covenants. The rights embodied in these conventions have been supplemented in many specialized agencies like the International Labour Organization (ILO) and the United Nations Education, Social and Cultural Organization (UNESCO). Article 14 of the European Convention on Human Rights, Article 1 of the Inter-American Convention on Human Rights and Article 2 of the African Charter on Human Rights prohibit discrimination on grounds of sex. There has been and remains a tendency to frame clauses to do with women specifically in terms of 'protection'; for example, the Fourth Geneva Convention talks of protecting women's 'honour', against rape, enforced prostitution or assault. However, long-standing practices of discrimination against women, based on the assumption of female dependency, have also been addressed. The UN now has a Commission on Status of Women, which is active in preparing recommendations for the Economic and Social Council (ECOSOC) for the promotion of women's rights in political, social and educational fields and for immediate attention in the domain of human rights law. See Chinkin, 'Gender, Inequality and International Human Rights Law'.

63  Women use their position and experiences as a point of departure from which to reflect critically upon global political and economic processes which have an impact on their everyday lives and struggle to change the material conditions of their lives, particularly, though not exclusively, as a result of the UN Decade for Women. A variety of women's groups, feminist groups and NGOs are lobbying states and institutions like the IMF and World Bank on concrete issues to do with the distribution of resources, working conditions, welfare and security.

64  So, for example, in India women's groups have been at the forefront of campaigns in the field of health, where there has been a proliferation of amniocentesis clinics and a rise in female foeticide. In this way, women's groups have extended the parameters of debates about 'human rights' to incorporate women's experiences and concerns. Barnett R. Rubin, 'Human Rights and Development: Reflections on Social Movements in India', in Forsythe, *Human Rights and Development.*

65  Religious authors have tried to adopt the notion of human rights in reinterpreting ancient modes of thought and transforming them into rights discourse. See James Piscatori, 'Human Rights in Islamic Political Culture', in Kenneth W. Thompson, *The Moral Imperatives of Human Rights* (Washington, DC, University Press of America, 1980); A. A'la Mawdudi, *Human Rights in Islam* (London, Islamic Foundation, 1980); Fatima Mernissi, *The Veil and the Male Elite: A Feminist Interpretation of Women's Rights in Islam*, rev. edn (London, Al Saqi, 1985).

66  Wilson, *Human Rights*, p. 18.

67  Ibid.

68  Chinkin, 'Gender, Inequality and International Human Rights Law', p. 47.

69   Ibid., p. 47.
70   Ibid., p. 48.
71   Ibid.
72   Critics argue that NGOs can have depoliticizing and deradicalizing effects on social movement politics. Alvarez argues that neo-liberal social and economic adjustment policies, state downsizing and changing international regimes have dramatically altered the conditions under which feminist and other struggles for social justice are unfolding. States and IGOs are turning NGOs into 'gender experts' rather than citizens' groups advocating on behalf of women's rights. This reduces political-cultural interventions in the public debate about women's citizenship into largely technical issues. See Alvarez, 'Advocating Feminism'.
73   See, for example, Steans, *Gender and International Relations* (ch. 2); V. Spike Peterson, 'Transgressing Boundaries: Theories of Knowledge, Gender and International Relations', *Millennium: Journal of International Studies*, 21 (2) (1992), pp. 183–206.

# 5

# Developing Inequality
## *A Global Fault-Line*

## Caroline Thomas

### Introduction

A key feature of the landscape of international relations post-1989 has been the universal mainstreaming of liberal economic ideology via the Washington consensus.[1] This ideology informed the approach to development promoted by the G7 countries and the International Monetary Fund and World Bank in the 1980s. In the 1990s we witnessed the expansion of this ideology across the globe, and the intensification of its application via the policy prescriptions of a growing number of global governance institutions.

A second key feature of the post-Cold War global landscape has been the intensification and reconfiguration of pre-existing inequalities of an economic, political and social nature. This chapter is most concerned with material polarization, though the economic, political and social cannot easily be separated. The growth of material inequality is evident between states, within states, and between private actors.

The nature and geographic configuration of this inequality leads me to believe that post-1989 the Third World, far from disappearing, is becoming global. The promise of the peace dividend raised expectations that material inequalities would be ameliorated as more resources would be diverted to accelerate development, but this has not been borne out in practice. Moreover, and more important, the dynamic of economic-driven globalization characteristic of the most recent stage of capitalism is resulting in the global reproduction of Third World problems. The demise of the communist bloc and the associated rejection of 'real existing socialism' as a mode of economic organization have provided a specific additional fillip to the reconfiguration of the 'Third World'. Thus, notwithstanding the demise of the bipolar Cold War context, the collapse of communism and the associated Second World, and the abandonment of a Third World development strategy based on the state sector, the term 'Third World' still has resonance today.[2]

Characteristics which distinguished Third World states a quarter-century ago now apply to a wider group of states than previously. At a broad level, and despite marked heterogeneity, the current Third World grouping now embraces the former Second and Third World states.[3] But equally the term embraces groups of people, irrespective of their geographical location, who are failing to benefit from the process of globalization. Growing inequality is arguably now the most significant global fault-line.

The chapter is divided into four sections. The first section examines the global architecture which drives and legitimates this differentiation process. The second section maps the globalization of inequality at the inter-state, intra-state and private company levels, and suggests some important links between the globalization process and this deepening inequality. The third section highlights contending ideas within the policy community about global economic integration. The conclusion offers some suggestions as to how the discipline of international relations might respond to the transformation under way in world politics evident in the globalization of the Third World.

## Global architecture

The 1980s, and more particularly the 1990s since the demise of communism, have witnessed the near-universal mainstreaming of liberal economic ideology via the policies of an expanding global network of institutions, public and private. These policies reflect a particular brand of liberalism which privileges freedom defined in terms of private power and the individual; it attacks the public realm and associated ideas of collectivity and society. Global economic integration has been presented as the best, the most natural and the universal path towards growth and therefore development for all humanity. This is to be promoted through liberalization of trade, production and finance. The blueprint has been marketed with the powerful language of 'There Is No Alternative' or TINA, and to a large extent it has been accepted by Third World governments desperate for external finance. Dissenting voices have been neutralized, often by the incorporation of the language of opposition into the mainstream presentation.

An increasingly conscious co-ordination of policies is evident in the work of the IMF, the World Bank, other regional multilateral development banks, the World Trade Organization (WTO) and a growing number of other arms of the UN system, most recently the UN Development Programme (UNDP) and the UN Conference on Trade and Development (UNCTAD). To different degrees and in different ways, these key international institutions have been adapting their general orientation, their institutional structures and their policies to facilitate movement towards a world in which for private finance, if not for people, national economic sovereignty is an anachronism.[4] Within this vision, inequality in itself is not a problem, and may even be desirable, as it will unleash entrepreneurial abilities which will contribute to maximizing global wealth creation. Ultimately everyone will benefit.

The scope, depth and speed of the changes that are being effected via the policies of this network of institutions are breathtaking; their legitimacy is open to question,[5] and the future of billions depends on them. The rest of this section is devoted to a brief outline of some of the key aspects of their policies.

### Structural and institutional reform of national economies by the IMF and World Bank

The IMF is the linchpin in the implementation of the vision. Going beyond its original mandate to provide short-term balance of payments support, it has co-ordinated with the World Bank in the 1980s and 1990s to promote fundamental structural and institutional reforms of national economies worldwide to better reflect the dominant vision of market-led rather than state-led development. These changes redraw the social as well as the economic map, profoundly altering the relationship between state, market and citizen. Beginning with Latin America and Africa in the 1980s in the context of the debt crisis, the IMF and the World Bank turned their attention to the economies in transition post-1989, and more recently to East Asia.

Conditioned structural adjustment loans[6] have enabled these institutions to advance the role of the market, and redesign the role of the state to support the creation of an enabling environment for the private sector.[7] Key components of IMF and World Bank packages include privatization of public services and public assets, liberalization of trade, finance and production, deregulation of labour and environmental laws, and the destruction of state activism generally in the public realm. The export-led growth expected from these changes would generate the foreign exchange income necessary to keep up debt repayments. Essentially these institutions have been applying a blueprint, a standard remedy for problems which may in fact be different depending on the specific country. This blueprint is very clear in the IMF's handling of the East Asian crisis, based on the incomparable experience of Latin America over a decade earlier.[8]

### Trade liberalization

IMF/World Bank structural adjustment policies are in tune with their vision of the emerging world trade system as supportive of the maximal welfare of all, and of free trade as necessarily desirable. James Wolfensohn has remarked that 'together, we [the IMF and the World Bank] must work with and support the work of the World Trade Organization which is so critical to the trading arrangements and future of our client countries'.[9] The global push for trade liberalization is reinforced and supported by the movement towards increased regional liberalization, for example the North American Free Trade Agreement (NAFTA). From 1948 to 1997, seventy-six free trade agreements were created or modified, and more than half of these came into being after 1990.[10] The momentum is increasing.

In the 1980s the central role of trade was evident in the liberalizing trend of the Uruguay Round, and more recently in the WTO. The Uruguay Round brought down barriers to agricultural trade, instituted trade-related investment measures (TRIMs) and trade-related intellectual property rights (TRIPs). A new round of trade talks is being sought under the WTO by the First World states, keen to bring even more new areas into the agreement. The EU Commission is pushing for a new 'Millennium Round' of comprehensive trade negotiations. Topics under suggestion include investment and competition policy and government procurement. It is interesting to note that the First World states, having failed to get an agreement on investment at the Organization for Economic Cooperation and Development (OECD),[11] have identified the WTO as the appropriate locus for this issue. In discussions in the WTO working group on investment, First World states have pushed for new rules to make it mandatory for all WTO countries to give foreign investors the right to enter and establish themselves with 100 per cent ownership, for foreigners and foreign firms to be treated at least as well as locals, and for prohibitions on the restrictions of free flow of capital.

## Finance

Public overseas development assistance is at its lowest level in fifty years, and falling sharply: in 1998, the figure stood at $33 billion, 40 per cent down on 1990, and equivalent to 0.25 per cent of the GDP of First World countries.[12] Most Third World countries find it exceedingly difficult to raise money or attract foreign direct investment (FDI). (Indeed, in 1997, 58 per cent of FDI went to OECD countries.) But, as public finance has been dwindling, private flows have soared, with private lenders and investors taking advantage of opportunities created by the financial deregulation pursued by Third World governments in response to the policy prescriptions coming from the IMF and G7.

A very useful assessment of these private flows has been undertaken by Anderson and her colleagues.[13] Several key points emerge from their study, and these are outlined here. First, they show that the volume of private flows, plus their proportion of overall flows, has surged. Private flows grew from $US44 billion in 1990, to $US256 billion in 1997. By 1996 they accounted for over 85 per cent of resource flows, dwarfing public flows. Second, they suggest that short-term portfolio flows have been the fastest growing, surging from US$3.2 billion to US$45.7 billion. These short-term flows are speculative rather than long-term and productive, and as such have been concentrated in twelve countries – the 'emerging markets', the preferred terminology of the World Bank's International Finance Corporation. The rest of the Third World countries have been unable to attract private funds. Third, they point to a huge proliferation of new financial instruments and institutions in the 1980s and 1990s. The leverage they can exert is significant, with the potential to pose a challenge not only to individual countries, but to the stability of the entire global financial system.

Some international supervision of private finance has developed, but this has not kept pace with financial deregulation. Efforts are under way to build on the Basle Capital Accord of 1988 which provided a minimum standard for bank health,[14] but as yet these have not resulted in concrete developments because of disagreement about how to measure risk.[15] Supervision of non-bank private finance is meagre, existing mainly within the national domain. The January 1999 Basle Committee for Banking Supervision Report on Highly Leveraged Institutions, commissioned by the central bankers of the industrialized countries following the collapse of the US hedge fund Long Term Capital Management (LTCM), advised sounder risk management practices by banks and other lenders to highly leveraged institutions. It did not recommend regulation of the hedge funds themselves. When LTCM collapsed in September 1998, the US Federal Reserve Bank hosted a meeting of creditor banks. While it has denied putting public money into the rescue, its precise role is very sensitive and open to question.

The general thrust of the above policies is being replicated by other arms of the UN. Space does not allow examination of these. In the next section I shall examine the configuration of global inequality since 1989.


## Developing inequality

In the words of the UNDP, 'the past decade has shown increasing concentration of income, resources and wealth among people, corporations and countries'.[16] In this context, we can say that the Third World is becoming global. At the state level, the Third World, far from disappearing, has increased numerically and in terms of geographic spread. Third World state status has effectively been globalized. The picture is highly differentiated, but the central characteristics of material poverty of significant sectors of the population, vulnerability to the workings of the global market, and lack of meaningful influence in global governance institutions are shared by a growing group of states. The gap between these states and a handful in the First World is growing across all these indicators. The *World Development Report 2000/01* reveals stark inequalities.[17] A recent US intelligence report suggests that the inequality within and between states is likely to grow over the next fifteen years.[18] Yet an exclusive focus on the inter-state level, characteristic of traditional international relations analyses, hides the increasingly global social configuration of inequality, risk and opportunity. Globalization of the Third World can be seen in the life experience of people, as well as in the experience and condition of states.[19] There is a First World within Third World states, and increasingly there is a Third World within First World states. In identifying where the Third World is now, we must be mindful of this intra-state polarization (see table 5.1).

## Inter-state polarization

The general pace of globalization in the 1980s and 1990s, and the particular trajectory of capitalist expansion, have increased inequality and risks for a broader group of countries. The UNDP suggests that the income ratio between the fifth of the global population living in the richest countries, and the fifth living in the poorest countries, has changed from 30:1 in 1960, to 60:1 in 1990, to 74:1 in 1997. This reflects a similar trend to that experienced in the last three decades of the nineteenth century when rapid global integration was also taking place. In the nineteenth century, inequality defined by income between the top and bottom states increased from 3:1 in 1820, to 7:1 in 1870, to 11:1 in 1913.[20] In addition to income gap, inequality is evident in other spheres (see table 5.2).

Growing inter-state inequality post-1989 is evident when we consider global policy-making. Only a handful of states exert meaningful influence in global governance institutions such as the IMF, World Bank or WTO. The G7 drives the global economic policy agenda (see table 5.3).

**Table 5.1**   Global polarization at the end of the twentieth century

- OECD countries, with 19% of the global population, have 71% of global trade in goods and services, 58% of foreign direct investment and 91% of all Internet users.
- The world's richest 200 people more than doubled their net worth in the four years to 1998, to more than $1 trillion. The assets of the top three billionaires are more than the combined GNP of all the least-developed countries and their 600 million people.
- The recent wave of mergers and acquisitions is concentrating industrial power in megacorporations – at the risk of eroding competition. By 1998 the top 10 companies in pesticides controlled 85% of a $31 billion global market, and the top 10 companies in telecommunications controlled 86% of a $262 billion market.
- In 1993 just 10 companies accounted for 84% of global research and development expenditures and controlled 95% of the US patents of the past two decades. Moreover, more than 80% of the patents granted in developing countries belonged to residents of industrial countries.

*Source*: UNDP, *Human Development Report 1999*, p. 3

**Table 5.2** Concentration of global income, resources, wealth 1999

|  | 20% global population in highest income countries | 20% global population in lowest income countries |
|---|---|---|
| % of world GDP | 86 | 1 |
| % of world export markets | 82 | 1 |
| % of foreign direct investment | 68 | 1 |
| % of world telephone lines | 74 | 1.5 |

*Source*: Adapted from UNDP, *Human Development Report 1999*, p. 3

The G7 countries, plus the rest of the European Union, represent a mere 14 per cent of the world's population, but control 56 per cent of the votes in the IMF Executive Board. 'The rest of the world is called upon to support G7 declarations, not to meet for joint problem-solving.'[21] The US is still the only state which can exert unilateral veto power at the IMF.

Trust has been further eroded by the handling of the recent financial crises in East Asia, Russia and Brazil. South Korea, for example, perceives a lack of distance between IMF and US policy agendas. It regards the US as having taken advantage of the crisis to work through the IMF to push through its pre-existing trade and investment agenda.[22] IMF restructuring of East Asian economies has enabled First World companies to take advantage of bargain-basement-priced East Asian companies. In 1998, US and European companies mounted over $30 billion in takeovers of Asian companies – a fourfold

**Table 5.3** Global economic governance 1997

| Title | Institutional grouping | Membership | % World GDP | % World population |
|---|---|---|---|---|
| G7 | Western economic powers | Canada, France, Germany, Italy, Japan, UK, US | 64.0 | 11.8 |
| G77 | Developing and some transition countries (not Russian Fed. or Poland) | 143 members | 16.9 | 76.0 |

*Source*: Adapted from UNDP, *Human Development Report 1999*, p. 109

increase on 1997.[23] This has been described by one commentator as 'the greatest global asset swindle of all time'.[24] The Asian crises have also heightened awareness of the ability of a handful of relatively new private financial actors such as hedge funds to exert such leverage that they can force currency devaluations at a breathtaking pace, undermine national economic policy and erode national development.

It is sobering to reflect that no former Second or Third World country has joined the ranks of the First World countries in a solid sense. While a handful have significantly increased their economic power – and this is a very important achievement – this has not been matched by influence in key global governance institutions. Global success in massively increasing consumption is not being reflected in access of the majority of states to the benefits of this growth. The UNDP reports that: 'No fewer than 100 countries – all developing or in transition – have experienced serious economic decline over the past three decades. As a result per capita income in these 100 countries is lower than it was 10, 20, even 30 years ago.'[25] There was a moment when the achievement of East Asian states suggested that the economic gap between First and Third World states could be closed, but recent crises have shattered that hope. GDP growth in East Asia as a whole fell from 4.3 per cent to −6.2 per cent in the short period 1997–8.[26] The UN Economic and Social Commission for Asia and the Pacific (ESCAP) 1999 regional survey shows that, over the same period, the percentage of population in poverty has risen dramatically, as labour market displacement has been massive. For example, in Indonesia the proportion in poverty has risen from 11 to over 40 per cent, and unemployment from 4.7 per cent to 21 per cent. This is particularly tragic given the unique gains that had previously been made in the region to promote growth with equity and lift millions of people out of poverty.

The transition of central and eastern Europe and the Commonwealth of Independent States (CIS) from centrally planned to market economies has on the whole propelled these states more towards the ranks of Third World rather than First, although some – such as Poland – are faring much better than the rest. These states have acquired the characteristics of extreme vulnerability to the workings of the global market, and deepening poverty and inequality. Output in most of them remains below pre-transition levels, and unemployment is very high and rising. The Russian economy was expected to decline by 8.3 per cent in 1999. The painful process of transition has been undertaken without the cushion of public provision previously in place, and in the case of Russia with the disadvantage of highly corrupt government officials committed to capital flight of public funds for private enrichment. The number of people in poverty in Russia has increased from 2 million to well over 60 million over the last decade.[27] By 2000, it reached 20 per cent of the population.

Significantly, no First World country has joined the ranks of the Third World. Yet, even for First World states, the risks accompanying globalization have been brought into sharp relief[28] – witness the contagion effect in financial crises, the collapse of LTCM in September 1998, and job losses due to mergers, efficiency gains and even the withdrawal of Asian investments. Importantly, however, First World states enjoy a voice in global governance.

## Intra-state polarization: inequality, risk and opportunity

Over the last fifty years, and more particularly so over the last decade, differentiation/stratification has increased at the intra-state as well as inter-state level. With a few exceptions such as the East Asian tigers, the success of states, measured in terms of GDP per capita, has not been reflected in their societies at large. This is as true for the First as for the Third World countries. Since the 1980s, for example, all OECD countries except Italy and Germany experienced an increase in wage inequalities, and this was worst in the UK, US and Sweden. In the UK, the number of families below the poverty line increased by 60 per cent from the early 1980s to the early 1990s.[29] Nick Davies's shocking book, *Dark Heart*, paints a shocking portrait of the UK.[30] Concentration of wealth, and social exclusion, seem to be part of a single global process. The dynamic of economic-driven globalization has led to a global reproduction of Third World social problems, while at the same time aggravating socio-economic divisions within weak states. In the CIS and eastern Europe, transition has been accompanied by large changes in the distribution of national wealth and income – indeed the biggest ever recorded change in the case of the Russian Federation and the CIS.

This intra-state differentiation increasingly reflects the degree of integration of various social classes and geopolitical regions within the emerging global economy. Thus, for each human being, their respective position in the global economy has an enormous impact on their perception and their experience of risk, vulnerability and opportunity.

In defining the Third World from the human aspect, our concern is with those human beings for whom poverty is the norm, for whom vulnerability and risk are defining features of their daily existence, wherever they are located territorially. Their search for security is not just about the fulfilment of basic material needs. It is also about the achievement of human dignity, which includes personal autonomy, control over one's life, and unhindered participation in the life of the community. Human security is pursued as part of a collective, most commonly the household, sometimes the village or the community, defined along other criteria such as caste or religion. At the global level the state is the community which is given legitimacy to represent the interests of human beings and further their search for security. Such human security is indivisible – it cannot be pursued by or for one group at the expense of another.[31]

Global economic integration is directly impacting on human security. Patterns of systemic inclusion and exclusion of people can be mapped with reference to the means of economic sustenance. Cox provides a useful categorization of the world's producers in a global economy:[32] a core workforce of highly skilled people integrated into the management process; a second level of precarious workers located where business is offered the greatest incentives in terms of lowest labour costs or environmental controls; and the rest, the expanding pool of people in the First and Third World states who are excluded from international production – the 37 million unemployed plus the low-skilled in the rich countries; and the 1 billion under- or unemployed, the marginalized in the poor countries.[33]

The core refers to those people who are able to take advantage of the opportunities which global economic integration presents. James Gustave Speth of the UNDP has written that 'An emerging global elite, mostly urban based and interconnected in a variety of ways, is amassing great wealth and power, while over half of humanity is left out.'[34] Within this group also sit the super-rich. The world's richest 225 people have a combined wealth equal to the annual income of 47 per cent of the world's people.[35] The three richest people have assets exceeding the combined GDP of the forty-eight least-developed countries. Eighty-three of these ultra-rich people, that is, over a third, are non-OECD citizens (see table 5.4).

The core of people who are already reaping the benefits of the globalization process will be able to advantage themselves further by their ability to exploit lifelong learning opportunities, and to tap into ongoing technological advance and the related communications revolution. The highly mobile and well-paid global professional elite, composed, for example, of corporate executives and scientists, has the potential to be self-sustaining.

**Table 5.4**   The ultra-rich, by origin, 1997

| Region or country group | Distribution of 225 richest people | Combined wealth of ultra-rich ($US billions) | Average wealth of ultra-rich ($US billions) |
| --- | --- | --- | --- |
| OECD | 143 | 637 | 4.5 |
| Asia | 43 | 233 | 5.4 |
| Latin America and the Caribbean | 22 | 55 | 2.5 |
| Arab states | 11 | 78 | 7.1 |
| Eastern Europe and CIS | 4 | 8 | 2.0 |
| Sub-Saharan Africa | 2 | 4 | 2.0 |
| Total | 225 | 1,015 | 4.5 |

Source: UNDP, Human Development Report 1998, p. 30

The ESCAP Survey 1999 identifies the future as Internet commerce. Yet, out of the world's 6 billion population, there are only 50 million Internet users, and over 90 per cent of Internet hosts are in North America and western Europe. Eighty per cent of people worldwide still do not have access to a telephone.[36] A quarter of countries do not yet have a teledensity of one, that is, one telephone line per 100 people. The cover of the UNDP's *Human Development Report 1999* provides a graphic illustration of the geographic spread of the 'global enclave of Internet users' superimposed on a pie diagram showing the regional distribution of global population. 'Geographic barriers may have fallen for communications, but a new barrier has emerged, an invisible barrier that is like a world wide web, embracing the connected and silently – almost impercept-ibly – excluding the rest.'[37] Noticeably, significant pockets of Internet users exist in Latin America, East Asia, South-East Asia, eastern Europe and the CIS. Sub-Saharan Africa and South Asia are poorly served. Yet even in those regions, particularly South Asia, pockets of technical expertise and access exist and a global labour market operates. Within India, the state government of Bangalore has tapped into the global market by developing software pro-gramming.

Cox's second category, precarious workers, comprises those people who may gain temporarily from the globalization process by job creation, but who remain very vulnerable due to the pace of change in the demand for skills, and labour market conditions. In Latin America, for example, we have seen job creation accompanying growth, but 85 per cent of those new jobs are in the informal sector. Globally, the numbers of new jobs are disappointing, as is the level of security associated with them. The pressure of global competition drives employers wherever they are located to adopt flexible labour practices, and often in association with a change in national employment laws, for example the UK, South Korea, Peru and Ukraine.

Some writers have argued that we are witnessing a feminization of the workforce as global trade integration increases women's share of paid employ-ment. In some countries, such as Bangladesh, this is evident. There, the share of women participating in the labour force has increased from 5 per cent in 1965 to 42 per cent in 1995. The women have been employed in the garment export industry. Yet that particular industry is very competitive internationally, so employment opportunities can disappear overnight. Moreover, the opportun-ity for such employment is a mixed blessing for the individual women con-cerned, for in contrast to men their amount of unpaid work does not diminish significantly on account of their paid work.[38] Also the conditions of employ-ment are often undesirable.

Transnational corporations directly employ only 3 per cent of the global labour force.[39] Export processing zones provide opportunities, but the condi-tions of employment are poor. Moreover, these zones act as a magnet for migration, and this can create social problems when the expected opportun-ities do not materialize. For example, in China, deepening differentiation between the export-oriented coastal region of the east and the rest of the country is stark, and there is a growing problem of urban unemployment. The human poverty index is just under 20 per cent for the coastal regions, but more than 50 per cent in inland Guizhou province.

The push to liberalize trade results in capital seeking out the location where it can reap the best advantage. This pits country against country, and even divides individual states – and therefore citizens – within a federal structure. An example of the latter is Brazil. When the new Governor of Rio Grande Do Sul decided to try to renegotiate contracts with Ford, other states within Brazil were quick to compete for the investment by offering more attractive loans and infrastructure to the company.

The globalization process is resulting in more mergers and acquisitions, and these are consuming an increasing proportion of foreign direct investment (85 per cent of the global total in 1997, and 67 per cent of the total going to the Third World countries). Unlike greenfield investment, these often result in job losses rather than job creation, thus fuelling the precarious nature of employment in the current era.

The outlook for Cox's third category, the expanding pool of people marginalized by the process of global economic integration, is bleak. For them, risk and vulnerability are increasing, and there do not appear to be opportunities. In the words of ILO director General Michel Hansenne: 'The global employment situation is grim, and getting grimmer.'[40] Social exclusion of the most vulnerable – the old, the young, the disabled, ethnic minority groups, the less skilled – is intensifying, and across all these groups there is a bias against women.[41]

Education and training can create opportunities to overcome labour market exclusion. The OECD classifies 25–40 per cent of its adults as 'functionally illiterate', that is, without the necessary skills to function in the modern work environment, and thus excluded from the advantages globalization offers.[42] If this is the situation in countries where virtually all children have the opportunity to go to primary and secondary school, the scenario for the rest of the world is very frightening indeed. Some 125 million primary-school-age children worldwide never attend school. Another 150 million drop out before they can read or write.[43] Globally, this is over a quarter of the world's children. Yet there is marked differentiation across region, country and districts, and along other fault-lines such as gender. In Sub-Saharan African states, 50 per cent of school-age children are not enrolled in schools. The average man in Africa has less than three years' schooling, the average woman less than a year. Given that the greatest population growth takes place amongst the poor who have least access to education, then without immediate remedial action we can expect differentiation to become more entrenched and to cascade into future generations. The potential for poor people to exploit learning opportunities will be affected by their malnutrition, which impacts on learning ability.

The survival risks endured by marginalized people particularly in Third World states result not only through exclusion from the economic globalization process, but also by the way in which that process directly undermines their ability to be self-sufficient. An example is the privatization of the commons.[44] A notorious recent example is the redrafting of the Mexican constitution in the context of liberal restructuring in the run-up to the NAFTA. This was done to stop government redistribution of land to the landless, and to facilitate privatization of previously communal land. While the resulting Chiapas uprising hit the global headlines,[45] other examples can be cited from all over the world illustrating the violation of the rights of indigenous communities, landless peasants and fishing communities in order to further the interests of the holders of capital.

## Polarization in the private sector

Developing inequalities which we have seen between and within states are being repeated in the private sector, where capital is becoming more concentrated globally. There is a trend towards the merger of huge corporations, and this is often occurring across territorial borders. The UNDP *Human Development Report 1999* gives details.[46] Examples cited there include Exxon and Mobil, Chrysler and Daimler, and Hoechst and Rhône-Poulenc. Over the period 1990–7, cross-border mergers and acquisitions more than doubled, from 11,300 to 24,600. In 1997, they accounted for 59 per cent of total foreign direct investment, compared with 42 per cent in 1992.[47] In 1997, 58 transactions exceeded $1 billion each. The increase in total value of mergers and acquisitions has been startling in particular sectors (see table 5.5).

In the global drive for efficiency, many small and medium-size firms are disappearing. In the particular context of the East Asian crisis, many local firms were bought up by foreign companies in what has been described as the 'greatest asset swindle of all time'.[48]

**Table 5.5**  Total value of mergers and acquisitions, $US billions

| Sector | 1988 | 1998 |
| --- | --- | --- |
| Computers | 21.4 | 246.7 |
| Biotechnology | 9.3 | 172.4 |
| Telecommunications | 6.8 | 265.8 |

*Source*: UNDP, *Human Development Report 1999*, p. 67

## Globalization and inequality: a cause for concern?

What has been the reaction of global governance institutions, and the IR academic community, to deepening inequality in the post-1989 era? Is this inequality a central issue on the global political agenda, and is it central to the research and teaching agendas of IR scholars? What relationship do students and practitioners perceive between global economic integration and deepening inequality?

In the immediate post-Cold War period, euphoria abounded, as people and policy-makers put their faith in the ability of global economic integration to deliver material improvements for all. The end of history had arrived. The IR academic community, confused and undermined at its failure to have foreseen momentous events, hardly provided a note of caution.

A decade later, we are witnessing the sudden flowering of discussions about the principles, practice and outcomes of global economic integration. Civil society groups, concerned about the actual and potential costs of global economic integration, throughout the 1980s and 1990s called for reform of global governance institutions and the policies they promote. What is new now is that debate is taking place among concerned champions of existing strategies. Global financial crises, spreading from East Asia in mid-1997 to Russia in 1998 and Brazil in 1999, have been the catalyst for growing concern amongst supporters of liberalization that the process may be taking place too fast, or that the situation may get out of control, hence threatening the stability of the global financial order. Former US Treasury Secretary Robert Rubin, for example, remarked in 1999 that the crisis heightened the broad-based awareness of the risks and opportunities of a global economy.[49]

Disagreement has arisen within the IMF and the World Bank, and also between these institutions, particularly over the handling of the Asian crisis. There were differences between influential mainstream academic economists (mostly American) who moved in and out of government and international organizations, such as Joseph Stiglitz, Jeffrey Sachs, Paul Krugman, Lawrence Summers and Stanley Fischer. Within the G7, disagreement also surfaced. For example, former Japanese Finance Minister Eisuke Sakakibara, who was involved in IMF decisions on the financial crises of Asia, accused the US of market fundamentalism and dominance of the IMF which he believed mishandled the Asian, Russian and Brazilian crises. Differences emerged between the EU and Japan, on the one hand, and the US, on the other. Yet again, there were differences within individual industrialized countries. In the US, the Wall Street–Treasury complex[50] emerged as a term to refer to the closeness between the US Treasury Department and Wall Street investment bankers, a closeness not necessarily supported by other sectors of the US government. There is a growing recognition across a broad spectrum of opinion that the rewards of globalization have been enjoyed by a few, the gains have been made at the expense of stability, and the quality and sustainability of the growth itself are open to question.[51] We are also witnessing a growing uneasiness about this situation.

A critical assessment of the Washington consensus was offered in January 1998 by Joseph Stiglitz, Senior Vice-President and Chief Economist at the World Bank. In a public lecture entitled 'More Instruments and Broader Goals: Moving Toward the Post-Washington Consensus', Stiglitz argued that:

> We seek increases in living standards – including improved health and education – not just increases in measured GDP. We seek sustainable development, which includes preserving natural resources and maintaining a healthy environment. We seek equitable development, which ensures that all groups in society, not just those at the top, enjoy the fruits of development. And we seek democratic development, in which citizens participate in a variety of ways in making the decisions that affect their lives.[52]

This position was reiterated a year later in a discussion document put out by James Wolfensohn, President of the World Bank.[53] Using the analogy of a balance sheet, Wolfensohn suggested that the left-hand side presented the language of finance ministers, that is, macroeconomic data such as national income accounts, balance of payments and trade statistics, while the right-hand side presented social, structural and human aspects. The emphasis in the 1980s and 1990s was on the left-hand side; in the twenty-first century, we must consider both sides together. In other words, growth is necessary but not sufficient. This is evident in the World Bank's Comprehensive Development Framework, which aims to better balance the macroeconomic and human aspects of development, and to increase ownership by broad-based consultation with stakeholders. It is evident too in the evolution of enhanced structural adjustment facilities (ESAFs) into the Poverty Reduction and Growth Facility (PRGF). National Poverty Reduction Strategy Papers are to reflect the views of civil society, not just governments.

Broadly speaking, we can identify reformist and transformist positions on what might be done to address the problem of globalization and inequality, though neither group is monolithic. The former, emanating from the G7, the World Bank and the IMF, is more limited in scope and nature, focusing mostly on technical modifications to existing policies and general risk management. It is supported by various academics, particularly in the US, who via consultancy work are involved in policy prescription and move easily between work for global institutions and governments and their academic obligations. The transformists, emanating from civil society groups in First and Third World states, and a few academics/researchers who move between academic obligations and campaigning/activist activities, tend to be more imaginative, far-reaching and directed at changing structures. At base, the reformist approach is informed by 'the fundamental belief that a market-based system provides the best prospect for creating jobs, spurring economic activity, and raising living standards in the US and around the world'.[54] Transformists do not share the fundamental belief in the market system. For them, 'The global financial crisis presents an opportunity to rethink and reshape the rules of the international economy so that they benefit people and the environment.'[55] What is at stake is the relationship between market, state and society. Transformists support the agenda articulated in 1974 by Third World states in the Charter of Economic Rights and Duties of States (CERDS), but they go further: they want national and local authorship and ownership of, and control over, development policies.

These two basic positions can be identified across a range of issues that currently highlight the inequality problem. These include the debt question, in particular the HIPC (heavily indebted poor countries) initiative; questions about the legitimacy of drawing new areas into a new round of trade negotiations; issues of finance, foreign direct investment and corporate accountability.[56] For reformists, global economic integration must be pushed ahead, as this is the best means to foster growth, create employment opportunities and wealth for the global good. However, there is increasing acknowledgement that globalization must develop a human face. For the transformists, global economic integration is not the most important and overriding policy goal. Values other than growth are important – human rights, the environment, gender concerns. For them, governments must have the right to determine the extent and pace of integration. They must have the right to trade, and not to trade. These different approaches are illustrated by discussions in the latter half of the 1990s about the debt of the poorest countries. Reformists continued to advocate the macroeconomic reform strategies designed by the IMF and World Bank, which tied debt reduction to proper implementation of ESAFs. For transformists, those ESAFs were seen as part of the problem, and could not be part of the solution. They do not regard the new PRGF loans as any better. For them, any solution to the debt problem must be delinked from IMF macroeconomic reform programmes.

At the beginning of the twenty-first century, the Washington consensus is losing ground, and the reformist approach is gaining ground, in policy circles and academia. The transformist position, however, remains on the periphery of both.

## Conclusion

The IR academic community, if it is to remain in touch with developments on the ground, must build bridges with scholars in other disciplines better equipped to map the outcomes of global economic integration for human beings. Development studies, anthropology and human geography have much to offer us in our quest to move away from the limitations of a predominantly state-centric analysis and to capture the relationship between the global and the local. Working with colleagues in these other disciplines, we will all be better able to understand the development of inequality.

What will we choose to do with this knowledge? Is it enough simply to understand the world better? Do we want to legitimate the existing order of things? Do we seek to change the existing order? Townsend has written that: 'Liberal-pluralists who have been influenced by the classical, neo-classical and monetarist approaches in economics, the functionalist and post-industrialist approaches in sociology and the democratic pluralist approaches in political science adopt a relatively compliant approach to the continuation of widespread and severe poverty.'[57] The same can be said of their attitude to deepening inequality. This liberal approach dominated the discipline in the 1990s and, apart from the Coxian school, there were few voices among the Northern IR academic community calling for significant change. With US intelligence reports now arguing that inequality will increase both within and between states over the next fifteen years,[58] surely the time has come to say that global economic integration in the twenty-first century is a legitimate goal only if it works in favour of global redistribution of resources.

## NOTES

1   The term 'Washington consensus' was coined by John Williamson of the Institute for International Economics. It refers to a particular recipe for development growing in popularity in the 1980s and especially in vogue in the 1990s. It has been explained and summarized succinctly by Paul Krugman in 'Dutch Tulips and Emerging Markets', *Foreign Affairs*, 74 (1995), pp. 28–9: 'By "Washington" Williamson meant not only the US government, but all those institutions and networks of opinion leaders centred in the world's de facto capital – the International Monetary Fund, World Bank, think tanks, politically sophisticated investment bankers, and worldly finance ministers, all those who meet each other in Washington and collectively define the conventional wisdom of the moment. ... One may ... roughly summarize this consensus ... as ... the belief that Victorian virtue in economic policy – free markets and sound money – is the key to economic development. Liberalize trade, privatize state enterprises, balance the budget, peg the exchange rate.'

2   See any edition of the monthly publication *Third World Resurgence* (Penang, Malaysia, Third World Network); Eric Toussaint, *Your Money or Your Life: The Tyranny of Global Finance* (London, Pluto, 1999); Julian Saurin, 'Globalisation, Poverty and the Promise of Modernity', *Millennium*, 25, 3 (1996); Ankie Hoogevelt, *Globalisation and the Post-colonial World* (Basingstoke, Macmillan, 1997); Caroline Thomas and Peter Wilkin (eds), *Globalisation and the South* (Basingstoke, Macmillan, 1998); Caroline Thomas, 'Where is the Third World Now?', *Review of International Studies*, 25 (1999), pp. 225–43.

3  See Christopher Clapham, 'Degrees of Statehood', *Review of International Studies*, 24 (1998), pp. 143–57; Laszlo Andor and Martin Summers, *Market Failure: Eastern Europe's Economic Miracle* (London, Pluto, 1998).

4  For a critical assessment of the changing focus of the IMF, see Martin Feldstein, 'Refocusing the IMF', *Foreign Affairs* (March/April 1998), pp. 20–33; also Devesh Kapur, 'The IMF: A Cure or a Curse?', *Foreign Policy*, 77, 2 (1998), pp. 114–29.

5  See several contributions on transparency and accountability of the IMF, World Bank and WTO in John Cavanagh, Daphne Wysham and Marcos Arruda (eds), *Beyond Bretton Woods* (London, Pluto, 1994).

6  The literature on structural adjustment is extensive, and the arguments will not be rehearsed here for lack of space. See the two volumes of theory and case studies by Paul Mosley, Jane Harrigan and John Toye (eds), *World Bank and Policy-Based Lending* (London, Routledge, 1991).

7  The Corner House, *The Myth of the Minimalist State* (Dorset, Corner House, 1998), Briefing No. 5.

8  For more on this see Kevin Watkins, *Economic Growth with Equity: Lessons from East Asia* (Oxford, Oxfam, 1998).

9  James Wolfensohn, 'A Proposal for a Comprehensive Development Framework: Discussion Draft' (Washington, DC, World Bank, 21 January 1999).

10  United Nations Economic Commission for Latin America and the Caribbean, 'Summary of Global Economic Developments', *UN Focus in the Caribbean: Newsletter of the UN System in the Caribbean* (January–June 1997), pp. 6–7.

11  For a critique of the Multilateral Agreement on Investment proposed by the OECD, see Caroline LeQuesne, *Reforming World Trade: The Social and Environmental Priorities* (Oxford, Oxfam, 1996), p. 21.

12  James Wolfensohn, Press Conference, Washington, DC, World Bank, 22 April 1999.

13  For a useful assessment see Sarah Anderson, Tom Barry and Martha Honey, 'International Financial Flows', *Foreign Policy in Focus*, 3, 41 (December 1998). The figures in this paragraph are taken from ibid.

14  See Bill McDonough, Chair, Federal Reserve Bank of New York and Chair, Basle Accord, 'Issues for the Basle Accord', Federal Reserve Bank of New York, 1998 Annual Report, pp. 3–12; and 'Capital Ideas: What's Cooking in Basle', *The Economist*, 17 April 1999, p. 12.

15  'Basle Brush: Banking Regulation', *The Economist*, 1 May 1999, p. 115.

16  UNDP, *Human Development Report 1999* (New York and Oxford, Oxford University Press), p. 3.

17  World Bank, *World Development Report 2000/01: Attacking Poverty* (Washington, World Bank, September 2000).

18  Inter Press Service, 20 December 2000.

19  UNDP, *Overcoming Human Poverty* (Oxford and New York, Oxford University Press, 2000).

20  Ibid., p. 3.

21  Jeffrey Sachs, 'Stop Preaching', *The Financial Times*, London edn, 1, 5 November 1998, p. 22.

22  See Feldstein, 'Refocusing the IMF', p. 32.

23 Walden Bello, 'The TNC World Order: Will It Also Unravel?', paper prepared for the Democracy, Market Economy and Development Conference, Seoul, Korea, 26–7 February 1999.
24 Robin Hahnel, 'The Great Global Asset Swindle', *ZNet Commentary*, 23 March 1999.
25 UNDP, *Human Development Report 1998* (New York and Oxford, Oxford University Press, 1998), p. 37.
26 United Nations Information Services, 8 April 1999.
27 James Wolfensohn, World Bank President, described this increase as 'enormous'. See press conference at the beginning of the spring summit of the IMF and the World Bank, 22 April 1999.
28 For a very interesting discussion of how in this era of advanced modernity, when genuine material needs can be satisfied, risks are being produced in society to an extent previously unknown, see Ulrich Beck, *Risk Society* (London, Sage, 1992).
29 UNDP, *Human Development Report 1999*, p. 37.
30 Nick Davies, *Dark Heart: The Shocking Truth about Hidden Britain* (London, Vintage, 1998).
31 For more on this see Caroline Thomas and Peter Wilkin (eds), *Globalization, Human Security and the African Experience* (Boulder, CO, Lynne Reinner, 1999); Caroline Thomas, *Global Governance, Development and Human Security* (London, Pluto, 2000).
32 Robert Cox, 'Civil Society at the Turn of the Millennium: Prospects for an Alternative World Order', *Review of International Studies*, 25, 1 (1999), p. 9.
33 International Labour Organization, *World Employment Record 1998–99* (Geneva, ILO, 1999), p. 1.
34 Speth quoted in B. Crossette, 'UN Survey Finds World Rich–Poor Gap Widening', *New York Times*, 15 July 1996, p. 55.
35 UNDP, *Human Development Report 1998*, p. 30.
36 *African Development Bank Report 1998*, p. 172.
37 UNDP, *Human Development Report 1999*, inside cover.
38 Ibid., p. 81.
39 Panos Institute, *Globalisation and Employment*, Briefing No. 33 (London, Panos Institute, May 1999), p. 6.
40 Cited in ibid., p. 5.
41 International Labour Organization, *World Employment Report 1998–99*, p. 9.
42 Panos Institute, *Globalisation and Employment*, p. 5.
43 Oxfam International, *Education Now, Break the Cycle of Poverty* (Oxford, Oxfam, 1999).
44 See Michael Goldman (ed.), *Privatizing Nature* (London, Pluto, 1998).
45 On the Chiapas uprising see Lynn Stephens, 'Between NAFTA and Zapata: Responses to Restructuring the Commons in Chiapas and Oaxaca, Mexico', in Goldman, *Privatizing Nature*, pp. 76–101.
46 UNDP, *Human Development Report 1999*, p. 32.
47 Ibid., p. 31.
48 Robin Hahnel, 'The Great Global Asset Swindle', *ZNet Commentary*, 23 March 1999.

49   US Treasury Secretary Robert E. Rubin, 'Remarks on the Reform of the International Financial Architecture to the School of Advanced International Studies', Princeton University, 21 April 1999.

50   See Jagdish Bhagwati, 'The Capital Myth: The Difference Between Trade in Widgets and Dollars', *Foreign Affairs*, 77 (May/June 1998).

51   David Korten, *When Multinationals Rule the World* (London, Earthscan, 1995). See also an interesting collection of views on the differential benefits of trade liberalization in Annie Taylor and Caroline Thomas (eds), *Global Trade and Global Social Issues* (London, Routledge, 1999).

52   Joseph Stiglitz, 'More Instruments and Broader Goals: Moving Toward the Post-Washington Consensus', WIDER Annual Lectures, 2 (Helsinki, United Nations University, 1998), p. 31.

53   Wolfensohn, 'A Proposal', 1999.

54   Rubin, 'Remarks', April 1999.

55   'A Citizens' Agenda for Reform of the Global Economic System', sometimes referred to as the 'Declaration on the New Global Financial Architecture' (Friends of the Earth-US, Third World Network, Institute for Policy Studies (US), December 1998).

56   These ideas are developed further in Thomas, *Global Governance, Development and Human Security*.

57   Peter Townsend, *The International Analysis of Poverty* (London, Harvester Wheatsheaf, 1993), p. 6.

58   US Intelligence Report 'Global Trends 2015', published 18 December 2000, Washington, DC, and reported by Jim Lobe, 'Wider Gaps Between Haves and Have Nots', in Inter Press Service, 20 December 2000.

# 6

# Taming Economics, Emboldening International Relations
## *The Theory and Practice of International Political Economy in an Era of Globalization*

## *Richard Higgott*

If war is too important to be left to generals, then globalization is too important to be left to economists and markets are too important to be left to free marketeers.

## Introduction

International political economy (IPE) – perhaps best seen as a 'field of inquiry' or 'a set of questions'[1] – is more focused on the theory and practice of globalization than other areas of inquiry in international relations (IR). This is increasingly so irrespective of the approach to the study of IPE adopted (realist, liberal institutionalist or Marxist) or the issue area (production, trade, finance or development) under investigation. A core question that besets all IPE under conditions of globalization is simple in its posing: how do we understand and explain the relationship between an increasingly non-territorial and globalized economic system on the one hand and the extant territorially delimited hierarchical state system on the other? But it is a question not so easy in the answering. It is a question for all students of IR, but nowhere does it come into sharper relief than in the study of IPE and nowhere does the study of world politics, more broadly, intersect with contemporary practice than in the global political economy.

IPE must therefore play a larger role in shaping the study of IR than in the past if other theoretical currents are to have more than just scholarly interest in the early years of the second millennium. As the theme of this volume implies, this is a time of both challenge and opportunity for IR. Its popularity as a discipline within the university community has never been stronger but, by contrast, the influence of the scholarly-cum-research community over the policy process has never been weaker. This is all at a time when the need for good normative and analytical scholarship in IR to inform the policy debate has probably never been higher.

Nowhere does this assertion have sharper clarity than in comparison of the fortunes of IR as a discipline with those of economics. Under conditions of globalization, the influence of economics over the policy process has never been higher, while the normative poverty of economic theory – especially in the wake of the recent economic crises in Asia, Latin America and Eastern Europe – has never been weaker. Yet, while economics is ripe for challenge, IR theory – a potential contender to score telling points – seems all too often immersed in insular ontological and epistemological self-evaluation. It's time for a change.

Let me say what this chapter is not. It is not yet another review of the 'state of IPE' nor another foray into the critical theory versus problem-solving debate. Nor do I suggest we can, or indeed should try to, move to settled positions. IR is a contested discipline, as many have told us,[2] especially over questions of epistemology, ontology and terrain. Rather, I am suggesting that this should not stop us from striving to identify those areas of common concern at the interface of IR and IPE that are now in much starker relief than they might have been before the collapse of the Berlin Wall.

It is not sufficient merely to bolt IPE on to IR. As Susan Strange long ago noted, there is more to IPE than the recognition of economic interdependence and the growth of transnational actors as add-ons to inter-state politics. There are serious structural dynamics at work – in the domains of security, production, finance and knowledge – that are the stuff of IR and should be studied accordingly.[3] And while, by deciding the state was redundant as a meaningful unit of analysis in international relations, she over-egged her pudding,[4] to the end her basic point remained valid: much IR theory today, to its cost, still has little or no understanding of, or interest in, economic interdependence and the power of markets in general or, more importantly under conditions of globalization, the financial markets in particular.[5]

The first section of this chapter looks at the relationship between globalization and economics as discipline and practice. The communication revolution means that globalization *is different* from previous eras of economic internationalization and integration. Neo-classical economic theory has been its intellectual handmaiden and the dominant mode of policy thinking in economics sees progress as economic liberalization and resistance to it as anti-progressive. Neo-classical economic scholarship identifies a rationality of methodological individualism and the notion of equilibrium as its core tools. But it has hit a brick wall with the growing resistance to globalization that has emerged, especially since the Asian crises of 1997.

The following discussion attempts to identify the bones of a normative agenda for IPE. In recognition of the manner in which globalization has exacerbated inequality within and between states, it does so by focusing on the themes of governance, justice and the prospects of the provision of important global public goods. It is an avowedly reformist agenda that will not be to the taste of either the IR mainstream or its various radical fringes.

## Globalization and the hegemony of economics

Early understandings of globalization, especially economic ones, were primarily 'process' or 'flow' definitions – identifying the increasing mobility of factors such as capital, labour, information and technology brought about by liberalization, privatization and deregulation. These activities are not historically 'new'.[6] But their volume, scope, depth, speed and clustering are unprecedented. Market reform and the retreat of the state may have occurred in previous historical eras, but not in combination with a rapid growth of foreign direct investment (FDI), multilateral institutions and the spread of a single ideology. Early definitions demonstrated an optimistic, progressive, modernist teleology exemplified in the cartography of a borderless world in which the nation-state becomes increasingly irrelevant.[7] Globalization became a 'normalizing discourse' of power conditioning the policy responses of governments to the perception, if not always the reality, of global market integration. Nowhere is this better exemplified than in those analyses that see a revolution taking place not only in relations between the state and the economy, but also within civil society.

> [New] technology will lead to big productivity increases that will cause high economic growth – actually, waves of technology will continue to roll out through the early part of the 21st century... and a new ethos of openness... will transform our world into the beginnings of a global civilization, a new civilization of civilizations, that will blossom through the coming century.[8]

This view is influential among representatives of the 'networked economy' of international managerial policy elites vertically linked into the global economy in a flexible fashion. It is a technologically driven, economistic definition. But it is bereft of any sense of the limits of liberalization or any serious political theory that might lead to a realization of the problematic nature of the teleology espoused. Before the economic downturns of 1997 it demonstrated little appreciation of any of the downsides of globalization or, indeed, the countervailing pressures that globalization might call forth.

It is also a triumphalist view of globalization.[9] The first triumph, of the West over state-controlled collectivism in the Soviet empire, was followed by a second triumph over heterodox capitalist development strategies. Following the first wave of the Asian economic crisis of late 1997, the Anglo-American economic model was deemed to have triumphed over Asian developmental statism. For many in 'the West' the 'Asian way' was getting its come-uppance. Wall Street, Washington and the international financial institutions initially saw the Asian crisis as a 'window of opportunity'. Indeed, Michel Camdessus, managing director of the IMF, initially saw it as a 'blessing in disguise' that would sweep away crony capitalism and free up markets along 'Western' lines.[10]

The commitment to liberalization had spread geographically from Europe and North America and in the last quarter of the twentieth century to other parts of the world, notably East Asia and the other parts of the Americas and, since the end of the Cold War, to eastern and central Europe and even China, albeit in the context of a dual system logic. Experiments with protectionism and import substitution had been progressively abandoned. The empirical record on the alleviation of human suffering in the late twentieth century, notwithstanding the remaining human hardship, was, according to Harvard economist Richard Cooper, 'unambiguously positive'. Things may be worse in Africa, he argued, but, as a result of improvements in China and India, 'the fraction of the world's population living in poverty has gone way down'.[11]

So, with such a track record for success, why does liberalization's victory not seem final? With two billion people living on less than $US2 a day and almost as many without access to clean water, the benefits of liberalization are not unambiguous, especially since the currency collapses and ensuing economic crises of 1997. Further, there is a strong and growing body of non-state actors – NGOs and global social movements – increasingly capable of articulating the case against globalization. The information revolution may ensure that the rich get richer, and do so faster, but it also connects the dispossessed in a more articulate fashion than in the past.

At the theoretical level the very strength of liberal economics is also a major weakness. Far from being the 'dismal science', when it examines globalization, economics appears as an excessively optimistic science. Its concentration on the goal of openness and growth at the expense of non-economic factors has led to a parsimony of theorizing that no other social science can match. This has parallels in practice, the effect of which is to minimize the salience of all other aspects of the policy process and make much economic analysis insensitive to the complex politics that constitutes the downside of economic liberalization. Further, economic theory has only a limited moral sense and ability to understand social relations.

Sound rationalist economic logic on its own is not sufficient to contain what is variously called the 'globalization backlash' or 'globaphobia'. This is not confined just to one country. Nor is it even confined to poor countries. In the US more than 50 per cent of Americans in a recent survey believed that globalization 'does more harm than good'.[12] This is less a critique of economic theory than an assertion of the limits of economic theory.[13] But rapid aggregate increases in global wealth and production have been accompanied by a corresponding political and social naïvety as to the effects of these processes on the civil polities of developed and developing societies alike and (*pace* the Battle of Seattle) the closing years of the second millennium witnessed the first post-Cold War 'crisis of globalization'. It became understood that economic analysis alone was not well equipped to deal with this crisis.[14] In order to understand why, a brief excursion into the historiography of economics might be useful.

Contemporary economics is dominated by a neo-classical approach that flourished from the time of the marginalist revolution in the 1870s which separated economics out from classical political economy and was largely responsible for the bifurcated manner in which the social sciences developed over the next hundred years. In methodological terms, political economy became the application of economic analysis to the various arenas (domestic and international) of politics. To the extent that political economy – and IPE – became sites at which the social sciences met, when this happened it was invariably on the terms of the dominant actor – the economics discipline.

At one level, this is maybe how it should be. The central concerns of economics – material production, distribution and exchange – are the central activities of life. Most social sciences started out as political economy until economists came to believe that their modes of analysis could exist as some kind of disembodied study and disciplinary specialization began to take over.[15] For a hundred years or more, the other social sciences became, and remain, largely irrelevant to economics. Points of contact only really began to re-emerge over the last two decades as other social sciences on the one hand recognized that they needed to take on board economic methods in order to become 'scientific' and, on the other, because some economists felt that they wished to, and could, colonize the issues areas of 'social' and 'political' life, traditionally the preserve of sociologists and political scientists.[16] But economics made no attempt to come to grips with other social sciences on other than their own terms.[17]

Other disciplines, especially IR, are seen through the lenses of the 'economic approach' stressing the primacy of the equilibrium. This concept is basically a belief that change in economic systems will, over time, result in independent actors converging on a more or less common point. Convergence is achieved through the actors pushing their own interests and notwithstanding the constraints under which they might operate. By contrast, IR has used the language of differentiation, anarchy and path dependence rather than convergence. The difference, until rational choice theory gained hegemonic status in American political science (and by extension IR[18]), was a reflection of the opposing modes of reasoning of economics and IR (and most social sciences other than economics).

Because of this, some economists reject all other social sciences because they lack the power to generalize like economics.[19] Other social sciences are weak because they assume instability and unpredictability of activity rather than patterned behaviour. Their *ad hoc* nature is merely a disguise for analytical failure.[20] Even Barry Eichengreen, who is not quite as dismissive as others, argues that IR 'needs to move in the direction of formulating parsimonious models and clearly refutable null hypotheses, and towards developing empirical techniques that will allow these hypotheses to be more directly confronted by the data'.[21] In the 'economic approach' anything that is not predictable or patternable is taken to be exogenous. Of late, some branches of political science have aided and abetted economics. In his now classic defence of rationalist method, Keohane insists on the need to focus full square on 'substantive rationality', if we are to avoid 'diversionary philosophical construction'.[22] In short, we have seen an intellectual hegemony of an almost unchallenged faith in rationality. Rationality is not unimportant but it needs to be complemented or countered by other variables such as morality, power, culture and psychology.

In the US, where IR scholarship has addressed the 'economic', it has done so largely by copying its methods and has therefore made IPE the handmaiden of the intellectual hegemony of economics.[23] The test of good IPE in the US nowadays is largely the degree to which the IR scholar can learn and handle the tools of rationalist method found within economics. To be critical of this often over-eager and sometimes slavish mimicking of economic method is not to deny the importance of what economists do well. They well understand the technical dynamics of global markets (while IR scholars generally do not). But they are invariably blind to the normative implications of much of their work, especially when removed from 'developed world' contexts and the temporal parochialism of the present. Historical and wider spatial (developing country) contexts find more sympathetic treatment, or recognition, in IR scholarship.

But the 'economic approach' performs another function unmatched by any of the other social sciences. Modelling the market and, more importantly, securing the transformation of capitalism into a more precise representation via scholarly models, has given economics a detached authority. In so doing, it puts at one stage remove the less savoury overtones of capitalism as a system of economic production and exchange. The appeal to expert economic knowledge as a source of policy advice, at the IMF or the World Bank, for example, is an appeal to ideologically neutralized or sensitized rhetoric.

Behind this scholarly and theoretical detachment is to be found the power of institutions. As an ideological project, neo-liberal economics is an attempt to create as self-regulating a global market as possible. And attempts to install market freedom implicitly, indeed explicitly for some, represent a challenge to the institutions of the nation-state. The privileging of the self-regulating market relieves economic activity from any notion of political citizenship or duty. Nowhere is this better illustrated than in the initial IMF responses to the Asian crises.

In the implementation of the 'rescue packages' we saw the hand of the economic theorist operating within the glove of institutional power. Abstract economic theory became actual political and social reality for the recipients of the packages. In this regard, the power of international financial institutions represents, especially for the student of IPE, the transformation of 'abstractionism' from scholarly inquiry to political power with massive practical effects. And it has been allowed to do so because of the ability of economics to intimidate other social sciences.

This has left the way clear to economists in most policy fields and the international domain under conditions of globalization in particular. While many IR scholars have been preoccupied with epistemological and ontological questions, the economists have swept all before them. This is where postmodernism presents us with a paradox. In providing (often plausible) reasons to question rationality-driven 'economic science', postmodernism has often tossed the baby out with the bathwater. IR has done so with a radical veneer, but one with no practical effect on 'real' issues such as poverty, exploitation and justice. For the last decade or so the IR theorist has often preferred the role of heroic critic on the margin rather than address central policy issues.[24]

The crucial thing for the scholar of IPE is to make sure that the flight from postmodernism does not return it to the arms of the abstracted virtualism of high neo-classicism. This is not hard-headed materialist political economy but a false abstracted rigour. Economistic theories of choice have no way of explaining how choice is affected by the social meaning of objects and actions. It is here that advances in social theory of a constructivist genre find their way into IR and become so important for advancing IPE.

If there is one thing that emerging processes of globalization have taught us – and especially the events following the financial crises in Asia – it is that monocausal explanations of international economic phenomena lack sufficient explanatory power. Such a view holds currency not simply among Third World economic nationalists and radical academic critiques of the neo-liberal agenda, but also within the mainstream of the international policy community.[25] What is needed is an IPE grounded in history and the 'material' but with a critical policy bent attuned to a strong normative agenda of 'order'; not an order that is simply a euphemism for the absence of open conflict and the presence of control, but one underwritten by strong policy impetus towards issues of enhancing justice and fairness under conditions of globalization.

## The normative poverty of economics and new agenda for IPE

I have suggested that the very success of liberal economic hegemony under conditions of globalization may hold within it the seeds of its own downfall. That the integration of the international economy – especially demand for goods, capital and services – is a strong secular tendency in the contemporary era is well understood. That these demands are changing the traditional economic practices of many societies is also well understood. A hyper-globalization thesis argues that there has been a shift in the relationship between state authority and market power. The increase in capital mobility – arising from financial deregulation and revolutions in technology and communication – has meant that governments have shifted the cost of the welfare state from capital to the recipients in order to prevent capital exercising exit options offered by the deregulation process.[26] The urge for free markets and small government has created asymmetries in the relationship between the global economy and the national state that have undermined John Ruggie's 'embedded liberal compromise'.[27]

But these changes are increasingly resisted. More groups are recognizing that, when pursued in combination, free markets and the reduction of compensatory domestic welfare are a potent cocktail leading to radical responses by the dispossessed.[28] There are several reasons for this. For one thing, globalization – with the substitution of workforces in one part of the world for those in other parts in an era of increasing mobility of capital and technology – alters employment relationships. The skilled and the mobile are privileged at the expense of the unskilled.[29]

Further, as it has become more difficult to tax capital, it is also more difficult to run welfare states. Thus it is harder for governments – even if they so wish – to provide the compensatory mechanisms that underwrite social cohesion in the face of changing employment structures. The internationalization of trade and finance ceases to be simply sound economic theory. It also becomes contentious political practice. Rather than being recognized just for its ability to enhance aggregate overall wealth, it is seen also for its negative redistributive consequences that disturb prevailing social structures. Increasingly articulate NGOs voice objections to the side-effects of unfettered liberalization. In contexts where communities attach value to means as well as ends, these groups exhibit genuine concerns about the socially disintegrative effects of liberalization.

Securing domestic political support for the continued liberalization of the global economy requires more than just the assertion of its economic virtue. If the benefits of the rapid economic growth of the last few decades are not to be jeopardized, then how social cohesion is maintained in the face of liberalization will be a major issue. As Garrett notes, embedded liberalism is probably more important to political stability and economic prosperity now than it has ever been.[30] Can Ruggie's embedded liberal compromise be maintained or revivified? More importantly, can it be globalized? The importance of embedded liberalism has never been as well appreciated in the economics community as it has in political science. Economics has always demonstrated a political and social naïvety as to the effects of these processes on the civil polities of developed societies. Its views of the state have always been astonishingly simplistic.

From a neo-classical economic perspective, government – especially the welfare state in the post-World War II era – is inefficient. Thus, beyond the provision of basic public goods – the rule of law and external security – the dismantling of the public economy must come sooner or later in an era of globalization. But much economic analysis fails to recognize the manner in which domestic political institutions still have assets capable of mediating the effect of global economic activity in their own territorial space. While the debate in the 1990s focused more on the question of good governance, it did so largely with a limited neo-classical economic and neo-liberal political 'night watchman' view of the state. There is still an unwillingness in the international economic policy community to see that functioning markets, as socio-political constructs, require legitimacy and support within civil society and that welfare statism might be important for the stability of an open international economy.

In contrast to a strong globalization thesis of a neo-liberal genre, the state is not in retreat on all fronts, let alone dead. There is still no substitute for the state as the repository of sovereignty and rule-making and as provider of national security. It remains the socializer of risk of last resort and the orchestrator of co-ordinated policy responses to the challenges thrown up by globalization. The task is to analyse the nation-state in a 'process of adaptation', not decline.[31]

Moreover, the economic crises since 1997–8 have presented an opportunity to go beyond free market hegemony. The urge to move beyond the 'Washington consensus', to challenge the 'winner takes all' outcomes and the growing inequality that has accompanied globalization, provides a space for a more ethically driven IPE. 'Market civilization'[32] is an abstraction as well as a material reality. It is difficult to argue with the materiality, but it is challengeable as an ideological abstraction if, but only if, an alternative vision can be put in its stead. This should be the task for IPE in the twenty-first century.

## Analysing globalization: from economics to IPE

One role for IPE as praxis is to challenge the assumption that politics and society can be governed by market assumptions alone. Changes in government in Europe, crises in Asia, Latin America and central Europe, and the increasing volatility of financial markets have seen a rethinking of the merits and utility of the state not fashionable since the collapse of Keynesianism. The state is seen less as an unwieldy public drag on the economy and more as the pivot in a relationship between public and private domains charged with developing more efficient and just forms of private provision. The crucial thing about a new normative IPE is that it would add the justice and accountability dimension of governance to the efficiency and managerialist dimension.

This form of thinking, which informs the domestic policy process, must also inform the international process under conditions of globalization. Indeed,

policy thinking in the more progressive of the international financial institutions – to wit, the World Bank – has seen a recognition of the salience of the
state (governance, human capital and capacity-building) as well as the market.
Market bias at the IMF in the wake of the recent crises has also been tempered,
albeit less so. James Wolfensohn at the World Bank, and even Michel Camdessus at the IMF, acknowledged the dangers of globalization without equity.
As Wolfensohn noted in an address to the Board of Governors of the Bank
(October 1998), 'if we do not have greater equity and social justice, there will
be no political stability and without political stability no amount of money put
together in financial packages will give us financial stability'. An economic
system viewed as unjust will not long endure.[33]

The IMF has seen its policies of structural adjustment, stabilization and
deregulation fail to prevent the kinds of shocks in Third World markets experienced over the last few years. In essence Krugman, Soros and others triggered a
debate about the utility of capping market forces to allow governments the
breathing space to 'sort things out'.[34] In so doing, they opened up a policy
space that not long previously had been firmly off limits. As the globalization
backlash gathered momentum throughout 1998, this space expanded from a
once hegemonic neo-liberal discourse, across the social democratic terrain
towards a reconstituted Keynesianism and, for some, even back towards
Marxism which, in the 150th year since the *Communist Manifesto*, saw
adherents keen to point out (once again) that capitalism may have reached
its last crisis. This is intellectually interesting speculation, but probably premature.

What the period 1997–9 witnessed was less a crisis of capitalism, more a
crisis of free-market fundamentalism. Moreover, the crisis is less an economic
one than one of governance, or more specifically the absence of international
economic institutional governance since the collapse of Bretton Woods.
Beyond short-term survival strategies, we are now seeing the emergence of a
genuine debate in domestic and international policy circles and, in academic
communities, on potential means of 'managing' or 'governing' globalization.
Evidence at present suggests that the future trajectory of policy will reflect an
abandonment of the more dogmatic elements of the neo-liberal discourse in
favour of more flexible and heterodox approaches to economic management at
both the global and national levels.

At the global level, even Washington policy circles in the late 1990s recognized that the push for capital liberalization fostered the vulnerabilities that
were an underlying cause of the economic crisis in Asia and Latin America.[35]
Perhaps more important in the longer term, emerging economic theory is
beginning to accept that early capital account liberalization has been a mistake
and crisis prevention requires proper sequencing and the minimization of
short-term lending to poorer countries.[36] Other suggestions – be they Tobin-
style taxes; changes in capital adequacy requirements that favour long-term
rather than short-term investment; eliminating the protection of portfolio

investors to remove moral hazard considerations in investment strategies; or even finding ways to break the 'mass psychology' of the herd mentality in financial markets – have found their way into the policy debate since the Asian crisis.[37] This intellectual change of heart can be seen in large parts of the international policy community.

I do not want to oversell this case, but the consideration of such reforms has wider implications. We may not be witnessing a revolution in thought but we are seeing a stylistic and substantively significant policy change from the assertiveness and hubris characteristic of the 'Washington consensus' days of the 1990s. If the momentum of a reformist agenda can be maintained, then it might eventually evolve into a wider agenda focusing on equity and justice considerations too. With the right intellectual support, a reformist IPE might fight off the worst excesses of the 'economic approach', and enhance coalition formation and agenda-building that ensures the reform process continues. IPE as *critical problem-solving* – articulating the normative arguments to underwrite this agenda – could at the very least provide a mitigating effect on the worst excesses that have emanated from neo-classical economics.

There are other ways in which the 'economic' can meet the 'political' in IR. Keynes posed a question for us that should be as normatively and analytically central to the scholar of international relations today as at the time he was writing in 1931: 'The political problem of mankind', he asserted, 'is to combine three things: economic efficiency, social justice and individual liberty.'[38] This is as much a normative agenda for an economically sensitized IR as it is economics.[39] The integration of IPE within the core of IR, rather than being seen simply as a subfield, offers one opportunity to move the agenda along. This requires a willingness within the IR community to grasp an intellectual nettle that it has shown little inclination for. The recent intellectual and policy failures of economics offer a window of opportunity. But we should not be naïve about this nor underestimate sites of resistance – within certain sects of IPE (along the critical theory/problem-solving divide) on the one hand or within certain theoretical traditions (old and emerging) in IR theory on the other. So-called incommensurability (often a euphemism for 'it's too hard to think about dialogue') and lack of comprehension across specialized disciplines present enduring difficulties to multi-disciplinary research. They need to be transcended in IR as much as in economics.

IPE, like all exercises in understanding and explanation, has to cope with 'abstractionism', or what David Miller has recently called 'virtualism'[40] in thinking that has accompanied the development of knowledge societies and especially the economic abstractionism of the market under conditions of globalization. We need to think of economics beyond the market and beyond the 'economic approach'. We need to think again of IPE as substantive historical narrative as well as method – this is where the work of Robert Cox, and his better groupies, is so essential to the study of IPE in particular and indeed IR in general.[41]

In this regard, IPE must be a site of contest and interaction between grand narrative (in the current context 'globalization') and sites of particularist resistance (be these states, classes, regions or other localist levels). How useful, we should ask, are grand narratives of globalization that rest solely on an understanding of 'Western capitalist' development and that treat East Asia or Latin America as but 'add-ons'? The intellectual response of the scholarly economics community to the crises of the late 1990s was, with the exception of the simplistic identification of 'cronyism', mainly a response to 'technical problems' such as 'asset bubbles', 'moral hazard' and 'sequencing' in financial deregulation.

The myopia of economic analysis to the growth of the sites and styles of resistance to globalization was at times breathtaking in the late 1990s. There was little or no room in 'the economic approach' for an appreciation of the changes that non-rational, non-economic agents driven by a normative agenda can bring about. There is no room in economic analysis for the role of those non-state actors (NGOs and global social movements) that play an increasingly telling role in global policy processes.[42] There is clearly space here for IPE as an intellectual site for a study of the dynamic interactions of the state–market–civil society nexus. Above all, however, we need to secure the normative and idealist core of IPE.

## IPE beyond the Washington consensus

I have tried to make a case to suggest that the unadulterated neo-liberal moment may be passing. This is due to the impact of the Asian and other financial crises. The 'Washington consensus' (WC) that governed multilateral thinking for much of the last twenty years is now a moving feast as the major financial institutions, at odds with each other over the appropriate policy responses to the financial crises and the need to create a new financial (indeed economic) architecture, search for a new role, or paradigm even. The contours of this new approach are now emerging. The original well-known buzzwords of the WC were liberalization, deregulation and privatization. To these the post-Washington consensus (PWC) now adds civil society, capacity-building, governance, transparency, a new international economic architecture, institution-building and safety nets.

Add to the post-Washington consensus UNDP initiatives on 'governance' and 'global public goods'[43] and the UN's 'global compact'[44] with the private sector to promote human rights and raise labour and environmental standards and we now have a new rhetoric of globalism to accompany globalization as a process. That the 'global compact' reads like an attempt to globalize embedded liberalism is hardly surprising. The intellectual architect of this agenda is John Ruggie, former Assistant UN Secretary-General.

The details of the PWC – especially its emphasis on governance, civil society and safety nets – cannot and need not be spelt out here save to note that its understanding of governance is underwritten by (1) a managerialist ideology of effectiveness and efficiency of governmental institutions and (2) an understanding of civil society based on the mobilization and management of social capital rather than one of representation and accountability – not, *pace* Robert Cox's recent reformulations of the concept, as a site of resistance.[45] While both factors represent a sharp departure from the narrowly economistic and technocratic decision-making models of the WC, they do not reject the WC's emphasis on open markets. Rather, the PWC should be seen as an attempt to embed institutionally, and even maybe humanize, the earlier elements of the WC.

Given that the PWC holds a very sanitized view of the socio-political dimensions of the development process, why is it significant for IPE? Because, at base, *it is a recognition that politics matters*. It demonstrates a sensitivity to the political difficulties inherent in the economic reform processes. While, to date, the PWC and the economic literature show little cognizance of the difficulty of understanding politics, they offer a starting point for an agenda for justice under conditions of globalization that did not exist in the mid-1990s.

Theorists are still groping for a universally acceptable definition of 'social and economic justice'. But, while that continues, we are now fairly certain that globalization in its unadulterated form enhances inequality and unequal treatment for some states and, more importantly, exacerbates poverty for many sections of the weakest members of international society. At this stage poverty alleviation has a stronger claim than equality in prevailing definitions of justice.[46] One key question for IPE to address is: what is the relevant community or society to which 'social justice' pertains and in what domains should the question of justice be addressed? This question has traditionally been understood in the contexts of the values that actors attach to their behaviour within market structures. But markets are not the only actors. The 'domain' issue is at the core of the 'global governance' question.


## Conclusion: an agenda for justice and global governance

Why is it important that students of IPE focus on global governance? Because, if we accept the argument that the transnationalization of market forces is exacerbating inequality, then one of the only avenues for mitigating this gap lies with a radical reformist agenda for the global rules and norms that underwrite the current international institutional architecture. To date, the governance agenda has largely excluded questions of power, domination, resistance and accountability from the debate. To the extent that international institutions recognize that resistance is a legitimate part of the governance equation, it is something that is to be overcome by governance, not something that is a perpetual part of the process. In this respect, for many key players, global governance is not about politics. There are no problems that good governance cannot contain or 'govern away'. This critique is not a plea to reject a major role for international organizations in developing a justice agenda. Rather, it is a suggestion that we need to look beyond our traditional understandings of them simply as agents of order.

If social and strategic relationships are not merely the aggregate of self-interested calculation (as both realist and neo-liberal approaches would affirm), then international organizations will not simply reflect the preferences of states, they must also be vehicles for moulding and adapting state preferences. They will then become much more important actors than in the past. This is extremely important for IPE in the twenty-first century. This is not to suggest that international organizations will become more important than states, or indeed multinational corporations. In contrast to states, or indeed firms, international organizations have no natural constituencies with primary loyalties. Economic life may be increasingly global, but everyday socio-political life for most people remains firmly embedded in national and local settings.

The financial crises have shaken the IMF's belief in the idea that there may be some 'one size fits all' view of best practice in macroeconomic and financial management. The early years of the twenty-first century will be crucial in confirming an agenda that allows for difference and complexity rather than one that reasserts the economists' normative and analytical preferences for convergence. But, while the Asian crises may have been a spur to rethinking global governance, mainstream demands to date have been largely for an incremental reform of a new financial architecture.[47]

The post-Washington consensus that is emerging does not represent radical reform but it does represent a recognition of the limits of the market fundamentalism of the 1980s and 1990s. It is a recognition that global markets are only likely to remain open in the context of an efficient regulatory, and just, environment. Let me thus come out of the closet. At one level I am calling for a normative IPE that attempts to globalize the Keynesian compact as a way of recivilizing capitalism after the period of a neo-liberal hegemony that shattered it. Why? Because the renewal of such a compact appears, in contrast to unfettered market fundamentalism at least, to be the most progressive *economic system* of wealth production, distribution and exchange that is compatible with the prevailing realities of an *international political system* in which the state remains the dominant unit of analysis and the key decision-making actor.

This leads to two ironies. The first is that, in rejecting the Keynesian compact, free-market fundamentalists have attacked and reduced the effectiveness of those very structures that allowed them to operate so successfully and profitably over the last few decades. The second is that, in calling for the development of a global Keynesian compact, reformers may be trying to reinstate a system that may well be necessary to ensuring the survival of open liberalism; thus saving free-market ideologues from their own excesses. Let us not forget that the initial Keynesian compact did not simply reflect the current state of economic theorizing. It was also an exercise in normative political theory. It represented a bargain struck between the state and the rapacious capitalism of the first half of the twentieth century that would allow for the continuance of free markets accompanied by mechanisms that would prevent repeats of the Great Depressions of the inter-war years and provide compensatory support systems for those most dispossessed by free markets.

The ideology of the 1980 and 1990s was increasingly ill disposed to such measures and strongly in favour of the globalization of financial market deregulation. When crisis struck in the emerging markets of East Asia and Latin America, the policy response, dictated largely by the public and private sector econocrats of the Wall Street–Washington axis[48] – raising taxes and interest rates, cutting welfare systems and so on – were *exactly the opposite* of what one would have expected under a Keynesian compact in a developed state. But, Krugman notes, the crisis in the financial system is only marginally explained by economic theory. Rather it was driven by what he calls 'amateur psychology'.[49] But what Krugman sees as 'amateur psychology' (and 'amateur sociology', but never 'amateur economics') is the stuff of what should be IPE – basically a complex form of analysis in which it is recognized that choices made by policy-makers are always likely to be sub-optimal and will always be driven (implicitly or explicitly) by particular ideological views and specific actor interests.

We must start with a recognition that the global system does not treat all actors equally. Markets operate double standards. Rich, developed countries when they stray from the straight and narrow of 'market fundamentals' tend to get the benefit of the doubt that allows them to pursue reform policies at a pace and with a freedom that is never extended to the developing world. As a consequence, IPE as problem-solving must have as its key normative goal an agenda for mitigating the market vulnerabilities of the weaker members of the international system. This might seem a reformist agenda, but, in the context of a neo-liberal hegemony, it is a radical one.

While the softening and widening of the Washington consensus to include those elements of a post-Washington consensus might represent one step on the learning curve for the international policy community, it is unlikely to address the justice and poverty questions on the international agenda. The absence of a wide-scale acceptance of its 'legitimacy' in the developing world remains, for quite appropriate reasons, the major challenge to globalization. It is not just Mahathir who sees globalization as a new form of imperialism or colonialism. Unless the world's poor secure a stake of their own in the global economy, the gains to the developed world may yet still fall victim to global disruption. North–South conflicts over questions of distributive justice at the global level represent perhaps the major potential source of widespread conflict in the post-Cold War world. Their analysis should be at the core of IPE scholarship in particular, and IR scholarship in general.

## NOTES

Thanks to my colleague Dr Nicola Phillips for her comments on this early draft. Needless to say, I alone am responsible for the mistakes.

1 See respectively James Caporaso, 'International Political Economy: Fad or Field', *International Studies Notes*, 3, 1 (1987), and Robert Gilpin, *The Political Economy of International Relations* (Princeton, NJ, Princeton University Press, 1987).

2 Most recently see Thomas Biersteker, 'Eroding Boundaries, Contested Domains', *International Studies Review*, 1, 1 (1999), p. 3.

3 Susan Strange, *States and Markets* (London, Pinter, 1988).

4 Susan Strange, *The Retreat of the State* (Cambridge, Cambridge University Press, 1996), and especially 'The Erosion of the State', *Current History*, 96 (1997).

5 See her critique of several key IR texts in Susan Strange, *What Theory? The Theory of Mad Money*, Working Paper No. 18 (University of Warwick, ESRC Centre for the Study of Globalization and Regionalization, December 1998) at http://www.csgr.org.

6 See Karl Polanyi, *The Great Transformation: The Political and Economic Origins of our Time* (Boston, MA, Beacon Press, 1944).

7 Kenichi Ohmae, *The End of the Nation-State: The Rise of Regional Economies* (New York, Free Press, 1995), and Kenichi Ohmae, *The Borderless World* (New York, Fontana, 1990).

8 Peter Schwartz and Peter Leyden, 'The Long Boom: A History of the Future, 1980–2020', *Wired* (July 1997), p. 116.

9 See Mortimer Zuckerman, 'A Second American Century', *Foreign Affairs*, 77, 3 (1998), pp. 18–31.

10 For insightful discussions see Waldon Bello, 'East Asia on the Eve of the Great Transformation', *Review of International Political Economy*, 5, 3 (1998), pp. 33–6.

11 Cited in Jim Hoagland, 'Is the Global Economy Widening the Income Gap?', *International Herald Tribune*, 27 April 1999, p. 8.

12 Gary Burtless, Robert Z. Lawrence, Robert E. Litan, Robert J. Shapiro, *Globaphobia: Confronting Fears About Open Trade* (Washington, DC, Brookings, 1998).

13 I have discussed this at length in Richard Higgott, 'Economics, Politics and (International) Political Economy: The Need for a Balanced Diet in an Era of Globalization', *New Political Economy*, 4, 1 (1999), pp. 23–36.

14 See, for example, Dani Rodrik, *Has Globalization Gone Too Far?* (Washington, DC, Institute for International Economics, 1998); Joseph Stiglitz, 'Towards a New Paradigm for Development: Strategies, Policies and Processes', the 1998 Prebisch Lecture (Geneva, UNCTAD, 19 October 1998). To be found at http://www.worldbank.org/html/etme/jssp101998.htm; Paul Krugman, *The Return of Depression Economics* (London, Allen Lane, 1999).

15 Robert Heilbroner and William Milberg, *The Crisis of Vision in Modern Economic Thought* (Cambridge, Cambridge University Press, 1995), p. 6.

16 See Ben Fine, 'The Triumph of Economics: Or, Rationality Can Be Dangerous to Your Reasoning', in James G. Carrier and Daniel Miller (eds), *Virtualism: A New Political Economy* (New York, Berg, 1998).

17  See Barry Eichengreen, 'Dental Hygiene and Nuclear War: How International Relations Looks to Economics', *International Organization*, 52, 4 (1998), p. 993.

18  See Jonathon Cohn, 'What Did Political Science Forget About Politics?', *The New Republic*, 25 October 1999, pp. 25–31.

19  Gary Becker, *Accounting for Tastes* (Cambridge, MA, Harvard University Press), p. 61.

20  Ibid., p. 49.

21  Eichengreen, 'Dental Hygiene', p. 1012.

22  Robert O. Keohane, 'International Institutions: Two Approaches', *International Studies Quarterly*, 32, 4 (1988), p. 382.

23  See, for example, Lisa Martin and Beth Simmons, 'Theories and Empirical Studies of International Institutions', and Helen Milner, 'Rationalizing Politics: The Emerging Synthesis of International, American and Comparative Politics', both in *International Organization*, 52, 4 (1998).

24  Best exemplified in Richard Ashley and R. B. J. Walker, 'Speaking the Language of Exile: Dissident Thought in International Studies', Special Issue, *International Studies Quarterly*, 34, 3 (1990).

25  Stiglitz, 'Towards a New Paradigm for Development'; see also his 'More Instruments and Broader Goals: Moving Towards a Post Washington Consensus', the 1998 WIDER Lecture (Helsinki, 7 January 1998).

26  For an empirical discussion of how direct taxes on capital have declined in the major economies since the 1980s see Rodrik, *Has Globalization Gone Too Far?*

27  John G. Ruggie, 'At Home Abroad, Abroad at Home: International Liberalization and Domestic Stability in the New World Economy', *Millennium: Journal of International Studies*, 24, 3 (1995), pp. 507–26.

28  See Vincent Cable, *The World's New Fissures: The Politics of Identity* (London, Demos, 1994).

29  See Marina Wes, *Globalization: Winners and Losers* (London, Institute for Public Policy Research, Commission on Public Policy and British Business, 1995).

30  Geoffrey Garrett, 'Global Markets and National Politics: Collision Course or Virtuous Circle', *International Organization*, 52, 4 (1998).

31  See Linda Weiss, *The Myth of the Powerless State* (Ithaca, NY, Cornell University Press, 1998).

32  Stephen Gill, 'Globalisation, Market Civilisation and Disciplinary Neo-Liberalism', *Millennium*, 24, 3 (1995), pp. 399–423.

33  Ethan Kapstein, 'Distributive Justice and International Trade', *Ethics and International Affairs*, 13 (1999).

34  George Soros, 'The Case for Global Finance', *The Economist*, 12 September 1998, pp. 19–20.

35  See Richard Higgott and Nicola Phillips, 'Resisting Triumphalism and Convergence: The Limits of Liberalization in Asia and Latin America', *Review of International Studies*, 26, 3 (2000), pp. 359–79.

36  C. Wyplosz, 'Global Financial Markets and Financial Crises, Coping with Financial Crises', in *Developing and Transition Countries: Regulatory and Supervisory Challenges in a New Era* (Amsterdam, Forum on Debt and Development, 16–17 March 1998), p. 4.

37   For a discussion see Ariel Buira, 'An Alternative Approach to Financial Crises', *Essays in International Finance*, no. 212 (Princeton University, Department of Economics, February 1999).

38   John Maynard Keynes noted in *Essays in Persuasion* (London, Hart-Davis, [1931] 1951).

39   This argument is developed in Richard Devetak and Richard Higgott, 'Justice Unbound? Globalization, States and the Transformation of the Social Bond', *International Affairs*, 75, 3 (1999).

40   Daniel Miller, 'A Theory of Virtualism', in James G. Carrier and Daniel Miller (eds), *Virtualism: A New Political Economy* (Oxford, Berg, 1998).

41   See Robert Cox, *Power, Production and World Order* (New York, Columbia University Press, 1987); Robert Cox with Timothy J. Sinclair, *Approaches to World Order* (Cambridge, Cambridge University Press, 1996), and Randall Germain, *The International Organization of Credit: States and Global Finance in the World Economy* (Cambridge, Cambridge University Press, 1997).

42   See Cecilia Lynch, 'Social Movements and the Problem of Globalization', *Alternatives*, 23, 2 (1998).

43   See UNDP, *Governance for Sustainability and Growth* (New York, July 1997), and Inge Kaul, Isabelle Grunberg and Marc A. Stern (eds), *Global Public Goods: International Co-operation in the 21st Century* (New York, Oxford University Press for the UNDP, 1999).

44   'Business Leaders Advocate Stronger UN and Take up Secretary General's Global Compact' (New York, UN Press Release, 5 July 1999).

45   Robert Cox, 'Civil Society at the Turn of the Millennium: Prospects for an Alternative World Order', *Review of International Studies*, 25, 1 (1999).

46   See the excellent paper by Ngaire Woods, 'Order, Globalization and Inequality', in Andrew Hurrell and Ngaire Woods (eds), *Inequality, Globalization and World Politics* (Oxford, Oxford University Press, 1999).

47   For example, see Barry Eichengreen, *Towards a New International Financial Architecture: A Practical Post Asian Agenda* (Washington, Institute for International Economics, 1998).

48   See J. N. Bhagwati, 'The Capital Myth', *Foreign Affairs*, 77, 3 (1998), pp. 7–12.

49   Paul Krugman, *The Return of Depression Economics* (London, Allen Lane/The Penguin Press, 1999), p. 113.

# 7

# The Global Politics of the Environment

## Lorraine Elliott

### Introduction

Contemporary environmental insecurities are well documented, as are their social, political, economic and ecological causes and impacts. Environmental degradation is now taken as evidence of a globalized world, bound up in the economic practices of globalization, demonstrative of the ecological 'one-ness' of the planet and invoking the imperatives of global governance in the face of a state in the throes of a crisis of capacity and legitimacy. The insinuation of such concerns on to the agenda of world politics has arisen variously as a response to environmental accidents and disasters, to increases in scientific knowledge, to activism and lobbying by non-governmental organizations and grassroots movements, and to heightened public consciousness. The reason for concern is twofold. First, scientific evidence supports the proposition that ecological damage is occurring at a rate faster than it has ever done in the past and that it is doing so because of human (and corporate) activity. Second, environmental changes have the potential for severe and possibly irreversible impacts not only on the ecosystem but on the social and economic development of people and states.

The prevailing image of the global politics of the environment is that of a liberal politics of the environment. International political responses to the globalized challenges of environmental change have been accommodated within and informed by neo-liberal values and modalities. This neo-liberal orthodoxy has been confirmed by the dominant analytical and theoretical responses to the environmental agenda within the discipline of international relations, informed by neo-liberal institutionalism and its dialects. At the same time, however, the political and economic structures and practices of a liberal world order, and their impact on environmental degradation and its consequences, have been subject to greater critical scrutiny. This chapter turns first to a brief and necessarily selective tour of the key themes of the contemporary politics of the agenda of environmental change.

## The environmental agenda: transiting the end of the Cold War

The inscription of environmental degradation on the international public policy agenda is not a simple by-product of the 'fall of the Wall', if that stands as a metaphor for the ending of superpower politics. By the end of the Cold War, environmental concerns were already firmly on the international agenda as shared, common and global problems. Environment and economics were conceptually, although hardly operationally, entwined in the concept of sustainable development, and environmental degradation was being linked to debates about broader conceptions of security.

The political globalization of environmental change dates at least to the 1972 United Nations Conference on the Human Environment (the Stockholm Conference). The momentum of Stockholm did fade rather quickly but picked up again in the early 1980s when the UN General Assembly established an independent expert commission – the World Commission on Environment and Development (known as the Brundtland Commission) – to propose 'long-term environmental strategies for achieving sustainable development to the year 2000 and beyond'.[1] The Commission's 1987 report established sustainable development as the leitmotif of the international environmental lexicon and, in its title, gave credibility to the notion that the future was one held in common, echoing the common security theme of the Palme Commission.[2] A sense of urgency characterized the political rhetoric of the late 1980s. In 1989, the G7 called for 'decisive action to understand and protect the earth's ecological balance'[3] – a call, incidentally, they could hardly themselves be accused of heeding – and the General Assembly declared the deterioration of the environment to be 'one of the main global problems facing the world today'.[4]

The willingness of governments to turn their post-Cold War attention to the problems of environmental degradation seemed confirmed by the United Nations Conference on Environment and Development (UNCED), established by General Assembly resolution in December 1989 and convened in Rio de Janeiro in 1992. The agreements adopted at Rio (all of them non-binding) confirmed the rhetoric of an equitable and global partnership for sustainable development.[5] They also confirmed the rhetoric of compromise, finessing difficult problems with diplomatic language or diverting them for negotiation at a later date, and fudging completely the crucial issues of institutional reform and financial support for developing countries.

For the most part post-Cold War (or post-Rio) global politics of the environment are a continuation, confirmation and intensification of the trends of the pre-1989 period. The political debates have become more complex and the diversity of political locations in which those debates take place has expanded. Since UNCED, the multilateral terrain of global environmental politics has become congested with conventions, protocols, declarations, statements of principle, committees, commissions, expert working groups, *ad hoc* working groups, open-ended working groups, intergovernmental panels, high-level advisory boards, scientific committees, convention secretariats, conferences of parties, intersessional meetings, ministerial summits and so on. However, this activity has not produced the kinds of agreements which are required to mitigate and reverse environmental decline or to protect those peoples most severely affected by the local and global impacts of that decline. The consensus demands of international diplomacy ensure that multilateral environmental agreements are often characterized by permissive compliance and verification mechanisms, few effective sanctions, and lengthy grace periods or deferred target dates. Political and economic interests continue to take precedence over environmental ones. International environmental institutions such as the United Nations Environment Programme (UNEP) and the Commission on Sustainable Development have limited mandates, lack substantive powers and are poorly resourced.

The traditional post-Stockholm cast of actors – environmental agencies, scientific organizations and environmental NGOs – has been transformed by a partial democratizing of environmental diplomacy and by the rebadging of the problem as sustainable development rather than environmental protection. It now includes all the major international economic institutions (especially the World Bank and the WTO), regional organizations, international business and industry organizations, most of the UN specialized agencies and programmes, trade unions, local government networks and the military as well as a range of grassroots organizations such as indigenous peoples' and women's networks. They take their place on the stage as activist 'stakeholders' in international environmental negotiations, as convenors of conferences and as initiators of policy strategies. The multilateral environmental agenda has also become much more than one of conservation, protection and 'end-of-pipe' regulation. It now includes trade and the environment; emissions trading and green taxes; sustainable consumption and production; debt, development assistance and foreign direct investment; sustainable tourism; urbanization and sustainable cities; sustainable development of small island states; telecommunications and the environment. Environmental scarcity is posed as a new threat to peace and security, providing a rationale for new defence missions and continued militarization even in the face of non-military insecurities.[6]

The global politics of the environment remains firmly embedded in inequities. Inequities in causes and impacts between rich and poor countries (and people), unequal trade and capital transactions, the paucity of international development assistance in pursuit of basic human needs, and the ever-growing burden of developing country debt are entwined with environmental degradation in a complex cause-and-effect relationship. Those who are most immediately and disproportionately hit by environmental decline and its economic and social consequences are those who are already economically and politically marginalized – the poor, indigenous peoples and women, especially but not exclusively in the developing world. Those countries which are already ecologically and economically vulnerable are less able to control the causes or mitigate the impacts of environmental change without assistance.

Affluence rather than poverty remains the primary cause of global environmental decline. While the visible consequences of environmental degradation – deforestation, desertification and air pollution, for example – are concentrated more in developing countries, the invisible causes are embedded in the ecological shadow cast by the industrialized countries. These causes arise from the practices of industrialization and the pursuit of economic growth, unsustainable patterns of production and consumption, and extensive and excessive exploitation of living and non-living resources. In 1998 the industrialized world comprised about 20 per cent of the world's population but accounted for 86 per cent of total private consumption expenditure, consumed 58 per cent of total energy, owned 87 per cent of the world's vehicle fleet, and emitted 53 per cent of the world's carbon dioxide emissions.[7] Tensions between developed and developing countries therefore remain a central feature of the global politics of the environment and concerns about inequities are revisited in political debates about commitments, obligations, and the provision (or otherwise) of financial and technical resources.

The rhetorical urgency which characterized the transition across the end of the Cold War has not been much in evidence in practice. Certainly there has been little transfer of resources from Cold War security budgets to post-Cold War environmental expenditure, despite promises of a peace dividend. There has been little beyond a declaratory commitment to important cross-sectoral issues of financial and technology transfer, debt, unequal trading relationships and poverty alleviation. Despite an increase in the number of environmental agreements, conferences and other modalities of international debate, and despite greater attention to environmental problems in many countries, the state of the global environment continues to deteriorate as UNEP's first *Global Environmental Outlook*, published in 1997, demonstrated.[8] By 1997, and the United Nations General Assembly Special Session (UNGASS) to review the implementation of Agenda 21, the spirit of Rio had been substantially weakened. At UNGASS, governments were unable to reach consensus on a political statement and, despite adopting a Programme for Further Implementation, could find little of real substance to agree on except that 'five years after the Rio Earth Summit, the planet's health is generally worse than ever'.[9]

## The hegemony of neo-liberalism

The post-Rio challenges are embedded in the intensification of globalization and its political and normative consequences. The central theme, admittedly more obvious in some cases than in others, is the dominance of neo-liberal interpretations and explanations in international political practice and in the discipline of international relations as it attends to the agenda of environmental change. This neo-liberal orthodoxy has animated a reformist approach to global politics of the environment, one akin to Robert Cox's characterization of problem-solving theory and practice. As Cox observes, this 'takes the world as it finds it, with the prevailing social and power relationships and institutions into which they are organized, as the given framework for action. The general aim of problem-solving is to make these relationships and institutions work more smoothly.'[10] Resolving the environmental crisis becomes synonymous with making the existing political and economic order – states and markets – work more efficiently and effectively. This may articulate some basis for reform but it does not invoke any challenge to the fundamental assumptions upon which that order is based. These assumptions look to the value of international institutions based on the sovereign state, decision-making informed by democratic pluralism, a commitment to the market and economic growth (albeit of the 'right' kind) and a belief in the importance of objective science and technology. Mobilized by these kinds of concerns, the dominant approach to the global politics of the environment within international relations is that 'global environmental issues can best be understood by studying environmental movements, ecological parties, international organizations and regimes, international law and the problems of policies of specific nations in different regions of the world'.[11]

This neo-liberal problematic has, at best, provided an incomplete and partial picture of the global politics of the environment. At worst, it has been discursively complicit in sustaining particular hegemonic ideologies and practices that serve to conceal the fundamental causes of environmental degradation and the relations of power and powerlessness which result in inequitable social and economic impacts of environmental decline. In other words, there is a kind of meta-politics at play. This exposes a different environmental problematic both in the practice of international politics and in the discipline of international relations. The global environment is more than an issue area. Rather, it is 'an arena in which fundamental conflicts over power, wealth and control are played out'.[12] The ideologies and practices of the contemporary liberal world order are bound up with the ways in which environmental problems are articulated and understood, as well as with the causes of the environmental crisis. In a critical global politics of the environment, prevailing power relationships which reflect and constitute that world order – states and markets – are ecologically dysfunctional: a cause of the ecological crisis and a barrier to its resolution.

In order to consider this proposition further, I examine three 'sites' which are simultaneously interconnected and in tension in the patterns of and debates about globalization – the global, the state and the market. First, what sense is to be made of the 'global' in the context of the policy and intellectual agenda of environmental politics? Second, what sense is to be made of the international politics of environmental governance and, particularly, the role of the state? Third, what sense is to be made of the international political economy of the environment in an era of globalization? There is, however, a fourth site – the local – that is consistently ignored or downplayed in these debates. The local is most often excluded from the realm of the international and paid little attention in the conventional mainstream of the discipline of IR. Where it is acknowledged, neo-liberal faith assumes that local voices and concerns will be heard and represented through the processes of democratic pluralism, and effective solutions will arise as an axiomatic outcome of the contemporary international political and economic order – a kind of political ecology 'trickle-down'. Yet, as much of the critical literature demonstrates, the local is disadvantaged by the globalized order but also constitutes a site of resistance activism opposed to that order.

## Site 1:  Locating the global

The representation of environmental degradation and unsustainable development as urgent, global and shared was strengthened by the transition to a post-Cold War environmental politics. The image of a shared vulnerability to and responsibility for global environmental insecurities captured in 'our common future'[13] is reproduced in the metaphors of the 'global partnership'[14] and 'our global neighbourhood'.[15] It appears again in the principle of 'common but differentiated responsibilities' which were intended to moderate tensions between developed and developing countries over relative responsibilities and obligations. It appears also in the 'common heritage of humankind', reworked from its original concern with sharing the benefits of resource exploitation to one which expresses (in theory at least) the imperatives of environmental stewardship.

Yet the 'global' has been defined as much politically as ecologically and in a way that has served to advantage the privileged interests of the few rather than the collective interests of the many. Problems such as climate change and ozone depletion clearly have a global dimension: the atmosphere *is* a global commons and the impacts of atmospheric pollution and degradation will be felt, indeed are being felt, planet-wide. In many cases, however, the imbalance between impacts and contributions to the problem is substantial – the low-lying Pacific Island states are a case in point. Industrialized countries such as the United States and Australia have, however, insisted on invoking the 'global' to demand that *all* countries – including developing countries – should commit to mitigation strategies and targets in the face of a 'common' problem such as climate change because of anticipated future emissions. This neatly avoids the fact that the 'global' and 'common' problem remains one created and sustained very much by the activities of a few.

Tensions over the global are also key to the international politics of (tropical) deforestation and loss of biodiversity. Developing countries are host to much of the world's biodiversity and tropical forests. These debates, which illuminate disputes over the claiming of sovereign 'resources' – forests and individual creatures – as the common heritage of humankind, have given further grist to G77 arguments about the inequities of what is defined as global and in whose interests. The 'global' value of the world's biodiversity has been determined to lie primarily in its utility value for pharmaceuticals and agriculture, much of which is still exploited by Northern-based corporations.[16] The 'global' consequences of tropical deforestation lie in the double assault on climate change – the release of stored $CO_2$ and the destruction of a carbon sink. Developing countries have perceived the focus on deforestation as an infringement of sovereign rights, the imposition of Western environmental priorities, and as a way for industrialized countries to minimize or divert *their* climate change responsibilities. The causes of deforestation are caught up as much in the globalized economy, through trade and investment, as they are in local practices, although the impacts of local corruption and illegal logging activity should not be overlooked. The expectation that developing countries will shoulder much of the economic burden associated with management of forests for the 'common good' exacerbates the impression that burden-sharing is a bit too one-sided. The global principles of burden-sharing are much less in evidence when the interests of industrialized countries are less clearly engaged, as in the case of desertification for example. The negotiations for that convention were notable for US and EC resistance to having desertification defined as a 'global' problem – despite the fact that it affects up to 35 per cent of the world's land surface and up to one-quarter of the world's population.

The limits of the global have been most clearly spelled out in the mandate for the Global Environment Facility (GEF) which establishes something like a two-stage selection process. Its priorities are confined to four issues: protection of biodiversity, the mitigating of global warming, the control of pollution in international waters and the management of stratospheric ozone. The GEF's terms of reference restrict it further to funding only the incremental costs of the global component of environmental projects in each or any of these four areas, on the basis that it is possible to determine what is of benefit to the world at large and exclude what is of 'local' benefit only.

Environmental concerns which do not meet the privileged criteria of global are thereby excluded from the arena of responsibility of the world community of states, narrowing rather than expanding the agenda. It is difficult to resist entirely the argument that the 'hegemony of globalism' articulates the interests of the industrialized 'North' in influencing the developing 'South' for the purpose of risk prevention for the rich.[17] Global burden-sharing comes to represent something of a one-way transaction – what's mine is mine, what's yours is mine.[18] Shiva argues that the global, as presently constructed, does not represent universal human interests but rather a 'particular local and parochial interest which has been globalized through the scope of its reach'.[19] Whose common future, then, are we talking about? Those 'local' environmental problems which affect the largest proportion of the planet's people – who just happen to live in developing countries – do not count as global. Yet the difference between a global problem and what is confined to the category of local (and therefore not part of the agenda of the 'international') is often a matter of degree. As Lipschutz and Conca point out, 'phenomena such as soil erosion and land degradation that are depicted as "local" – and thus relegated to a lesser sense of urgency – are ... [nevertheless] linked by economic, political and social institutions of much broader, and often global, extent'.[20] Reclaiming the local has become the focus of resistance to globalization and the centralizing of the global. In particular, the demands of 'relocalization' have provided a vehicle for reasserting sustainable development as a local practice based on small(er)-scale economies, democratic decision-making, local reinvestment and self-reliance.

## Site 2:   The state – globalizing governance

Debates about the state and sovereignty are central to the global politics of the environment. Environmental change, no longer (if it ever was) easily accommodated within the politically bounded space of the state, calls into question the reality and utility of sovereignty as a fundamental international norm and draws attention to debates about the adequacy and authority of the state. Environmental change has become synonymous with globalization and deterritorialization – and globalization 'has seriously reduced [states'] scope for independent action'.[21] The territorial integrity of the state appears increasingly precarious in the face of environmental challenges. The capacity of the state to respond unilaterally and effectively is weakened in the face of the increasing trans-boundary nature of environmental degradation. Doubts about the state's ability to fulfil the social contract to provide its citizens with security and justice, in this case a secure environment and environmental justice, or to defend same citizens against environmental threats from 'outside', create ambivalence about its normative appeal as the basis for political community.[22]

The limitations of sovereignty as a key organizing principle of international politics and the increasing frailty of territorial boundaries (at least in the environmental context) are openly acknowledged in the face of the interdependencies revealed by trans-boundary and global environmental degradation. The World Commission on Environment and Development provided the most apt aphorism – 'the Earth is one but we are not'.[23] Debates about environmental governance have sought, however, to rehabilitate the state as the agent of more effective international co-operation, and to encourage institutional reform under the banner of collective sovereignty masquerading as global multilateralism. Two explicit assumptions are in force here. First, the state is the '*sole* legitimate source of public policy'.[24] Second, international institutions, which 'necessarily follow the principle of state sovereignty', can be made to function more effectively and efficiently.[25] No more is expected of an effective institution than that it will 'nudge countries further along [the] continuum of commitment and compliance...promote concern among governments [and] enhance the contractual environment by providing negotiating forums'.[26] Success is most often defined in terms of institutional rather than environmental outcomes: reaching an agreement is concrete evidence of the cooperative spirit at work, even if the agreement is environmentally inadequate.

There is a general liberal optimism about the increasing web of multilateral environmental regimes and new norms. The apparent willingness of states to accept and articulate concepts such as intergenerational equity or (more controversially) environmental rights, concepts which widen the scope of those to whom obligations are owed in international law beyond states and present generations, is taken as evidence of the sophistication and the confidence of the state. In other words, the state (or, one assumes, governments) retains authority while at the same time casting the governance net more widely and supposedly more effectively.

This optimism has thus far been largely misplaced or, at the very least, overstated. The normative interests of the state remain evident in the dominance of sovereignty claims which are pursued at the expense of cosmopolitan values *and* at the expense of the environment. This is not states acting as local agents of the common good.[27] The primacy of sovereign state interests is sustained rather than challenged in environmental governance. The principle that 'states have...the sovereign right to exploit their own resources pursuant to their own...policies' appears as standard fare in almost all multilateral environmental agreements and pre-dates most other contemporary norms of international environmental law. In some cases (the 1972 Stockholm Declaration and the 1992 Rio Declaration for example) sovereignty rights are balanced against a requirement that states have a 'responsibility to ensure that activities within their jurisdiction or control do not cause damage to the environment of other States or of areas beyond the limits of national jurisdiction'. Just as there is extensive evidence of states' commitment to their sovereign rights, there is equally extensive evidence of the almost total disregard of this second principle of trans-boundary and extraterritorial stewardship.

The dominance of sovereignty concerns has been further reinforced by the particularistic definitions of the global outlined above. In the face of common heritage claims to developing country 'resources', but in the absence of firm multilateral commitment from developed countries to the provision of financial and technological assistance, developing countries have reasserted sovereignty to protect, as they see it, their right to development. And who can forget ex-President George Bush's claims at UNCED in 1992 that the American lifestyle was not up for negotiation! Thus sovereignty and the pursuit of national interest remains normatively strong (although intuitively problematic) even as the role and capacity of the state are being challenged and reworked by the processes of globalization and environmental change.

Despite this continued emphasis on the state and some form of collective sovereignty, liberal concerns with 'better governance' have been responsible for a greater democratization of environmental diplomacy and politics. Rio did not herald the beginning of non-governmental participation in environmental negotiations (that dates at least to the 1972 Stockholm Conference) but it did broaden the rules of participation. Maurice Strong, Secretary-General of UNCED (as he had been of Stockholm, twenty years before), was insistent that representation in the preparatory process and at the conference 'proper' would accommodate NGOs who could demonstrate that their interests were directly relevant to the UNCED agenda. As a result, 1,400 NGOs (including scientific and industry organizations) were officially accredited to the Rio process although their opportunities for involvement in the detail of the agreements fluctuated depending on the stage of the negotiations. The extent to which they were able to influence outcomes remains a matter of some conjecture, even among the NGOs themselves. What they did provide was a degree of transparency, accountability and expertise. In this sense, they were not simply the objects of democratization: they were its subjects, they helped to create it, and in ways that some governments might not have expected or even necessarily welcomed.[28] Environmental agreements and the strategies they advocate also suggest a more inclusive politics. In Agenda 21, for example, governments devoted nine chapters to the so-called 'major groups' whose participation in the global partnership for sustainable development was deemed crucial.[29] Other agreements point to the importance of consulting with local communities, with NGOs and with other groups within society.

The creation of political space in the global politics of the environment for actors other than states is justified and supported on the grounds of democratic pluralism, efficiency and effectiveness. Decision-making by governments and the implementation of environmental agreements is argued to be more effective if all stakeholders are represented, if the legitimate interests of other actors are recognized and if agreements acknowledge that, in particular circumstances, they have a role to play. This logic of pluralist analysis is reinforced in the conventional wisdoms of the discipline. The *theoretical* importance to the global politics of the environment of non-state actors, particularly non-governmental organizations and the scientific community, lies in the way they 'exercise authoritative knowledge',[30] and in their ability (or otherwise) to influence the patterns of state-based decision-making and behaviour, to affect the distribution of power among them or to order behaviour among other actors. This resource mobilization theory of social movements tends to focus on elite dynamics and on 'epistemic communities' rather than, say, the dynamic transnationalism of grassroots movements which often proceeds not simply as a response to statism but independently of the state. Global civil society is reduced to the rather anodyne 'slice of associational life that exists above the individual and below the state, but also across national boundaries'.[31] What is missing from this analysis is global civil society as a transformative political community, as an 'alternative organizing principle for world politics, based on new constitutive rules and institutional forms'.[32] In contrast with the centralized global of multilateral institutional practices, civil society represents a decentralized global, the integration of the 'locals' and the cumulative voice of locale-specific activism.

This is not to deny in any way the ecological and political diversity found within civil society nor to argue that NGOs are not at times beset by their own politics and interests. Nor does it overlook the fact that some environmentalist NGOs pursue a consumerist and technocratic discourse.[33] But it is to suggest that a neo-liberal emphasis on democratic efficiency and resource mobilization is intellectually one-dimensional. It runs the risk of ignoring or misunderstanding the political structures of inclusion and exclusion, and overlooking those very groups and voices whose participation *on their own terms* is essential to sustainable development and responses to the challenges of global environmental change. Participation therefore brings with it its own complexities for NGOs. To what extent does participatory multilateralism enhance the opportunities for NGOs to articulate change and to what extent does participation legitimize statist forms of governance? Strategies of participation reveal little about the power relationships which determine the extent or nature of that participation, and its assumptions about democratic outcomes are open to question. Whatever it is, democratic pluralism is not a cosmopolitan democracy. Whether it contains the seeds of cosmopolitan democracy, as the contradictions of state and civil society are worked through, is less certain and requires more thought and research.

The ambiguities of democratization are most forcefully played out over the gender politics of environmental degradation and the environmental politics of indigeneity. For both women and indigenous peoples, the disproportionate impact of the causes and consequences of environmental degradation on their daily lives and, in the case of indigenous peoples, their cultural and physical survival, is symptomatic of the biases of a more extensive structural inequality. Unequal and inequitable allocation of resources – including access to credit, rights to commons or traditional lands, decision-making authority over the resources and environmental services of daily life – simply compound the problem.

The Rio Declaration recognized quite specifically that women and indigenous peoples have a 'vital role' to play and that their 'full participation' (in the case of women) and their 'effective participation' (in the case of indigenous peoples) is essential to the achievement of sustainable development. A greater inclusiveness can only be welcomed as a precondition for sustainable development and more effective environmental outcomes. Yet the whole issue of rights and freedom from oppression is downplayed. For both women and indigenous peoples this emphasis on democratic efficiency and pluralist governance has ensured that they have been defined as objects to be acted upon, to be educated, consulted or informed, to be empowered from above or outside, or as a source of knowledge which can be appropriated and incorporated into the discourse of the 'global' as and when needed. Indeed, the rationale for inclusion is sometimes specifically expressed in those terms. A report for the World Bank suggests, for example, that 'it is in *our* interests and those of the planet to open a permanent space for these peoples and *their* values'.[34] The articulation of inside and outside, of them and us, is clear. The themes of emancipation and new visions of development which so often animate the outcomes of the collective global activism of women or of indigenous peoples on environment and development are, for the most part, absent.[35]

## Site 3:   The market – entrenching the liberal international economic order

The most obvious and confident articulation of liberal values in the global politics of the environment has been in the support for the practices and norms of a globalized world economy. A liberal international economic order – free(r) trade, the free movement of capital and limited interference in the market – is accepted with little question as essential for increased economic welfare, greater equity and, as a welcome consequence, the likelihood of greater environmental protection. The embedded normative assumptions are many. First, poverty is a major cause of environmental degradation. Second, unsustainable development is now primarily a developing-country problem. Third, the solution lies in economic growth – or 'high levels of productive activity', as the Brundtland Commission put it.[36] Fourth, economic growth can be achieved without environmental degradation. Fifth, economic growth and the successful pursuit of sustainable development can only be achieved within a supportive and open international economic system built on the cornerstones of free trade and investment. Sixth, market-based modalities that employ pricing signals to encourage better environmental behaviour and internalize environmental values and costs are more effective than command-and-control regimes. Seventh, the corporate sector is crucial to the pursuit of sustainable development and global environmental protection. The consequences: economic globalization is depoliticized and comes to be seen as part of the solution rather than part of the problem. Rather than being perceived as a cause of environmental degradation, economic growth and the production of wealth are offered as solutions to the problems of unsustainable development. Problems of ecology and politics are reduced to solutions of technology transfer and new and additional financial resources.

These assumptions and explanations are vulnerable to challenge. The demonizing of poverty as complicitous in unsustainable development because the poor have the 'propensity to engage in environmentally destructive patterns of behaviour'[37] not only casts the poor as perpetrators rather than victims but runs the risk of absolving the affluent of the same environmental crimes. As noted earlier, on almost any measure rich peoples and countries consume more resources and produce more waste than poor peoples and countries. Environmental and resource inequities are not simply a statement of geography. Past injustices, through the extractive practices of colonialism, have left the poorer countries less able to mitigate environmental degradation and less able to manage the impacts of that degradation, both local and global.[38] The industrialized countries continue to share in the burden of unsustainable development through disproportionately unsustainable patterns of production and consumption. If sustainable development is to start anywhere, it starts at home! The assumptions that economic growth – or what the United Nations Development Programme (UNDP) now prefers to call consumption growth – is the key to sustainable development because it will alleviate poverty detours the problem of continued inequitable distribution of wealth within and between countries. As the UNDP's own figures show, the increase in global consumption has not been accompanied by an increase in global income equity.[39] The logic that the consequences of the growth ethic have been environmental degradation and resource depletion remains powerful.

Concerns that patterns of free(r) trade and investment will continue to have severe environmental consequences and will do little to overcome poverty have not been ameliorated by the authoritative discourse of trade liberalization. As Postel and Flavin argue, 'much depends...on who gains from the added export revenue – peasant farmers or wealthy landowners...[and] on whether opening world markets would cause scarce land and water to be diverted from subsistence to export crops at the expense of the poor and of food self-sufficiency'.[40] Suspicion of free trade and investment strategies is heightened by concerns about the displacement of pollution-intensive industries which would allow industrialized countries to maintain the integrity of their own environments through exploitation of the raw materials and environments of other, primarily developing, countries.[41] Reliance on green corporatism engenders similar disquiet. The imperatives for better corporate practice cannot be overstated. Multinational corporate control over global wealth and resources is extensive and the consequences in terms of land-use, energy, deforestation, production and management of hazardous waste, emission of greenhouse gases, marketing and use of pesticides and other chemicals have been and continue to be widespread. But it is this record which should caution against corporate claims for the environmental benefits of self-regulation and voluntary initiatives.

To be fair, the liberal image of a globalized economy, articulated in key texts such as the Brundtland Report and Agenda 21, is not blind to the requirements of social justice and environmental degradation. The Brundtland Report made it clear that its purpose was to contribute to the building of a future that was 'prosperous, just and secure',[42] that we have a 'moral obligation to other living beings and future generations',[43] and that the natural systems that support life on earth should not be endangered by development.[44] However, globalization, to date, does not have a good record on social justice, environmental protection or the exercise of moral obligations. Rather than providing the basis for global economic growth and increased welfare, globalization has enabled major centres to draw on the ecological capital of other (usually developing) countries or poorer communities. The increase in global trading and direct investment has facilitated the export and displacement of pollution and environmental degradation from the industrialized world, both market and (prior to the 1990s) command economies. It has enabled high levels of consumption by the rich at the continued expense of the poor. The 'institutions' (in the broadest sense of the word) which have been most advantaged by the practices of globalization – the industrialized countries (though admittedly not all people within them), business and transnational corporate actors and global economic elites – are those most responsible for global environmental degradation.

## International relations and its (environmental) discontents

The global politics of the environment (GPE) are not simply confined to the world 'out there', as international public policy issues amenable to objective observation, description and analysis by scholars within the discipline of international relations. This is more than 'foreign policy and [international] current affairs', as Fred Halliday observed in his 1991 injunction that we 'look again at what constitutes this academic discipline'.[45] Certainly there is an analytical dimension. The matter of how to halt and reverse global environmental degradation and its ecological, social, political and economic consequences is a serious one. But the task for IR cannot be reduced to puzzling through 'which patterns lead to more rather than less cooperative behaviour'[46] or framing a research agenda around the questions 'how have [environmental] institutions fared, what functions have they performed well, and how can they be improved in the future?'.[47] The debate about global environmental change is fundamentally one of 'informed ethics and morality'[48] rather than simply strategy and efficiency. A critical global politics of the environment is already well established within IR, challenging international political practice and self-consciously 'subversive of the conventional wisdom of International Relations'[49] and mainstream theory. Three themes are central to this project, which has at its core a reinvigoration of the normative dimension of the study (as well as the practice) of international, or world, or global environmental politics.

The first refers attention again to the adequacy or otherwise of the disciplinary framework and, in particular, the inherited theoretical assumptions of the neo-liberal orthodoxy for thinking about the environmental crisis and for offering solutions and strategies. The arguments that neo-liberalism is for the most part mute on questions of power and powerlessness in the global politics of the environment – what Dalby refers to as the 'metaphysics of domination and control'[50] – and that it reproduces the 'industrial paradigm...as the privileged domain for analysis'[51] are now well examined in the literature. The question is, then, where to from here? In other words, if neo-liberalism is inadequate, what would a more theoretically rich and politically nuanced 'ecological IR theory' look like? One of the most fruitful roads to follow may well be the more specific incorporation of green political thought within IR, a project already articulated as one of 'radicalizing regimes'[52] and 'emancipating IR'.[53] Other compatible approaches which warrant further scrutiny are those which seek connections between the global politics of the environment and the cultural turn in IR,[54] those which explore the implications of feminist interventions for theorizing the global politics of the environment,[55] and those which adopt a more post-structuralist or specifically Foucauldian analysis.[56]

The second theme in a critical GPE poses questions about the degree of confidence or otherwise which can or should be afforded to the 'basic assumptions of modern western society'[57] and the 'capacity of western institutions to redress or reverse the environmental crisis'.[58] In other words, what sense should we make of modernity? This is hardly a new debate in the discipline. In the environmental context, the 'large-scale and systematic degradation [that] occurs from the ordinary and standard practices of modernity'[59] – the internationalizing of the sovereign state, the rise of global neo-liberalism and the spread of capitalism and industrialism – is now extensively examined in the environmental literature. But, again, where to from here? One possibility is a more intense contemplation of the implications for IR theory of the social and political theory literature on ecological modernization and risk society. Both are based on the rehabilitation of modernity as a more complex and reflexive phase of contemporary society and both are informed by the challenges of the ecological crisis of modernity. Such contemplation would also encourage a more detailed exploration of the ecological paradox of a globalized modernity. This includes the extent of our reliance on technology and science to expose the environmental consequences of modernization based on technological and scientific 'progress'; the extent to which the globalization of communications and perhaps even identity have facilitated the strengthening of global civil society as resistance to the impacts of economic globalization; the extent to which the state remains an assumed site of environmental implementation and regulation at the same time as its institutional and political capacity is being undermined by globalization.

The third theme in a critical GPE directs us to more specific concerns with justice, cosmopolitan values and the role of normative theory in IR. Debates about redistributive and environmental justice (to say nothing of ecological justice), moral obligations to those who are not co-nationals (and, indeed, to non-human species and to future generations), participatory and democratic governance, agency, and the whole issue of transnational harm which characterize contemporary cosmopolitan thinking are central to the global politics of the environment.[60] This cosmopolitan turn, or re-turn to be more precise, in IR is also likely to be hospitable to debates within the global politics of the environment about universalism versus particularism. These are manifest in concerns about eco-imperialism and the imposition of 'Western' values of environmental protection, but also (and often counter to the interests of developing country governments and elites) in the environmental politics of indigeneity, gender and (cultural) identity and the threads of justice and equity with which they are interwoven. Curiously this cosmopolitan path seems to be the least well-developed dimension of a critical GPE and yet it might perhaps offer the most productive opportunity for articulating a new ethic upon which to base a more equitable and democratic practice of global politics of the environment.

## NOTES

1    United Nations General Assembly, *Process of Preparation of the Environmental Perspective to the Year 2000 and Beyond* (A/RES/38/161), 19 December 1983, para. 8(a).

2    World Commission on Environment and Development, *Our Common Future* (Oxford, Oxford University Press, 1987).

3    Cited in A. J. Fairclough, 'Global Environmental and Natural Resource Problems – Their Economic, Political and Security Implications', *The Washington Quarterly*, 14, 1 (1991), p. 96.

4    United Nations General Assembly, *International Cooperation in the Monitoring, Assessment and Anticipation of Environmental Threats and in Assistance in Cases of Environmental Emergency* (A/RES/44/224), 85th Plenary Meeting, 22 December 1989.

5    See United Nations Conference on Environment and Development (UNCED), *Report of the UN Conference on Environment and Development*, Annex I: *Rio Declaration on Environment and Development* (A/CONF.151/26), vol. 1, 12 August 1992; UNCED, *Report of the UN Conference on Environment and Development*, Annex II: *Agenda 21* (A/CONF.151/26), vols 1–3, 12 August 1992.

6    For summaries of the extensive literature on environmental security see Lorraine Elliott, *The Global Politics of the Environment* (Basingstoke, Macmillan, 1997), ch. 9; Simon Dalby, 'The Politics of Environmental Security', in Jyrki Käkönen (ed.), *Green Security or Militarised Environment* (Aldershot, Dartmouth Publishing, 1994).

7    United Nations Development Programme (UNDP), *Human Development Report 1998* (New York, Oxford University Press, 1998).

8    United Nations Environment Programme (UNEP), *Global Environmental Outlook –1: Executive Summary* (UNEP, Nairobi, 1997). http://www.unep.org/unep/eia/geo1/exsum/ex2.htm.

9    United Nations Department of Public Information, 'Earth Summit Review Ends with Few Commitments', Round-up Press Release, DPI/1916/SD (July 1997). http://www.un.org/ecosocdev/geninfo/sustdev/es5final.htm.

10  Robert W. Cox, 'Social Forces, States and World Orders: Beyond International Relations Theory', in Robert O. Keohane (ed.), *Neorealism and Its Critics* (New York, Columbia University Press, 1986), p. 208.

11  Sheldon Kamieniecki, 'Emerging Forces in Global Environmental Politics', in Sheldon Kamieniecki (ed.), *Environmental Politics in the International Arena: Movements, Parties, Organizations and Policies* (Albany, NY, State University of New York Press, 1993), p. 1.

12  Ken Conca and Ronnie D. Lipschutz, 'A Tale of Two Forests', in Ronnie D. Lipschutz and Ken Conca (eds), *The State and Social Power in Global Environmental Politics* (New York, Columbia University Press, 1993), p. 3.

13  World Commission on Environment and Development, *Our Common Future*.

14  UNCED, *Rio Declaration*.

15  Commission on Global Governance, *Our Global Neighbourhood* (Oxford, Oxford University Press, 1995).

16  While the biodiversity convention does acknowledge multiple utility, the politics of biodiversity have become dominated by concerns about biosafety, genetically modified organisms, patent and intellectual property rights.

17  Wolfgang Sachs, 'Introduction', in Wolfgang Sachs (ed.), *Global Ecology: A New Arena of Political Conflict* (London, Zed Books, 1993), p. 17.

18  See Vandana Shiva, 'The Greening of the Global Reach', in Sachs, *Global Ecology*, p. 152.

19  Ibid., p. 150.

20  Ronnie D. Lipschutz and Ken Conca, 'The Implications of Global Ecological Interdependence', in Lipschutz and Conca, *The State and Social Power*, p. 331.

21  Andrew Linklater, 'Neo-Realism in Theory and Practice', in Ken Booth and Steve Smith (eds), *International Relations Theory Today* (Cambridge, Polity, 1995), p. 250.

22  The issue of capacity extends to the implementation of multilateral environmental agreements once adopted and in force. As Mische points out, if environmental commitments are to be put in place, a strong state may be required; see Patricia Mische, 'Ecological Security and the Need to Reconceptualise Sovereignty', *Alternatives*, 14, 4 (1989), pp. 389–427. Yet states are likely to have varying capacities to implement treaties and conventions in terms both of institutional and technological wherewithal and of the ability to oversee other actors whose behaviour might be more or less environmentally destructive.

23  World Commission on Environment and Development, *Our Common Future*, p. 27.

24  Marc A. Levy, Peter M. Haas and Robert O. Keohane, 'Institutions for the Earth: Promoting International Environmental Protection', *Environment*, 34, 4 (1992), p. 36 (emphasis added).

25  Ibid., p. 13.

26  Ibid., p. 14.

27  The phrase is Hedley Bull's; see Andrew Linklater, 'The Evolving Spheres of International Justice', *International Affairs*, 75, 3 (1999), p. 478.

28  Many of the smaller delegations, for example, whose human resources were stretched by the myriad of small working groups and corridor diplomacy, found

the daily publications produced by environmental NGOs valuable for helping them to understand what was going on.

29    The nine major groups identified in Agenda 21 are: women, farmers, young people, trade unions, business and industry, local authorities, scientists, indigenous peoples, and NGOs working in environment and development.

30    Peter M. Haas, 'Obtaining International Environmental Protection Through Epistemic Consensus', *Millennium*, 19, 3 (1990), p. 349.

31    Paul Wapner, *Environmental Activism and World Civic Politics* (Albany, NY, State University of New York Press, 1996), p. 4.

32    Conca and Lipschutz, 'A Tale of Two Forests', p. 9.

33    For a trenchant critique of environmental NGOs and consumerism see Timothy Luke, 'The (Un)wise (Ab)use of Nature: Environmentalism as Globalized Consumerism', *Alternatives*, 23, 2 (1998), pp. 176–82.

34    Shelton H. Davis, 'Introduction', in Shelton H. Davis (ed.), *Indigenous Views of Land and the Environment*, World Bank Discussion Paper no. 188 (Washington, DC, World Bank, 1993), p. xi (emphases added).

35    See, for example, Women's Action Agenda 21 or the representations by the Coordinating Committee for the Indigenous Peoples' Organizations of the Amazon Basin (COICA) to bilateral and multilateral funders and to environmental organizations, reproduced in Ken Conca, Michael Alberty and Geoffrey D. Dabelko (eds), *Green Planet Blues: Environmental Politics from Stockholm to Rio* (Boulder, CO, Westview Press, 1995).

36    World Commission on Environment and Development, *Our Common Future*, p. 44.

37    Mohamed T. El-Ashry, 'Development Assistance Institutions and Sustainable Development', *Washington Quarterly*, 16, 2 (1993), p. 84.

38    In some cases, of course, these structural difficulties have been further compounded by the legacy of years of repressive and corrupt regimes, many of which were actively supported by both superpowers during the Cold War.

39    See UNDP, *Human Development Report 1998*.

40    Sandra Postel and Christopher Flavin, 'Reshaping the Global Economy', in Lester R. Brown and Linda Starke (eds), *State of the World 1991* (New York, W. W. Norton Co, 1991), p. 180.

41    The most (in)famous articulation of environmental comparative advantage came from Lawrence Summers, former Chief Economist for the World Bank, who argued that 'the economic logic behind dumping a load of toxic waste in the lowest wage country is impeccable... underpopulated countries such as Africa [*sic*] are vastly under-polluted'; cited in Jim Puckett, 'Disposing of the Waste Trade: Closing the Recycling Loophole', *The Ecologist*, 24, 2 (1994), p. 53.

42    World Commission on Environment and Development, *Our Common Future*, p. 363.

43    Ibid., p. 57.

44    Ibid., p. 44.

45    Fred Halliday, 'International Relations: Is There a New Agenda?', *Millennium*, 20, 1 (1991), p. 57.

46    Robert O. Keohane, *International Institutions and State Power* (Boulder, CO, Westview Press, 1989), p. 11.

47  Joseph S. Nye, Jr, 'Foreword', in Peter M. Haas, Robert O. Keohane and Marc A. Levy (eds), *Institutions for the Earth: Sources of Effective Environmental Protection* (Cambridge, MIT Press, 1993), p. ix.
48  Lynton Caldwell, *Between Two Worlds: Science, the Environmental Movement and Policy Choice* (Cambridge, Cambridge University Press, 1990), p. xiii.
49  Caroline Thomas, 'Beyond UNCED: an Introduction', *Environmental Politics*, 2, 3 (1993), p. 5.
50  Dalby, 'The Politics of Environmental Security', p. 41.
51  Peter Doran, 'Earth, Power, Knowledge: Towards a Critical Environmental Politics', in John MacMillan and Andrew Linklater (eds), *Boundaries in Question: New Directions in International Relations* (London, Pinter Publishers, 1995), p. 194.
52  Matthew Paterson, 'Radicalising Regimes? Ecology and the Critique of IR Theory', in MacMillan and Linklater, *Boundaries in Question*.
53  Eric Laferrière, 'Emancipating International Relations Theory', *Millennium*, 25, 1 (1996), pp. 53–75; see also Eric Laferrière and Peter J. Stoett, *International Relations Theory and Ecological Thought* (London, Routledge, 1999).
54  See, for example, Hugh C. Dyer, 'EcoCultures: Global Culture in the Age of Ecology', *Millennium*, 22, 3 (1993), pp. 483–504.
55  See, for example, J. Ann Tickner, *Gender in International Relations: Feminist Perspectives on Achieving Global Security* (New York, Columbia University Press, 1992), and Lorraine Elliott, 'Women, Gender, Feminism and the Environment', in Jennifer Turpin and Lois Lorentzen (eds), *The Gendered New World Order: Militarism, Development and the Environment* (New York, Routledge, 1996).
56  See, for example, Luke, 'The (Un)wise (Ab)use'.
57  Sessions cited in Robert Paehlke, 'Environmental Values and Public Policy', in Norman J. Vig and Michael K. Kraft (eds), *Environmental Policy in the 1990s: Toward a New Agenda*, 2nd edn (Washington, DC, CQ Press, 1994), p. 350.
58  Frank Fischer and Michael Black, 'Introduction', in Frank Fischer and Michael Black (eds), *Greening Environmental Policy: The Politics of a Sustainable Future* (New York, St Martin's Press, 1995), p. xiii.
59  Julian Saurin, 'Global Environmental Degradation, Modernity and Environmental Knowledge', *Environmental Politics*, 2, 4 (1993), p. 46.
60  See, for example, Linklater, 'The Evolving Spheres of International Justice'.

# 8

# Meaning, Method and Practice: *Assessing the Changing Security Agenda*

## *K. M. Fierke*

### Introduction

The dramatic changes accompanying the end of the Cold War, and the reconfiguration of global politics since, impact more directly on security studies than almost any other area of international relations. This is because the subfield of security studies, as distinct from military strategy, is a child of the Cold War.[1] The emergence of the security concept in the post-World War II period corresponded with the transformation of departments or ministries of war to that of defence. Given the need to legitimize a new form of total warfare in a context of mass-based politics, the concept had an unquestionable propaganda appeal which is evident in its dominant metaphors: the prison and the family.[2] The nuclear arms race was a prison from which we could not escape; therefore deterrence was the only rational option. Security was provided by a hierarchical and dependent 'nuclear' family composed of a strong superpower and subordinate allies. In this respect the political language of security implied not only the threat of force but protection from it.

This language is consistent with several meanings of the words 'secure' or 'security' in everyday language: to protect against threat (deterrence was said to prevent any kind of war); to hold something in place (the Cold War froze the patterns of alliance formation in place); and to make something stable. Security has a 'soft' meaning (as in security blanket) in contrast to the hard reality of nuclear weapons. The concept of security was closely wedded to a particular historical context and a particular set of relationships centring around nuclear weapons. There is a much longer history of military and diplomatic history, as well as applied military strategy; but these were about war and the use of force. They were not defined explicitly in terms of security. While security and the threat to use force were joined during the Cold War, this was a unique combination, dependent on the logic of nuclear weapons.

Given this background, it should come as no surprise that the end of the Cold War gave rise to widespread questions about the meaning of security. In the last ten years the issue has become a cottage industry. The debate tends to revolve around two types of contrast. First, the earlier military definition of security is contrasted with a widening agenda which includes other areas such as the environment,[3] the economy,[4] migration[5] and human rights.[6] This widening is driven by an empirical observation that, particularly with the end of the Cold War, military security and deterrence no longer occupy centre stage as a source of or response to human or state insecurity. A second contrast, which is implied by the first, suggests the need to re-examine the referent object of security.[7] If the traditional literature focused on the state, the new agenda shifts attention to individuals,[8] society,[9] ethnic groups or nations,[10] international institutions or communities[11] and the globe.[12]

In this chapter I do not attempt to provide a definition of security or its referent object but instead approach the problem from a slightly different angle. I ask how we might know what security is in the post-Cold War world. If the definition of security has emerged from one era of international relations, by what criteria do we make claims about what security is or should be under dramatically altered conditions? One now established solution is to declare it an 'essentially contestable concept'.[13] Another, less fully explored, is to take seriously the task of examining how the concept of security is being used or how this is contributing to the construction of different post-Cold War contexts of international relations. The task, to quote Kolodziej, is 'to ask, at least, how published scholars, statesmen and national populations have posed the problem of security rather than pre-emptively to advance a particular answer to a question never fully raised, much less satisfactorily explored'.[14] Answering a question about the meaning of security in the post-Cold War world would involve a much larger excavation than is possible in this context. I therefore work through why the excavation itself is important and the significance of approaching it in a particular way.

## Why we want to know

Why approach the problem in this way? The short answer is because we no longer know what security is or should be. During the Cold War, security was not simply about the existence of a threat posed by the Soviet Union, but about the response to that threat, that is, nuclear deterrence. The security provided by deterrence was a response to the insecurity of the nuclear arms race. Security revolved around the paradox of the double image, that is, of being imprisoned by an arms race and secure in an alliance family whose actions were said to prevent any kind of war from occurring.

During the process of bringing the Cold War to an end, the meaning of security was decoupled from the threat to use nuclear force. In the 1980s, against the background of ex-President Reagan's bellicose rhetoric and renewed talk of a first-strike strategy and capability, critical movements in both East and West, concerned with peace or human rights, began to challenge the meaning of state practices – traditionally said to be expressions of protection and security. In the process, they renamed these practices a source of insecurity and called for 'emancipation' from two hierarchical alliances.[15] Somewhat later, in the academic sphere, security analysts such as Ken Booth, J. Ann Tickner and Chris Reus-Smit called for emancipation from traditional security assumptions and practices in more theoretical terms.[16] For the purposes of this argument, the most significant aspect of this debate was the effort to decouple the meaning of security from the threat to use force. The deterrent threat became a source of *insecurity*; the proposed response to this insecurity was explicitly *political* in the form of dialogue and disarmament. Gorbachev's New Thinking, for instance, was an explicitly political and normative articulation of security.

The changing security context of the ending Cold War offered a political solution to a changing security problem in place of the military solution of the Cold War. While nuclear proliferation is an ongoing issue, as are other arms races – such as that between India and Pakistan – it is safe to say that nuclear deterrence is no longer the defining feature of international relations or of security.[17] Further, as Chris Brown also points out in chapter 9, it is surprising, given the politicization of the 1980s, how uncontroversial – for the time being – nuclear weapons are, even though vast stockpiles remain.[18] The accelerated globalization of the 1990s has refocused attention on threats of economic collapse, environmental or ecological disaster and massive violations of human rights, to name just a few items on the new security agenda.

In these changed conditions, the narrow military definition of security is of questionable value. Consider one post-Cold War case where the use of force might be viewed as a security response: Kosovo. The security threat was posed by Serbian forces engaged in ethnic cleansing of Kosovars. The main referent object of security was the population of Kosovo. The potential respondent was NATO, whose acts were motivated less by national interest, at least in any apparent material sense, than by moral concern. The threat presented by NATO was intended less to deter than to compel the parties to reach an agreement. The threat did not work and at a certain point NATO had no choice but to follow through with the use of force. The threat was not, in itself, a source of protection, that is, it did not prevent conflict, as it was said to do in the Cold War. Once the threat had to be realized, it was hoped that Milosevic would, within days, give in to demands, which would result in greater protection and security. This was not the case and there are now serious questions about whether the prolonged use of force caused more suffering than security.

Ethnic cleansing by the Serbs increased dramatically after the bombing began, there were hundreds of direct – if accidental – casualties of NATO bombs, and the environmental consequences of the bombing could cause untold suffering over the long term. The properties of this 'security' context are of a much different nature from those existing in the Cold War. The link between the threat (of ethnic cleansing against Kosovars) and the 'security' response (bombing Serbian targets) is indirect. In any case, one can question whether the use of force in this context fits the category of 'security' or whether a different concept might be preferable.

A central concern of this context – as opposed to, for instance, one relating to the economy or environment – was the threat or potential use of military force. For this reason, cases of ethnic conflict, such as Kosovo, may be the post-Cold War phenomenon most compatible with the narrow military definition of security of the Cold War. Yet, as the comparison suggests, there is, at best, only a family resemblance between the two.

The difference only highlights the question of how we might identify the meaning of security or whether we should even be using the concept in a context of multiple threats, some of which do not, at this time, involve a security response, or others that involve an entirely different type of security response. The latter is interesting in regard to another type of post-Cold War context: that is, cases such as Northern Ireland, South Africa, the Israeli–Palestinian conflict – not to mention the end of the Cold War itself – where there has been movement out of a seemingly intractable conflict toward some kind of ongoing, if rocky, political dialogue.

This type of context is rarely included in the literature on security or referred to in these terms. However, if, during the short life-span of security studies, the threat of insecurity was closely tied to a security response, that is, a response which was said to increase the safety of the referent object, should we not refer to these processes of dialogue as security practices? The result of dialogue, at least in the showcase example of Northern Ireland, has been a marked reduction in fear for the referent object, that is, the people of Northern Ireland, as well as a dramatic increase in stability and prosperity, even though the situation remains somewhat precarious. The process of dialogue has brought greater security. Similarly, one might consider a global conference to reduce fossil-fuel emissions to be a security response in so far as it would lessen the threat of global warming.

Security analysts may be reluctant to incorporate these cases under the rubric of 'security'. Ole Waever, for instance, has made a distinction between securitization and desecuritization.[19] Securitization arises when elites name the existence of a threat which creates a state of high alert and justifies a crisis response. Desecuritization is normalization of a situation and a reduction of the crisis atmosphere. In this definition, political dialogue or agreement could never be a security response; it would instead be a move toward normalization and therefore desecuritization. However, like much of the literature on redefining security, this makes the naming of a security threat more central to the definition of security than the provision of security itself, in which case we might more accurately rename the field 'insecurity' studies.

The examples above raise several questions. The first is whether we *want* to develop new security practices. Post-structuralists, for instance, have put great effort into deconstructing existing concepts of security, pointing to the disciplining effect of security discourses and their role in constructing the power of the state to act.[20] From this perspective, the 'softness' of security disguises the dangers of the practice itself.[21] The second is whether security hasn't become a bit like NATO – its *raison d'être* no longer exists but some of us are so attached to the concept that we are searching for a new purpose. The third is whether the meaning of security necessarily extends beyond the naming of the source of insecurity to include how security will be provided. In this case, it is not self-evident that the most useful post-Cold War definition would revolve around the use of force. Here a distinction between the credible threat to use force, thereby preventing its use, and the actual use of force is important. But there may be other, largely unconsidered, security responses that require examination and elaboration. Do we need a toolbox of security responses and, if so, what would it include?

## Alternative ways of knowing

Scholars looking back at the origins of security studies often refer to a 'Golden Age' ending in the mid-1960s and a 'Renaissance' beginning in the mid-1970s.[22] In both of these Cold War periods, security was tied to the military domain and questions about the threat and use of force, especially as they related to nuclear deterrence. In the current discussion over the meaning of security, some look back with nostalgia to the clarity of this period, fearing the intellectual incoherence to which a broadening of the concept will inevitably lead.[23] If security can mean everything it means nothing.

If one reads between the lines of accounts of the Golden Age and the Renaissance, the nostalgia quickly disappears. On the one hand, the Golden Age was largely ahistorical and theoretically underdeveloped in its approaches,[24] while the Renaissance involved becoming both more historical and more theoretical. On the other hand, many believe that the last significant theoretical innovation in security studies was the deterrence and arms control theories of the late 1950s and early 1960s,[25] thus during the Golden Age. Both eras were noted for their ethnocentricity.[26] Most of the key concepts were defined by American scholars, concerned with American (or Western) problems of nuclear strategy within the Cold War.

Despite this questionable pedigree, traditional security analysts have responded to their constructivist and postmodern critics with an air of condescension regarding the superiority of their research programmes. The critics have often been accused of lacking either empirical pretensions or ability.[27] Yet security studies has been plagued by this problem from the beginning. As Nye and Lynn-Jones pointed out: 'In the fortunate absence of empirical data on nuclear exchanges, the field [of security studies] encourages non-empirical analyses.'[28] Given the dramatic changes in international politics, the questions of critical security analysts and constructivists, and the attempts to develop new approaches and answers, have arguably been more in tune with a changing world than their counterparts in the mainstream. As Krause and Williams document, critical security studies has given rise to a large number of studies within a fairly short period of time.[29] The main problem is that these scholars do not define 'empirical' in a way that fits within the research programmes of the mainstream and they are therefore not taken seriously. The difference regards a question of whether and how we might know the world we are analysing.

The old agenda assumed a given objective world within which law-like patterns could be identified. For neo-realists – the dominant model of the 1980s – this world was defined by the single game of anarchy.[30] Earlier realisms – as represented by, for instance, E. H. Carr or Hedley Bull in the English School, and to a lesser extent Morgenthau – created space for historical contingency and the political or the intersubjective;[31] neo-realism, in its search for elegance and parsimony, removed any traces of the human, the cultural or the political from international relations. States became billiard balls which possessed only the capability to act rationally to preserve their interest in survival within a structure of relations which was largely inescapable and dictated their moves. Neo-realism provided a general theory of international relations and a set of categories for formulating causal hypotheses which could then be tested against the world. If neo-realists explored the logic of anarchy in a larger sense, rational choice analysts, and particularly game theorists, explored the logics of distinct games within this anarchy.[32] As stated earlier, the empirical basis and application of both was often weak. None the less, both had resonance within the relatively stable context of the Cold War.

While rationalists treat the identities of actors – as individual maximizers – as given, constructivists posit that identities and interests are constructed in historically specific circumstances. Where the one assumes a static game, if only for analytic purposes, the other opens up a space for analysing how identities and interests (or preferences) change in the transition from one game to another. The shift to an understanding of international politics as a social and political construction expands the potential for formulating questions related specifically to processes of change, including how enemies transform their relationship into one of friendship or how the use of force is constructed. These questions are more empirically relevant to the changing contexts of the post-Cold War world than a general theory that assumes the sameness of international relations throughout time.

The constructivist turn in security studies was inspired by both the post-positivist Third Debate of the late 1980s and the problem of explaining change at the international level.[33] The Third Debate pitted two broadly conceived groups of 'positivists' and 'post-positivists' against one another. The post-positivist attack focused on a range of assumptions traditionally associated with the former. These include a Cartesian dichotomy between an external world and internal subjective experience, which presumes a separation between the material and the ideational, and a correspondence theory of truth and language.

More recently, the lines of debate have once again realigned. Post-structuralists have distanced themselves from constructivists who, they argue, have been seduced by the protocols of empirical social science at the expense of critical practice.[34] Constructivists have distanced themselves from post-structuralists, and their emphasis on language, in order to engage in dialogue with the American mainstream.[35] While maintaining the importance of the role of norms, ideas and social practice, many constructivists have reabsorbed a causal logic and an emphasis on first-order theory and testing, which implies a correspondence view of truth and language. In place of earlier debates between realists and liberals, or the debate between positivists and post-positivists that followed, a new debate between rationalists and constructivists has moved to the centre of the discipline, at least in the American context.[36] In the process the distinctions between the two have begun to blur, with scholars from both sides saying that they do not differ in any significant way in terms of epistemology or method.[37] In the next section, I will argue that this reorientation to a traditional social science definition of a research agenda not only generates philosophical inconsistencies, but undermines the potential of the constructivist turn to provide 'better' accounts of a changing world.

## Causes versus properties of security

Broadly speaking, rationalists and constructivists, as defined in recent debates,[38] are distinguished by two different ways of knowing, a causal and a constitutive. Alexander Wendt has written a very clear analysis of the distinction between the two.[39] To summarize very briefly, the causal argument, drawn from a natural science model, establishes a connection between two variables X and Y, such that X is temporally prior to Y and Y only occurs as a function of X. If X (for example, a threat from an aggressor state) occurs in a given set of circumstances, one can predict Y (acts that balance the power of the aggressor). Constitutive arguments, alternatively, 'account for the properties of things by reference to the structures in virtue of which they exist'.[40] While the causal argument establishes a unilinear connection between distinct variables, the constitutive establishes a systematic relationship by which, in the social realm, subjects and objects are invested with meaning.

One more familiar framework for the two is the distinction between explanation and understanding.[41] Hollis and Smith point out that the former has been granted superior scientific status over the latter. Wendt counters that this hierarchy relies on a misreading of the natural sciences and that both causal and constitutive models have a role in the natural as well as the social realms. On the one hand, constitutive theories can explain, although these explanations are not causal. On the other hand, natural scientists are as concerned as social scientists with the identification of the properties and the constitution of the structures they analyse. One model is not better than the other, in a scientific sense; rather, they raise different types of questions and are engaged in different tasks. The one asks a 'why' question and the other a 'how' or 'what' question. The one looks for causes and the other for properties or how things fit together.

The distinction and the observation that the two models involve different types of questions are useful. The argument contains a fundamental flaw, however. Wendt claims that 'although they have different truth conditions, this does not mean that causal and constitutive theories imply different "epistemologies"'.[42] Both kinds of theory are true or false by virtue of how well they correspond with states of the world. The assumption is that the correspondence theory of truth and language, directly related to the positivist tradition, works equally well in both cases. Both approaches allow us to 'observe' whether our theories correspond with the world.

This claim fails to recognize that the models, as they apply to social phenomena, belong to two philosophically opposed traditions.[43] The causal model – and the correspondence view – assume that theory, its derivative hypotheses, and the language from which they are formed are distinct from and independent of the reality to which they are compared. The constitutive model emerged from a critique of the former, and assumes the interwovenness of language and human practice. The latter refers to the thread with which a social fabric is woven, as contrasted with its more or less accurate reflection in a mirror.

Wendt says that post-positivists object to the correspondence theory of truth because human beings do not have direct access to how the world is constituted; however, the more salient formulation is that we *only* have access to our world through language. We cannot step outside of our language to compare it with that which it describes. The key question is whose language is to be preferred in the analysis. The causal model relies on categories and relationships formulated *by the scientist*, which are compared with the world; the other goes *directly to the contextual categories* by which social objects and practices are invested with meaning.

Take a completely unrelated example. Suppose we want to create a constitutive theory of marriage, delineating the properties and internal structure of marriage. In Wendt's line of thought, this theory could then be compared with the world to see whether they correspond. Proceeding in this way brings us back to the positivist problem with definition: how will we distil the essence of marriage in such a way that we can capture all instances of it? Such a definition is necessary if the goal is comparison with the 'real' world. We recognize a marriage when we see one, across cultures and across history; however, to construct a map of its properties we necessarily enter the realm of family resemblance rather than generalized theory. We need to 'look and see' the types of relationships that fit within the parameters of marriage (master and harem, a hierarchy of dependency, an equal partnership, a man and a woman, partners of the same sex – if only in Denmark), the types of acts that constitute a marriage (saying 'I do' or stamping a piece of glass), and the overlapping frameworks within which these distinct but related practices and identities are given meaning across context. Only in this way could we develop an empirically sound taxonomy of the categories and practices constituting marriage. As an investigation of *social* practices, an analysis of this kind necessarily takes the language of these practices seriously.

A similar problem is inherent in attempts to define security. From a correspondence view of truth and language, we would want to come up with a clearly bounded definition, like that of Stephen Walt, who defines security as involving the 'threat, use and control of military force'.[44] However, as the comparison in the first section demonstrated, the properties constituting the Cold War threat of force and the threat and use of force in Kosovo were distinctly different, to the extent that the label 'security' was questionable in the latter case. While the concept is arguably more applicable to other types of context in a globalizing world, the question of definition would seem to be less important in relation to Kosovo than one about how the use of force was constituted.

A more detailed analysis might reveal the evolution of Western action since the early stages of the Yugoslav crisis through the Kosovo campaign, and how the use of a particular concept of security constituted the non-use or use of force. For now it is useful to point to a major change. While the British government actively avoided intervention at the beginning of the crisis, not least because of a questionable national interest in the conflict, the Labour government, by the time of Kosovo, argued that the Yugoslav president, Slobodan Milošević, would understand no language except that of force and that there was a moral responsibility to intervene, from the air if not from the ground, for purely humanitarian goals. How this transition was constituted or how the use of force became possible in the absence of any clear national interest is an important question. An answer to the question would require a detailed analysis of how the properties of this context changed, that is, how its meaning and the range of possible responses were constituted over time. How it 'fitted together' and evolved is dependent on the categories by which the conflict itself was constituted.[45] If the definitions were prepared in advance, and then compared with 'reality', ignoring the language of the actors themselves, it is likely that the constitutive dynamics would be missed or misread. Definitions fix meaning; at issue in the above question is how the changing meaning of security in *use* contributed to the constitution of one outcome or another at different points of conflict in the Balkans.

## Language and context

Wendt ignores the dependence of the constitutive model on language and argues that both models rely on the correspondence view of truth. He further blurs the boundaries between the causal and constitutive accounts by implying a separation between ideas and material world or behaviour. Other construct-ivists in this genre have more explicitly discussed the relationship between ideas and the material world in causal terms.[46]

Colin Gray points to a similar problem in the writings of the third gener-ation of strategic culture theorists.[47] This third generation, some of whom are identified with the constructivists in the Katzenstein volume, *The Culture of National Security*,[48] are distinguished from earlier generations by their primary concern with researchability. While doing this well, they, in the process, make the mistake of positing a causal relationship between strategic ideas and behaviour. As Gray says:

> Anyone who seeks a falsifiable theory of strategic culture in the school of Johnston commits the same error as a doctor who sees people as having entirely separable bodies and minds. In his writings about Chinese strategic culture, Iain Johnston's apparently methodologically progressive determination to consider culture distinctively from behaviour for the purpose of studying the influence of the former on the latter transpires paradoxically to be a scholarly step or two backwards. There is an obvious sense in which positivistically he is seeking to explain how the cultural context (as 'that which surrounds') does, or does not, influence the realm of action. From the perspective of methodological rigour it is hard to fault him. The problem is that we cannot understand strategic behaviour by that method, be it ever so rigorous. Strategic culture is not only 'out there', also it is within us; we, our institutions, and our behaviour, are the context.[49]

The search for rigour (of a particular kind) leads to a separation between ideas and behaviour and a distorted conception of culture. Rather than a variable that can be treated as distinct, Gray argues that culture is outside us, in the context that surrounds us, and within us. While he does not make this further step, the glue by which this whole of culture is expressed, and by which a German or a British soldier cannot help but act as a German or a Brit, is socialization into a context and set of practices which precedes any individual and is communicated, learned and transmitted through – and therefore insep-arable from – language. The resulting unity of cultural influence and policy action, in his words, 'denies the existence of the boundaries needed for the study of cause and effect'.[50]

Culture is both inside and outside; it cannot be studied in terms of cause and effect. In this respect, neither the strategist nor the scholar stands apart from their context. The danger of the correspondence view in this situation is that we mistake our own cultural or contextually specific assumptions and preconceptions for reflections of an objective world. Here lies the difference between the constitutive and causal models in the natural and the social sciences. The natural scientist who undertakes a constitutive analysis *imposes categories and meanings where they did not previously exist*. Having named the properties of a system, a causal model might then elaborate why certain outcomes emerge from it. In the social realm, the constitutive analyst is confronted with social objects and practices that *already do have meaning in a time and place*. The issue is less comparison of his or her own categories with an objective reality than how the meanings of the subjects of analysis constitute their world and action within it. In so far as practices and patterns are woven into the language games of a culture, they are more akin to rule-following than the causal relationship between distinct variables. This is not to say that causality is absent from the social world; only that the two models rely on very different assumptions.

## Constructed agents

This chapter has not provided an answer to the question of what security in the post-Cold War period is. In concluding, I would like to argue that a premature effort to fix a new definition of security risks inadvertently reconstructing or reproducing patterns of the old agenda – or someone's agenda – in a new context where the consequences are potentially as or more dangerous than the Cold War.[51] The overlap, suggested earlier, between the meaningful practices of academics and political actors reveals the extent to which scholars are a part of the reality they analyse and construct. The key word here is inadvertent, that is, to avoid the assumption that our theories or definitions represent the world as it is when, particularly in a context of change, they may contribute to the constitution of it.

An alternative is to think of the analyst as a 'constructed agent'; constructed because embedded in a context and cultures (e.g. disciplinary, national, political, bureaucratic) which precede and into which one has been socialized. Thus, the challenge is to identify modes of analysis that make strange that which has become too familiar in order to see more clearly its constitutive properties. A space for agency and choice is created in the process.

Ken Booth warned that 'we live simultaneously, in our pasts, presents and futures. What we do is always shaped by the collision or collusion of memory and moment.'[52] The stories we tell about the past are often shaped by a present, and these stories likewise provide a guide to action in the future. The end of the Cold War is a case in point. Ten years ago, realist scholars –

and almost everyone else – were surprised and dumbfounded that the Cold War ended at all and that it ended as it did. Within a short space, many realists had forgotten this sense of surprise and gone on to make new predictions based on the same assumptions.[53] Others modified their theoretical assumptions to the point at which they were realist in name only.[54] Ten years later, we all carry around a language of the Cold War having been 'won' by the West. Our story of the end of the Cold War is one of winning and losing, a realist story of state survival and defeat that is hardly questioned any more. The success of the deterrence mission of the Cold War provides proof of the validity of NATO and a justification for threatening force. Knowledge of the past, present and future is in the process of being constituted – as opposed to caused – as this realist language seeps back into our intersubjective world, shaping the parameters of what is thinkable and therefore possible in entirely new circumstances.

If we instead 'look and see' how the properties of the end of the Cold War were constituted over time, it becomes difficult to sustain an argument that this was a case of winning and losing. As mentioned earlier – and contrary to arguments that NATO's deterrence or Reagan's military build-up 'caused' the end – the ten years prior to the sudden collapse of the Cold War saw a widespread challenge to the conceptualization of security in military terms. Nuclear deterrence and the arms race became a source of insecurity; in its place, there were widespread calls for more political alternatives, as expressed in the 'common security' of the Brandt Report or Gorbachev's 'New Thinking'. Even Reagan, in proposing the Strategic Defense Initiative (SDI), spoke of nuclear deterrence as a source of insecurity and strategic defence as a solution that would help the 'world sleep more secure'.[55] This conflict over the meaning of security opened a space for considering more positive-sum options that had been unthinkable at earlier stages; for example, disarmament became possible for the first time during the Cold War. The language of winning was imposed after the fact, and was less constitutive of the end of the Cold War itself, or the changes we associate with this, than of security relations in its aftermath.[56] By making the end of the Cold War strange – by stepping outside of the language that has seeped into our present consciousness – we create a space for becoming agents, for questioning the emerging necessities of the post-Cold War world.

The end of the Cold War is not a guide to what security will be in the post-Cold War period. In the period since its formal end was declared, a range of security practices have been constructed or reconstructed or are still in the process of being constructed. The process is ongoing. How we know will, cumulatively, shape what we do and what these practices become. Contrary to Wendt's claim that epistemology isn't, at the end of the day, important, and should be left to philosophers, it is crucial that the questions be asked and answered in a philosophically responsible way; not because we want to spend all of our time wrapped up in metatheoretical debates; rather because the questions are so fundamental to how we undertake analysis – and potentially to the constitution – of international or global security.

## NOTES

1   Franz Schurmann, *The Logic of World Power: An Inquiry in the Origins, Currents and Contradictions of World Politics* (New York, Pantheon Books, 1974), pp. 39–40. There was an older tradition of collective security which emerged along with the League of Nations.
2   For an analysis of the changing language of security in the context of the ending Cold War, see K. M. Fierke, *Changing Games, Changing Strategies: Critical Investigations in Security* (Manchester and New York, Manchester University Press and St Martin's Press, 1998).
3   Jessica Tuchman Matthews, 'Redefining Security', *Foreign Affairs*, 68 (1989), pp. 162–77; Patricia Mische, 'Ecological Security and the Need to Reconceptualise Sovereignty', *Alternatives*, 14, 4 (1989), pp. 389–427; Thomas Homer-Dixon, 'Environmental Scarcities and Violent Conflict', *International Security*, 19 (1994), pp. 5–40; Marc A. Levy, 'Is the Environment a National Security Issue?', *International Security*, 20 (1995), pp. 35–62.
4   Beverly Crawford, 'The New Security Dilemma and International Economic Inter- dependence', *Millennium*, 23 (1994), pp. 25–55; Theodore Moran, 'International Economics and National Security', *Foreign Affairs*, 69, 5 (1990–1), pp. 74–90.
5   Gil Loescher, 'Refugee Movements and International Security', *Adelphi Paper* 268 (London, International Institute for Strategic Studies, 1992); Ole Waever, Barry Buzan, Morton Kelstrup and Lierre Lemaitre, *Identity, Migration and the New Security Agenda in Europe* (London, Pinter, 1993); Myron Wiener, 'Security, Stability and International Migration', *International Security*, 17 (1992–3), pp. 91–126.
6   Brad Roberts, 'Human Rights and International Security', *Washington Quarterly* (Spring 1990), pp. 65–75.
7   Ronnie Lipschutz (ed.), *On Security* (New York, Columbia University Press, 1995); David Dunn, 'Peace Research versus Strategic Studies', in Ken Booth (ed.), *New Thinking about Strategy and International Security* (London, Harper Collins, 1991), pp. 56–72.
8   Roberts, 'Human Rights and International Security'; Loescher, 'Refugee Move- ments and International Security'; Mohammed Ayoob, 'Security in the Third World: The Worm about to Turn?', *International Affairs*, 60, 1 (1983–4), pp. 41–51; M. B. Nicholson, 'Security in the 1990s and Beyond', in Michael Clarke (ed.), *New Perspectives on Security* (London, Brassey's, 1993), pp. 104–17.
9   Waever et al., *Identity, Migration and the New Security Agenda in Europe*; Martin Shaw, 'There is No Such Thing as Society: Beyond Individualism and Statism in International Security Studies', *Review of International Studies*, 19 (1993), pp. 159–75.
10  Barry Posen, 'The Security Dilemma in Ethnic Conflict', *Survival*, 35, 1 (1993), pp. 27–47; Michael Brown (ed.), *Ethnic Conflict and International Security* (Prince- ton, NJ, Princeton University Press, 1993); Stephen van Evera, 'Hypotheses on Nationalism and War', *International Security*, 18 (1994), pp. 5–39.
11  Emanuel Adler and Michael Barnett, *Security Communities* (Cambridge, Cam- bridge University Press, 1998). This category would also include the vast literature

that since the end of the Cold War has reflected on the possibilities of an effective collective security system, under the auspices of the United Nations.

12   Michael T. Klare and Daniel C. Thomas, *World Security: Challenges for a New Century* (New York, St Martin's Press, 1994); Thomas Schelling, 'Rethinking the Dimensions of National Security: The Global Dimension', in Graham Allison and Gregory Treverton (eds), *Rethinking America's Security: Beyond Cold War to New World Order* (New York, W. W. Norton, 1992), pp. 196–210; Richard Falk, *Economic Aspects of Global Civilization: The Unmet Challenge of World Poverty* (Princeton, NJ, Princeton University Center of International Studies, 1992).

13   Barry Buzan, *People, States and Fear* (London, Harvester Wheatsheaf, 1983, 1991); Simon Dalby, 'Dealignment Discourse: Thinking Beyond the Blocs', *Current Research on Peace and Violence*, 3 (1990), p. 4.

14   Edward A. Kolodziej, 'Renaissance in Security Studies? Caveat Lector!', *International Studies Quarterly*, 36 (1992), p. 422.

15   See Fierke, *Changing Games, Changing Strategies*; K. M. Fierke, 'Changing Worlds of Security', in Keith Krause and Michael Williams (eds), *Critical Security Studies* (Minneapolis, MN, University of Minnesota Press, 1997).

16   Ken Booth, 'Security and Emancipation', *Review of International Studies*, 17 (1991), pp. 313–26; J. Ann Tickner, *Gender in International Relations: Feminist Perspectives in Achieving Global Security* (New York, Columbia University Press, 1992); Christian Reus-Smit, 'Realist and Resistance Utopias; Community, Security and Political Action in the New Europe', *Millennium*, 21 (1992), pp. 1–28. Implicitly or explicitly, these two processes, political and academic, constructed the security problem in terms of gender. In the political world, this was given meaning in terms of emancipation from a structure of alliance relations that was reminiscent of the 'nuclear' family. In the academic world, scholars analysed the public/private distinction and a masculinized logic of force as opposed to dialogue. For discussion of these themes, see also V. Spike Peterson, 'Security and Sovereign States: What is at Stake in Taking Feminism Seriously?', in Spike Peterson (ed.), *Gendered States: Feminist (Re)Visions of International Relations Theory* (Boulder, CO, Lynne Rienner, 1992), pp. 31–64; J. Ann Tickner, 'Revisioning Security', in Ken Booth and Steve Smith (eds), *International Relations Theory Today* (Cambridge, Polity, 1995), pp. 175–97; for a discussion of dialogue as an alternative, see Vivienne Jabri, *Discourses of Violence: Conflict Analysis Reconsidered* (Manchester, Manchester University Press, 1996).

17   Even NATO, whose original mission was defined by deterrence, now refers to itself less in terms of defence of the West and more as an anchor of stability. For an analysis of this evolution, see K. M. Fierke, 'Dialogues of Manoeuvre and Entanglement: NATO, Russia and the CEECs', *Millennium*, 28, 1 (1999), pp. 27–52.

18   The failure of the US Senate to ratify the Comprehensive Test Ban Treaty and the Cold War rhetoric of George W. Bush could change this.

19   Ole Waever, 'Securitization and Desecuritization', in Ronnie Lipschutz (ed.), *On Security* (New York, Columbia University Press, 1995), pp. 46–86.

20   R. B. J. Walker, 'Security, Sovereignty, and the Challenge of World Politics', *Alternatives*, 15 (1990), pp. 3–27; R. B. J. Walker, *Inside/Outside: International Relations as Political Theory* (Cambridge, Cambridge University Press, 1993); David Campbell, *Writing Security: United States Foreign Policy and the Politics*

*of Identity* (Minneapolis, MN, University of Minnesota Press, 1992, 1998); James Der Derian and Michael Shapiro (eds), *International/Intertextual Relations. Postmodern Readings of World Politics* (Lexington, Lexington Books, 1989).

21  In an analysis of the discourse of defence intellectuals, Carol Cohn pointed to a practice of 'patting nuclear missiles' as if they were soft, pet-like objects. Carol Cohn, 'Sex and Death in the Rational World of Defense Intellectuals', *Signs: Journal of Women in Culture and Society*, 12, 4 (1987).

22  See in particular: Joseph S. Nye, Jr, and Sean M. Lynn-Jones, 'International Security Studies: A Report of a Conference on the State of the Field', *International Security*, 12, 4 (1988), pp. 5–27; Stephen M. Walt, 'The Renaissance of Security Studies', *International Studies Quarterly*, 35 (1991), pp. 211–39; Kolodziej, 'Renaissance in Security Studies?'.

23  See, for instance, Theodore C. Sorensen, 'Rethinking National Security', *Foreign Affairs*, 69, 3 (1990), pp. 1–18.

24  Walt, 'The Renaissance of Security Studies', pp. 214–15; Nye and Lynn-Jones, 'International Security Studies', pp. 12–13.

25  Nye and Lynn-Jones, 'International Security Studies', pp. 12–13.

26  Ibid., p. 14.

27  Walt, 'The Renaissance of Security Studies', p. 23; John Mearsheimer, 'Back to the Future: Instability in Europe after the Cold War', *International Security*, 15, 1 (1990), pp. 5–56; Keohane, 'Two Institutions', 1988.

28  Nye and Lynn-Jones, 'International Security Studies', p. 13.

29  Keith Krause and Michael Williams, 'Broadening the Agenda of Security Studies: Politics and Methods', *Mershon International Studies Review*, 40, 2 (1996), pp. 229–54; Keith Krause and Michael C. Williams (eds), *Critical Security Studies* (Minneapolis, MN, University of Minnesota Press, 1997).

30  Kenneth Waltz, *Theory of International Politics* (Reading, MA, Addison-Wesley, 1979); see also Hayward Alker and Thomas Biersteker, 'The Dialectics of World Order: Notes for a Future Archaeologist of International Savoir Faire', *International Studies Quarterly*, 28, 1 (1984).

31  Dunne has argued that these traditions contained many constructivist assumptions. See Tim Dunne, 'The Social Construction of International Society', *European Journal of International Relations*, 3 (1995), pp. 367–89.

32  In the area of security studies, the most famous application of game theory is the work of Thomas Schelling, *Strategy of Conflict* (Cambridge, MA, Harvard University Press, 1960).

33  For a discussion of the Third Debate, see Yosef Lapid, 'The Third Debate: On the Prospects of International Theory in a Post-Positivist Era', *International Studies Quarterly*, 33, 3 (1989), pp. 235–49.

34  See, for instance, Campbell, *Writing Security*, 'Epilogue'.

35  See: Emanuel Adler, 'Seizing the Middle Ground: Constructivism in World Politics', *European Journal of International Relations*, 3, 3 (1997), pp. 319–63; K. M. Fierke, 'Critical Methodology and Constructivism', in K. M. Fierke and Knud Erik Jorgensen (eds), *Constructing International Relations: The Next Generation* (Armonk, NY, M. E. Sharpe, 2001).

36  Mainstream authors have recently referred to a reconfiguration of this debate, with rationalism and constructivism replacing realism and liberalism as the central

axioms. See Peter J. Katzenstein, Robert O. Keohane and Stephen D. Krasner, 'International Organization and the Study of World Politics', *International Organization*, 52, 4 (1998), p. 625. On the first point, see also Stephen M. Walt, 'International Relations: One World, Many Theories', *Foreign Policy*, 110 (1998), pp. 29–46.

37 Katzenstein et al. state that: 'On issues of epistemology and methodology...no great differences divide conventional constructivists from rationalists.' Katzenstein et al., 'International Organization and the Study of World Politics', p. 625. See also David Dessler, 'Constructivism within Positivist Social Science', *Review of International Studies*, 25 (1999), pp. 123–37; Alexander Wendt, 'Constitution and Causation in IR', *Review of International Studies*, 24, Special Issue (1998), pp. 101–18.

38 See, for instance, Katzenstein et al., 'International Organization and the Study of World Politics'.

39 Wendt, 'Constitution and Causation'.

40 Ibid., p. 105.

41 Martin Hollis and Steve Smith, *Explaining and Understanding International Relations* (Oxford, Clarendon, 1990). See also Michael Nicholson, *Cause and Consequence in International Relations* (London, Pinter, 1996).

42 Wendt, 'Constitution and Causation', p. 106.

43 The linguistic turn, which began with Wittgenstein's *Tractatus* and came to fruition in the *Philosophical Investigations*, is an important root of the constitutive approach. The correspondence or picture view of language articulated in his earlier work, the *Tractatus*, influenced the logical positivism of the Vienna Circle. His later work, the *Philosophical Investigations*, countered the picture view, arguing that language use is a form of action which is constitutive. See Ludwig Wittgenstein, *Philosophical Investigations* (Oxford, Basil Blackwell, 1958). When Wendt, one of the foremost constructivists, states that he is a positivist and a constructivist, he is claiming two traditions that have been defined in opposition to one another; it is akin to being both a Marxist and a capitalist.

44 Walt, 'The Renaissance of Security Studies', p. 212.

45 The problem, and our dependence on language for understanding how things 'fit together', was dramatically evident in the early stages of the conflict. In the immediate aftermath of the Cold War, Western leaders, faced with the breakdown of Yugoslavia, were at a loss for a proper response. After decades of interpreting every international event in terms of the Cold War conflict, they lacked a conceptual apparatus for observing Bosnia. The initial confusion concerning Bosnia illustrates that we do observe a brute reality but are fundamentally dependent on language. In the midst of the breakdown of an old world, and uncertainty about the new, leaders and populations only made sense of this context by situating it within one framework of past rules or another, by which they knew how to reason about what should be done. For the Conservatives, then in power, the only possible response was negotiations and unarmed peacekeepers, given the lesson of World War I, which began in the region. The fear was that any type of intervention would draw in the other great powers, escalating into a global conflagration. For the left and the peace movement, by contrast, intervention was the only option, given the existence of a new genocide in Europe after fifty years of saying 'never again'. The

US and NATO hoped to repeat the perceived success of the Gulf War, pushing back any aggressors by means of the threat of surgical strikes from the air; at the same time, the former had to avoid another imbroglio like Vietnam at all costs. For an expanded analysis of this issue, see K. M. Fierke, 'Multiple Identities, Interfacing Games: The Social Construction of Western Action in Bosnia', *European Journal of International Relations*, 2, 4 (1996), pp. 467–97.

46   See, in particular, Adler, 'Seizing the Middle Ground'. For a critique of this causal logic, see Campbell, *Writing Security*, 'Epilogue'.

47   Colin S. Gray, 'Strategic Culture as Context: The First Generation of Theory Strikes Back', *Review of International Studies*, 25, 1 (1999), pp. 49–70.

48   Peter J. Katzenstein, *The Culture of National Security* (New York, Columbia University Press, 1996). See also Adler and Barnet, *Security Communities*.

49   Gray, 'Strategic Culture as Context', p. 53.

50   Ibid.

51   As Baldwin points out, many of the attempts to redefine security were less concerned with the concept itself than with redefining policy agendas. David Baldwin, 'The Concept of Security', *Review of International Studies*, 23 (1997), pp. 5–26.

52   Ken Booth, 'Introduction', in Ken Booth (ed.), *Statecraft and Security: The Cold War and Beyond* (Cambridge, Cambridge University Press, 1998), pp. 1–26, esp. 1–2.

53   See John Mearsheimer, 'Back to the Future'. Charles Kegley provided an excellent analysis of the problems of testing realist and liberal theories related to the end of the Cold War. He points to the failure to recognize the overlap between political arguments and theoretically driven hypotheses and the resultant tendency to reproduce the former with an aura of scientific objectivity. At the time, 1993, realist explanations had already begun to move back into a dominant position. Charles Kegley, Jr, 'How Did the Cold War Die: Principles for an Autopsy', *Mershon International Studies Review*, supplement 1 (1993).

54   See William Wohlforth, 'Realism and the End of the Cold War', *International Security*, 19, 3 (1994–5), pp. 91–129.

55   Ronald Reagan, 'Life and the Preservation of Freedom', *Vital Speeches of the Day*, 52, 3 (1985).

56   For a more in-depth exploration of this argument, see Fierke, *Changing Games, Changing Strategies*. One might ask why this distinction is important, given that the West is now so apparently the victor; the Soviet Union has collapsed and the peoples of the former Eastern bloc have embraced Western values. The key issue is the constitutive features and consequences of the winning and losing framework. The end of the Cold War became possible as a more positive-sum solution to the East–West conflict became possible; to constitute the end in terms of winning and losing is to return to the military logic which had to be overcome for the changes to happen at all. There is also a normative and constitutive question about what we take away from these changes as lessons for what is possible in the future.

# Part III

# New Perspectives

# 9

# The Normative Framework of Post-Cold War International Relations

## *Chris Brown*

### Introduction

Both the actual framework of norms in international relations, and the discourses of normative theory, have been substantially affected by the ending of the Cold War, but then the role of norms in international relations has always been contestable, and while the ending of superpower conflict may have changed the context it has not altered the substance of this contest. Similarly, the discourses of normative theory have always responded to the frequent changes that take place within international relations theory more generally. In what follows, a necessarily limited initial examination of the nature of norms will lead into discussions of a number of interrelated topics: the use of force in international relations; the contrast between the Westphalian norm of sovereignty and the emerging international human rights regime; the fate of movements towards global distributive justice; and various challenges to Western universalism. In the final section, changes in the nature of the discourse of normative theory itself will be considered.

### The nature of norms

Norms are standards of behaviour; sometimes they describe how we *actually* behave but, crucially, they also tell us how we *ought* to behave. International norms perform this task for states or other international actors, and for us, as individual human beings, with respect to global issues. The first assumption of normative analysis – prior to discussion of the content of norms – is that individuals (and states) have a choice about what to do; they can follow a particular standard of behaviour or not. Machiavelli, for example, gives us an account of the standards of behaviour he expects from the successful Prince; in order to preserve power, the Prince ought to be prepared to lie, cheat, murder and so on.[1] Machiavelli is clearly engaging in normative thinking; he is telling us how the Prince ought to behave. What makes this a normative activity is the fact that, as he is well aware, princes very frequently do not follow the standards he is setting for them.

Because the ability to choose is a presumption of normative analysis, the real alternative to normative theory is provided by those accounts of human/state behaviour which deny that actors are capable of making effective choices. Thus, so-called 'structural' realists are often assumed to hold that state behaviour is determined by the imperatives of anarchy, in which case it does not make a great deal of sense to talk about action taking place on the basis of decisions taken in accordance with particular norms or standards. If actors have no choices, then the setting or advocacy of standards – of whatever kind – is a pointless exercise; to set standards and establish norms is to assume that action is goal-*directed* but not goal- (or otherwise) *determined*.

At this point, if not earlier, the student of international relations theory may well be feeling a little confused. A discussion on normative theory appears to have turned into an examination of the agent–structure debate. Moreover, the casual use of Machiavelli as an exemplary normative theorist apparently goes against the received view that he is a central figure within the realist tradition of international theory, a tradition that is conventionally taken to be anti-normative. Is not a more normal contrast that between 'normative theory', which tells us how things ought to be, and 'positive' theory, which tells us how things are? Such at least is the story that has dominated the discipline of international relations (IR) since the post-1945 triumph of 'realism', a triumph based on the claim of realists to be able to show how the world actually worked, an achievement they have taught us to value above the supposed normative task of showing how the world ought to work.

This normative/positive opposition *is* actually the usual way of setting up the project of normative thought, but this terminology is also the source of most of the confusion which surrounds normative thinking, and it is important to shake the hold of this way of thinking about the world. The idea that there is, or could be, a clear divide between normative and positive theory is profoundly misleading; all theories of international relations are, simultaneously, both positive and normative theories.[2] As suggested above, the only exceptions to this general proposition are those rare accounts of international relations which imply that questions of agency are entirely irrelevant, and that the actors in international relations are simply that, actors who give voice to a script (a script without an author).[3] The idea that it is possible to give an accurate account of how the world works without reference to norms, meanings and intentions is a non-starter, an import from the discipline of economics where the construction of highly elaborate and artificial models of economic behaviour comes close to achieving this feat, albeit at a high level of abstraction and under conditions which are unlikely to be replicated in political science.[4]

Once the illusion of a positive/normative divide is set aside, it becomes easier to identify the characteristic tasks of normative thought, and to specify more precisely what it is we are looking for when we compare the pre- and post-1989 normative agendas. First, the aim must be to identify the *declared norms* of the international order – what Mervyn Frost defines as the 'settled norms' of international society, those normative positions which are taken for granted and verbally endorsed even when apparently violated.[5] However, second, it is also necessary to try to identify the *actual norms* that govern state conduct, that is to say, the standards they actually follow, which may differ systematically and regularly from the declared norms of the system.[6] A good analogy to this task is the economist's employment of the notion of 'revealed preferences' – by studying what states actually do we may be able to deduce the standards they are applying.

The next, and most important, task of normative thought is to assess the underlying moral basis of the declared and actual norms of an international order. An analysis which stops at the process of identifying norms is bound to provide a justification for the status quo (although it may also identify some contradictions in that status quo when declared and actual norms are in serious conflict, or, indeed, when declared norms are in conflict with each other). It is only once the task of examining whether these norms can be related to a convincing moral account of the world is undertaken, and, in any event, asking whose interests they serve, that it becomes possible to engage in a genuinely critical exercise in which alternative ways of organizing the world come into focus. With these points in mind, shifts in the role of norms in the Cold War and post-Cold War period can now be examined, starting with the most basic subject for normative analysis, the role of force in international relations.

## Norms concerning the use of force

Declared norms concerning the use of force in the twentieth century (at least post-1919) centre on a legalized version of the 'just war' tradition. Originally, just war was a moral notion developed by Christian natural lawyers in the Middle Ages, its key feature being the idea that peace between individuals and communities was to be regarded as the norm of human affairs. The only circumstances in which violence could be justified would be to restore peaceful relations – and then only under very restricted circumstances. Force could only be directed to righting a wrong, as a last resort, and employed with 'right intention'. Force could only be authorized by a proper authority and then only if there was a reasonable prospect of a successful outcome; the force used must be proportional to the wrong done and the lives of the innocent must be protected at all times.[7]

In early modern Europe, this single idea was unpacked, and different aspects suffered different fates. The doctrine of state sovereignty gradually came to mean that the rulers of states were entitled to use force whenever, and for whatever purpose, they chose. 'Last resort' and 'right intention' disappeared as criteria, while a 'reasonable prospect of success' became a matter for calculation by the sovereign rather than a moral requirement; proper authority remained important but was vested solely in the sovereign state. A distinction, not found in medieval thought, between *'ius ad bellum'* and *'ius in bello'* emerged; the latter, based on the protection of the innocent, was translated into the notion of non-combatant immunity and, in the late nineteenth century, was accompanied by an emerging legal framework in which combatants themselves were assigned rights.[8]

By 1900 this latter, *ius in bello*, regime was extensive and elaborate, while the notion of *ius ad bellum* had become purely formal. However, the effect of the World Wars as well as the establishment of the League of Nations and, later, the United Nations has been to reinstall a legal regime governing the resort to force. Michael Walzer has helpfully summarized this regime as the 'legalist paradigm'. States form a society the law of which is based on the preservation of their territorial integrity and political sovereignty; the use or threat of force against this integrity or sovereignty is a criminal act of aggression; the only circumstances under which force may lawfully be used is in resisting this criminal act, either by a war of self-defence by the victim of the crime, or by a war of law enforcement by the victim and others.[9] Meanwhile, at least in principle, non-combatant immunity and the rights of combatants have been upheld and strengthened in the twentieth century, via successive Geneva and Hague Conventions and fuelled by public revulsion at the horrors associated with modern warfare.[10]

One important aspect of the declared norms concerning the use of force is the potential conflict between the rather strong doctrine of sovereignty those norms endorse, and the emerging international human rights regime. This issue – crystallized around the notion of 'humanitarian intervention' – will be examined below. The aim at this point is to examine the relationship between the declared norms and the actual norms operated by states, both during and after the Cold War. The simplest way of describing this set of relationships is to say that the gap between declared and actual norms has narrowed quite noticeably post-1989. During the Cold War years the high stakes involved in the ideological and military conflict meant that notions such as territorial integrity and political sovereignty could not be – or at least were not – approached in the legalist and formal way that the declared norms required. From Moscow's perspective the sovereign right of the East German, Hungarian, Czechoslovak or Polish states to determine their own internal political arrangements (much less their international stances) had to be exercised within very strict limits, and the so-called doctrine of the Socialist Commonwealth, enunciated after the Warsaw Pact's intervention in Czechoslovakia in 1968, defined those limits very strictly indeed. Within its own sphere of interest in the Caribbean and Latin America, the US attempted to operate a similar but anti-communist doctrine, symbolized by Dr Kissinger's *bon mot* that a country could not be allowed to go communist simply because of the irresponsibility of its people. The 'legalist paradigm' clearly could not operate in a world in which such mind-sets dominated.

Still, it would be a mistake to imagine that the end of the Cold War has done more than close marginally the gap between declared and actual norms in this area. It remains the case that states are very unlikely to treat all breaches of the declared norm with impartiality. Security and other considerations remain important in the post-Cold War environment and will still sometimes override a purely legalist reading of acts of aggression. Moreover, even when states can afford to be disinterested on the merits of a case, the costs of law enforcement in a world without a permanent police force are high, and this alone guarantees that there will always be a gap between the declared and actual norms of the system.

For all that, 1989 brought about a narrowing of this latter gap. This is probably a 'good thing', but not unambiguously so. Much here depends on the value attached to state sovereignty in itself, which will be discussed below in connection with humanitarian intervention, but the terms under which the gap has narrowed are also important. Because of the way in which the Cold War ended, with the effective elimination from a global role of one of the combatants, the enforcement of the declared norms of the current international order rests with the victors. In effect, the US and its closest allies alone have the capacity to determine when a norm has been broken, and what to do about it, and the possibility, not to say probability, that they will exercise this discretion in their own interests must be a matter for concern. This point, of course, applies to everything about the post-Cold War normative agenda.

One striking feature of the contrast between pre- and post-1989 norms on the use of force is the changing salience of nuclear weapons, an area where one set of problems has been exchanged for another. During the Cold War a great deal of thinking about norms was, understandably, focused on the possibility of a wholesale nuclear exchange in which, directly or indirectly, hundreds of millions of individuals might die, with the possibility that the earth could be rendered more or less uninhabitable. Here a massive gap between the declared and actual norms of the system was apparent. In principle, states subscribed to notions such as non-combatant immunity and discrimination in the use of force, but such discrimination is more or less impossible to achieve where nuclear weapons are involved. The official doctrine of many nuclear states was that nuclear weapons were for deterrent purposes only – although it should be noted that, given the Warsaw Pact's advantage in conventional forces, NATO refused to adopt a 'no-first-use' policy in the event of a European war – and this raised the interesting issue of whether it could be right to threaten to do something that it would be wrong actually to do. Many moral philosophers thought not, and regarded the actual defence policies of the major countries as in breach of the declared norms of the international order and potentially or actually criminal.[11] The nuclear powers, on the other hand, adopted the pragmatic position that the political and security risks of unilateral disarmament outweighed the remote possibility (as they saw it) that by retaining possession of nuclear weapons they could, ultimately, be complicit in mass murder. They reasoned that the caution nuclear weapons instil in their possessors was a more plausible road to peace than disarmament.

The extent to which moral discourse (and political action) on the use of force in international relations was dominated by this debate is striking, as is the speed with which it has more or less disappeared from the agenda. The nuclear arsenals of the superpowers remain substantial and potentially threatening but no longer attract a great deal of interest from either moral philosophers or anti-nuclear campaigners. The actual politics of nuclear weapons has now moved on to the issue of proliferation; in recent years India and Pakistan have joined the US, Russia, the UK, France, the China and Israel as nuclear powers of a sort, and few believe that the process will stop there. What is as striking as the disappearance of the issue of nuclear disarmament is the non-appearance of a great deal of overt moral concern at this development. The kind of heat generated during the debates of the 1980s has not returned, and there is no mass movement equivalent to CND in the UK (or even END in Europe) oriented towards this problem – which is strange, because the possibility of nuclear war is, surely, much greater in this century than it was in the 1980s. The suspicion must be that, as was argued by critics at the time, the anti-nuclear movements in western Europe in the 1980s were largely fuelled by anti-American (or perhaps anti-capitalist) sentiment rather than by a genuine involvement with the moral complexities of deterrence and disarmament.

## Human rights and humanitarian intervention

Underlying the contemporary (declared) norms regarding force in international relations is the doctrine of state sovereignty – broadly speaking, the notion that states are legally autonomous entities, entitled to run their own affairs without external interference, and obliged to acknowledge others as their equals.[12] Hence, the legal norms concerning the use of force refer essentially to inter-state war rather than to civil war or internal unrest (unlike the medieval doctrine of just war, which was, at root, about the role of force and violence in human affairs more generally). This reference point is unfortunate, given that in the post-1989 world (and for that matter even before 1989, although to a lesser extent) war has become an essentially 'domestic' affair – albeit quite frequently involving outsiders as well. The only *international* war fought under terms that illustrate the closing of the gap between declared and actual norms in the post-Cold War era was that begun by Iraq's invasion of Kuwait in 1990; every other conflict of the last decade has been, at root, a civil war.[13] The post-Soviet world has been riven by domestic conflicts, and elsewhere in the world, too, the restraints imposed by the conflict between East and West – where the possibility of a nuclear exchange imposed a degree of caution on everyone – have been lifted. In short, conflicts have been able to develop in ways that would not previously have been possible.

What is different about the post-Cold War period is that, in cases such as the collapse of the Somali state, outsiders have the opportunity to intervene on *humanitarian* grounds if they so wish. Nowadays choices have to be made – including the choice not to act – and not necessarily on strategic grounds; thus, norms become central. Unfortunately, current normative understandings about sovereignty and the circumstances under which intervention is legitimate are anything but clear. On the one hand, the current international normative order is based on the principle of state sovereignty, and, although the so-called Westphalia understanding of sovereignty is not quite as clear-cut as is sometimes taken to be the case, non-intervention is certainly a settled norm of that order. On the other hand, the post-1945 international human rights regime, composed of the Universal Declaration on Human Rights of 1948, various covenants, the Genocide Convention and an increasing volume of case-law, is clear that some of the ways in which governments might and do treat their own people are no longer defensible as acts of state sovereignty.[14] A large part of the normative agenda of the last decade has been concerned with the ways in which this contradiction has been negotiated.[15]

There is a great reluctance on the part of the majority of states to abandon the general norm of non-intervention. Poor, weak, states are only too well aware that the protection this norm gives them is already attenuated and often ineffective. Intervention is always an act of power, whatever else it is, and the powerless are understandably reluctant to legitimize it. This reluctance is often described in pejorative terms, on the principle that well-governed, non-oppressive states have nothing to fear from a doctrine of humanitarian intervention, while oppressive rulers do not deserve the protection of the law. There is some truth to this – it does sometimes seem to be the case that the people in a tyranny are prepared to put other considerations aside and welcome outside intervention, even forcible intervention.[16] But, in general, the argument is analogous to the weak rhetorical point sometimes made in domestic debates to the effect that only criminals ought to fear some new piece of legislation which undermines conventional understandings of civil liberties. The truth is that, in the (likely-to-be-prolonged) absence of some kind of global democracy, it is rich and powerful states – nowadays the US and its allies – who will, in practice, determine when intervention is appropriate or not; and one does not have to be an apologist for tyranny to see that this is not a particularly desirable state of affairs.

Perhaps surprisingly, states with the power to break the norm of non-intervention (including the US) tend to agree and it is only in rare circumstances that states have declared themselves to be intervening explicitly for humanitarian reasons – most notably in the case of the zone created for the safety of the Kurds in northern Iraq in 1991, and during Nato's campaign in Kosovo in the spring of 1999. The major countries are well aware that there would be no consensus behind the creation of a new statutory or customary rule to govern humanitarian intervention and thus, generally, give at least lip-service to the declared norm that intervention is legitimate only if approved by the UN Security Council in response to a potential threat to international peace and security. And, of course, since the major powers are more or less bound to be selective in the circumstances under which they will actually intervene, there is an obvious reluctance to lay upon themselves a general duty that they have no intention of meeting. Similarly, because the declaration that a genocide is taking place is widely held to generate an obligation to act, there is an equivalent unwillingness on the part of the major powers to use that term even when it is clearly appropriate, as in the case of Rwanda in 1994.[17]

The reluctance to enunciate an unambiguous doctrine of humanitarian intervention was partially overcome in 1999 during the Kosovo crisis. Whereas US government pronouncements on the rationale for NATO action were somewhat circumspect, some European states were more willing to go out on a limb. In Germany, perhaps surprisingly, the governing SPD/Green coalition was rather more enthusiastic for action to reverse the deportation of Kosovo's ethnic Albanians than their right-wing predecessors would have been. Doubtless this reflects the arrival in government of a generation of political leaders who had always been involved in human rights issues and, because of Germany's past, were preternaturally sensitive to the issue of genocide. Most members of the French Socialist government combined with their Gaullist President in a similar cause, while the British 'New Labour' government was the most bellicose of all. British Prime Minister Blair's 'Doctrine of the International Community', set out in a speech in Chicago, attempted to provide a framework for deciding under which circumstances humanitarian intervention would be justified – interestingly, many of the criteria of a just war appeared here (last resort, intention to right a wrong, proportionality, a reasonable prospect of success) but the issue of proper authority was glossed over (necessary in the absence of Security Council blessing for Nato's campaign), and the 'national interest' of the interveners was stressed in a way that would seem out of place in a just war context.[18]

In any event, the fall-out from Kosovo is very important in establishing the normative basis for future humanitarian actions, and it is clear that most states were determined that the precedent set by NATO's intervention should be as restricted and limited as possible. Although the campaign was judged a success, no one was keen to repeat the exercise, which was (and will be) extremely costly even for the victors. On the other hand, just as the US-led coalition in the Middle East in 1991 sent a clear message that such an extreme violation of international norms as the invasion of Kuwait in 1990 could not be tolerated, so the reaction to the blatant flouting of all humanitarian standards by the

Yugoslav regime may have sent a message that this kind of lawlessness also will not go unpunished.

One of the interesting features of the Kosovo campaign was the concurrent indictment of the Yugoslav leader Milosevic to answer war crimes charges, an indictment the significance of which may be comparable to the simultaneous attempts by Spain to extradite from Britain a former head of state, Senator Pinochet of Chile, on charges that he committed crimes against humanity. Both moves represent a trend in humanitarian law in which acts which might previously have been covered by the notion of sovereign immunity – the idea that one state is not entitled to hear cases which challenge the sovereignty of another – are deemed open to legal remedy. Although Pinochet was returned to Chile by the UK government on the grounds that he was mentally unfit to stand trial, in January 2001 he was indicted and placed under house arrest in Chile, on charges of alleged human rights abuses. On 1 April 2001 Milosevic was arrested and charged with domestic corruption, held in prison in Belgrade, and subsequently extradited to face trial in The Hague. Whatever the outcome of these events, a precedent has been set. Equally, the establishment of war crimes tribunals for Bosnia and Rwanda, and the likely birth of an international criminal court over US opposition, represent a real shift away from conventional notions of sovereignty.

Returning to the relationship between declared and actual norms, even when endorsing the norm of non-intervention, states have sometimes carried out interventions for quasi-humanitarian motives without admitting that this was what they were doing. This, surely, was partly the case when Tanzania invaded Uganda in 1979, citing threats to international peace and security, rather than the liberation of the Ugandan people as their motive – the relatively relaxed reaction of the rest of the world to this action rested on the widespread assumption that this was a convenient excuse for getting rid of a tyrant, Idi Amin, whose behaviour had become gross even by the worst of twentieth-century standards. This may be a case where, rather unusually, the actual norms are more morally palatable than the declared norms. In practical terms, a situation in which there is a general presupposition against international intervention, modified in extreme cases by action outside of the law, may be the best that can be hoped for given the difficulties involved in developing a new norm of humanitarian intervention.[19] In any event, this whole area is one where the arguments are changing quite quickly in response to events, and the new agenda of normative international relations theory is being created on a year-by-year basis. This process shows no sign of slowing down.

## Cosmopolitanism, universalism and global social justice

Humanitarian intervention and the international human rights regime challenge conventional notions of sovereignty, but are not without historical precedent. As Samuel Barkun and Bruce Cronin have demonstrated – and Stephen Krasner more recently – sovereignty has meant a number of different things over the past three centuries and only rarely an absolute right to do whatever the sovereign wished in domestic affairs.[20] The nineteenth-century suppression of the slave trade provided a precedent for later measures such as the Genocide Convention. However, there are some recent 'cosmopolitan' perspectives on normative international relations theory which cannot be provided with such a pedigree, most notably a concern for global *distributive* justice. The kind of economic inequalities which lead to differences of magnitude in quality of life indicators are the product of industrialization, and it is only since the decolonization process of the 1950s and 1960s that the 'less developed countries' (South) have been nominally equal members of the same international society as the 'developed' North. The idea that the North has an obligation to assist in the development of the South goes against the notion that sovereign states are responsible for their own welfare, while the idea that such transfers ought to be a matter of justice, as opposed to charity, is even more radical.

During the 1970s and 1980s such notions were advanced by the coalition of states that formulated demands for a new international economic order (NIEO) at the UN in the early 1970s, and supported by some liberal political philosophers who saw international social justice as a necessary accompaniment to the wave of theorizing about social justice begun by John Rawls in 1971.[21] The NIEO was not noticeably successful in changing international practice, but during the 1970s most states paid lip-service to the goals it represented. However, the arrival of Reaganomics, Thatcherism and, more generally, neo-liberal economics in the 1980s undermined the ideological foundations for the NIEO while high interest rates, which were a by-product of Reagan's fiscal policy, triggered the debt crisis. The latter shifted the practical agenda of North–South economic relations away from the NIEO and development, and towards crisis management and survival.

During these decades, just about the only real leverage the South had in its relationship with the capitalist North came from the existence of an apparently viable non-capitalist route to development in the form of communist industrialization; likewise, the communist states were an important source of political support. This card was rarely played with skill – apart from anything else, the communist world was lukewarm about the NIEO, arguing that Southern states should not rely on the capitalist world for assistance – but the very existence of an alternative to capitalism provided the rich with a reason not to push the poor too hard. Since about the mid-1980s, when it became unambiguously clear that this alternative was, in fact, no alternative, even this restraint disappeared. The move towards a stress on good governance and democratic politics as a precondition for assistance, and towards targeting such assistance to projects, policies and activities of which the North approved, could only have emerged with the strength it has in a world in which 'there is no alternative'. The ideological confidence with which the International Monetary Fund lays down its conditions has been amplified by the defeat of communism, while the pragmatic support that oppressive but reliably anti-communist rulers in the South could count on from the North (i.e., in this instance, the West) could no longer be relied upon. None of this is to suggest that the emphasis on good government and democracy is misplaced, or that many of the economic pre-scriptions of neo-liberalism are not sensible, but it is to point to the unchecked disparities of power that have allowed these positions to become so well established as the 'common sense' of contemporary international economics.

Here, then, is a sideways shift in the normative agenda post-Cold War. In the 1970s the NIEO called for an undermining of the doctrine of sovereignty by placing an obligation on the developed world to assist in the development of Southern states. In the 1990s the developed world is indeed undermining the sovereignty of these states, but in order to pursue its own version of their interests. In each case, the formal notion of sovereignty is preserved – after all, if states do not like the IMF conditions they do not have to take the IMF's money – but the reality is rather different.

One reaction to this situation has been the slow but significant growth of 'anti-systemic' movements in the South – that is to say, of social movements which attempt to avoid the poisoned chalice of a choice between Soviet-style enforced industrialization on the one hand, or Northern-sponsored neo-liberalism on the other, largely by rejecting conventional understandings of economic growth and development.[22] Perhaps the most dramatic manifest-ation of this shift has been the Chiapas revolt in Mexico, but the growth of peasant co-operatives in India and parts of sub-Saharan Africa is part of the same process.[23] This change is clearly related to the growth of environmental-ism and a general realization that the standards of 'development' taken for granted in the North most probably could not be generalized to the world's population as a whole (not, at least, with anything resembling existing tech-nology or energy requirements). Similar kinds of 'elective affinities' are found between these anti-systemic movements and the growth of the movement of indigenous peoples; at present the indigenous peoples who are most vocal are those who are fortunate enough to live in liberal democracies such as Canada, New Zealand, the US or Norway, but, in the longer run, UN support for these pioneers may well extend the movement into areas where local conditions are less propitious.

One of the things these diverse groups have in common is an ambiguous relationship towards the universalism they associate with Western thought.[24] Western notions of scientific rationality are challenged in the name of an allegedly less alienating relationship between human beings and their environ-ment, Western individualism is associated with acquisitiveness and greed, and the universal values summarized in documents such as the Universal Declar-ation on Human Rights are charged with a lack of respect for 'otherness', for the right to be different. However, there are ambiguities here: coping with environmental degradation without scientific rationality does not look too promising, and the desire for a longer, healthier life with a higher general standard of living is difficult to associate with the notion of greed. Perhaps most of all, the very notion of respect for the Other owes a great deal to Western thought; the idea, for example, of a worldwide movement of indigenous peoples would have made no sense to actual indigenous peoples prior to the arrival of universalizing Westerners. To take an example drawn from one of the most politically conscious of indigenous peoples, the word which was coined in the nineteenth century by indigenous New Zealanders (Aotearoans) to describe themselves, 'Maori', means 'normal people', implying the non-normality of the 'Pakeha', the Europeans, but also of *everyone* else including other indigenous peoples. The idea that all indigenous peoples have similar interests, let alone rights, would have been difficult, if not impossible, to explain to a Maori chief at that time.[25] The idea that we all have obligations to humanity as a whole as well as to our co-nationals and fellow citizens is largely the product of Western political and social thought – although, needless to say, the political practice of the West rarely lives up to this high ideal.

The Cold War era debates about human rights characteristically revolved around the difficulty of reconciling the classical, liberal, political conceptions of rights with the idea of social and economic rights.[26] These debates continue, but the 'rights of peoples' are now also at issue, and debates about the universal nature of rights as opposed to notions of, say, 'Asian' values are now coming to take centre stage.[27] This shift in normative debate in international relations is mirrored by intellectual challenges to the characteristic shape of normative international relations, and the final section of this essay is devoted to these challenges.

## Contemporary challenges to normative international theory

A central feature of modern moral philosophy has been a concern with establishing rules of conduct. 'Deontological' theories attempt to establish binding rules of conduct directly, as, for example, in the Kantian categorical imperative; 'consequentialists' are, in principle, opposed to this kind of thinking, but apply rules at a different level, as in the utilitarian 'felicific calculus', which tells us how to weigh up good and bad consequences. In any event, most consequentialists believe behaviour should be rule-governed but that the ultimate justification of a rule is that it has good consequences (for a Kantian this would be a hypothetical imperative).[28] Most of the approaches to normative international relations discussed in this chapter reflect this way of thinking; the idea of a norm implies a rule, and the idea that international relations is a norm-governed activity suggests that states follow rules. Thus, it seems natural to ask what rules ought to govern the act of humanitarian intervention; the implication is that we would not consider an act to be a humanitarian intervention unless it met certain criteria, and a further implication might be that we would expect these criteria to be general – in other words, the decision to intervene in one set of circumstances and not another ought not to be capricious, but to be rule-governed. Likewise, a concern for global distributive justice represents a desire to establish the criteria under which a particular distribution of resources might be considered to be justified, while the international human rights regime represents a set of rules that ought to be followed by states (and, sometimes, non-state bodies and individuals).

This way of thinking about moral issues is also reflected in much Marxist and left/progressivist thought, although Marxism has always been officially sceptical about bourgeois morality. Contemporary radical writers such as John Pilger and Noam Chomsky share this scepticism, but the charge of hypocrisy they so frequently make against the West relies on rule-oriented notions of consistency. Equally, to shift the emphasis somewhat, these radicals share with the majority of liberal political moral philosophers and writers the notion that it is possible to establish facts upon which moral judgements ought to be made – indeed the Chomskyian approach to international relations is dominated by an almost pathological belief in the importance of digging up the crucial facts which will establish US/Western guilt for almost all the problems of the world, while Pilger's journalism is devoted to the same end.

It is worth spelling out these points because some of the most influential work of the last decade rejects more or less completely both the emphasis on rules, and the concern to establish an inter-subjective factual base for moral judgements.[29] Many feminist writers on ethics privilege an 'ethic of care' above a rule-oriented, justice-based ethic and such notions are beginning to be applied to international issues.[30] Emmanuel Levinas has developed an ethic based on responsibility to and for the Other, and this 'ethics of encounter' has been applied to the Gulf War and the Bosnian conflict by David Campbell, and more generally by Michael Shapiro.[31] These movements have emerged in the context of a wider post- and anti-positivist trend; although, in fact, Foucault's genealogies, Derrida's deconstructions, the postmodernist writings of Jean Baudrillard and Paul Virilio and the narrativism of Hayden White have very little in common with each other, they have all contributed to the quite spectacular growth of 'new learning' in international relations theory in general, with obvious and important knock-on effects in the study of international norms.[32] And, of course, these trends fit in with the challenges to Western notions of universal values and rationality outlined at the end of the last section.

## Conclusion

A full assessment of the impact of all these changes would be beyond the scope of this chapter – or, rather, the chapter would have to have been devoted to this task rather than given over mainly to an overview of the conventional agenda. But it is clear that if these approaches become firmly lodged in the mainstream literature of international relations theory the consequences for normative thinking may be quite considerable, and in some areas the debates have begun.[33] In this concluding section, one or two pointers towards an assessment are worth making.

First, it seems very plausible that the rise of the 'new learning' is connected to the end of the Cold War, even though most of the intellectual sources of this work date back to the Cold War years, and even though a simplistic account of post-positivist writers as a kind of new 'New Left' clearly will not do.[34] The majority of late modern thinkers consider themselves to be on the left politically, but most lack the orientation towards economic issues of the old (new) left; for these writers the failure of communist command economies was not experienced as a setback (nor, for that matter, as a liberation). Their anti-capitalism is based on what capitalism shares with traditional socialism – its commitment to Enlightenment rationalism and conceptions of progress – rather than its distinctive features, a fact which explains why more conventionally left-oriented figures, such as the critical theorist Jürgen Habermas, regard them as 'young conservatives'.[35] Still, the ending of the Cold War certainly created a space for new thought, and the desire to break out of old ways of posing problems received a genuine fillip from the fact that moulds were being broken elsewhere in global politics.

Second, the same kind of ambiguity about the relationship between 'old' and 'new' learning is present, as was identified above in connection with challenges to Western notions of rationality. However much one is opposed to a rule-based account of moral behaviour, it is, in practice, exceedingly difficult to think about ethical issues without eventually employing some notion of rules, and, however sceptical one is about the value of positivist epistemologies, it is difficult to present an argument without some reference to the 'facts' of the case. The work of the best late modern theorists demonstrates – and indeed identifies and recognizes – this paradox. Thus, for example, David Campbell has presented three important studies over the past decade (of US national security policy, of the demonization of Iraq in 1990–1 and of 'national deconstruction' in Bosnia), each of which is prefaced by an account of the inherent unreliability of any single narrative and the dialogic need to recognize a multiplicity of points of view, but each of which eventually delivers a quite convincing narrative firmly based upon what, in other circumstances, one would be inclined to call the facts of the case.[36] A similar point might be made about the prescriptive element in these writings. Although manifesto statements of an orientation towards otherness, an ethics of encounter, or an ethics of care, abound in this literature, it is very difficult to find any actual prescriptions for the conduct of state (or individual) behaviour that have not been commonplaces of liberal thinking on international affairs for most of the twentieth century and part of the last.

If these generalizations – especially the latter – hold, then perhaps the shape of the normative agenda in the next decade will change rather less than might otherwise have been predicted. What does, however, seem to be a safe bet is that, one way or another, the issues raised by the challenge to universal categories posed both by late modern theory and the emerging political practice of new, anti-systemic movements will play a bigger role in normative thought about international relations in the next ten years than they have in the last ten, and that one of the major factors behind this shift will be the continuing impact of the end of the Cold War. Here, along with the politics of humanitarian intervention and the contest over the referent object of 'rights', is where the new agenda in normative international relations is to be found.

## NOTES

1   Niccolò Machiavelli, *The Prince*, ed. Quentin Skinner and Russell Price (Cambridge, Cambridge University Press, 1988).
2   Which is not to say that there are no such things as 'facts' or that it is not, in some circumstances, sensible to distinguish facts from values, on which see the final section below.
3   The clearest example of a thoroughgoing structuralist account of IR is provided by Immanuel Wallerstein's world systems analysis. See, for an overview, Immanuel Wallerstein, *Historical Capitalism*, rev. edn (London, Verso, 1996).
4   An emphasis on meanings and intentions is, nowadays, associated with 'constructivist' thought in international relations – for an overview, see the introduction to John G. Ruggie, *Constructing the World Polity* (London, Routledge, 1998), and for the most influential constructivist statement, see Alexander Wendt, *Social Theory of International Politics* (Cambridge, Cambridge University Press, 1999). This identification gives proper recognition to the efforts of scholars such as Ruggie, Friedrich Kratochwil, Alexander Wendt and Nicholas Onuf to combat the economism and neo-utilitarianism of the dominant modes of thought in US international relations but, for the most part, the position itself simply reiterates the commonplaces of recent epistemological thought in the social sciences. Post-Kant, we are all 'constructivists' in the sense that direct and reliable access to a reality 'out there' is generally recognized to be unavailable.
5   Mervyn Frost, *Ethics in International Relations* (Cambridge, Cambridge University Press, 1996).
6   Frost's account of 'settled norms' implies that while states often fail to act in accordance with these norms there are no other non-declared norms to which they do adhere. This implication seems unwarranted.
7   James Turner Johnson, *Just War Tradition and the Restraint of War* (Princeton, NJ, Princeton University Press, 1981); Terry Nardin (ed.), *The Ethics of War and Peace* (Princeton, NJ, Princeton University Press, 1997).
8   Adam Roberts and Richard Guelff (eds), *Documents on the Laws of War* (Oxford, Oxford University Press, 1983).

9    Michael Walzer, *Just and Unjust Wars*, 2nd edn (New York, Basic Books, 1992).

10   Geoffrey Best, *Law and War Since 1945* (Oxford, Oxford University Press, 1994), is a good guide to post-1945 legislation.

11   See, for example, John Finnis, Joseph Boyle and Germain Grisez, *Nuclear Deterrence, Morality and Realism* (Clarendon Press, Oxford, 1987), and Russell Hardin and John J. Mearsheimer (eds), 'Special Issue on Nuclear Deterrence and Disarmament', *Ethics*, 95, 3 (1985).

12   R. B. J. Walker, *Inside/Outside: International Relations as Political Theory* (Cambridge, Cambridge University Press, 1993); F. H. Hinsley, *Sovereignty* (London, Hutchinson, 1966). Stephen Krasner, *Sovereignty: Organised Hypocrisy* (Princeton, NJ, Princeton University Press, 1999), provides a much more sophisticated analysis of the different meanings of sovereignty than can be attempted in an essay of this scope.

13   The wars of former Yugoslavia sometimes involve sovereign states (or at least UN members), but have had many of the qualities of civil wars.

14   Hillel J. Steiner and Philip Alston, *International Human Rights in Context: Law, Politics, Morals, Texts and Materials* (Oxford, Clarendon Press, 1996).

15   Recent works include Thomas G. Weiss, *Military–Civil Interactions: Intervening in Humanitarian Crises* (Lanham, MD, Rowman & Littlefield, 1999), and Jonathan Moore (ed.), *Hard Choices: Moral Dilemmas in Humanitarian Intervention* (Lanham, MD, Rowman & Littlefield, 1998).

16   True, for example, in the case of the US intervention in Grenada in 1983.

17   Eventually the term was used, but too late to make a difference. See Philip Gourevitch, *We Wish To Inform You That Tomorrow We Will Be Killed With Our Families: Stories from Rwanda* (New York, Farrar, Straus & Giroux, 1998), for a brilliant account of events in Rwanda, and Linda Melvern, *A People Betrayed: The Role of the West in Rwanda's Genocide* (London, Zed Books, 2000), for the best analysis of the failure of the 'international community' to meet its obligations under the Genocide Convention of 1948.

18   Tony Blair, 'Doctrine of the International Community', speech in Chicago, 22 April 1999.

19   In the best book on the subject, Nicholas J. Wheeler, to whose thinking I owe a considerable debt, contests this particular judgement, arguing that a new norm of humanitarian intervention may be emerging: *Saving Strangers: Humanitarian Intervention in International Society* (Oxford, Oxford University Press, 2000).

20   Samuel Barkun and Bruce Cronin, 'The State and the Nation; Changing Norms and the Rules of Sovereignty in International Relations', *International Organization*, 48, 1 (1994); Krasner, *Sovereignty*.

21   For the former see, for example, J. N. Bhagwati (ed.), *The New International Economic Order: The North–South Debate* (Cambridge, MA, MIT Press, 1977), and, for the latter, Chris Brown, 'Theories of International Justice' (review article), *British Journal of Political Science*, 27, 2 (1997).

22   Giovanni Arrighi, Terence Hopkins and Immanuel Wallerstein, *Antisystemic Movements* (London, Verso, 1989).

23   Neil Harvey, *The Chiapas Rebellion: The Struggle for Land and Democracy* (Durham, NC, Duke University Press, 1998).

24  These concerns are more widely shared; see, for example, Stephen Toulmin, *Cosmopolis: The Hidden Agenda of Modernity* (Chicago, IL, University of Chicago Press, 1990).

25  James Belich, *Making Peoples* (Auckland, Penguin, 1996).

26  See, for example, Jack Donnelly, *Universal Human Rights in Theory and Practice* (Ithaca, NY, Cornell University Press, 1989), and Henry Shue, *Basic Rights: Subsistence, Affluence and United States Foreign Policy* (Princeton, NJ, Princeton University Press, 1980).

27  See James Crawford (ed.), *The Rights of Peoples* (Oxford, Clarendon Press, 1988), and Joanne R. Bauer and Daniel A. Bell (eds), *The East Asian Challenge for Human Rights* (Cambridge, Cambridge University Press, 1999).

28  See G. E. M. Anscombe, 'Modern Moral Philosophy', *Philosophy*, 33 (1958).

29  Neo-Aristotelian 'virtue ethics' also rejects the view that ethics is about what we should do, in favour of an account of what kind of people we should be; however, this kind of thinking has not yet penetrated deeply into the IR literature: see Chris Brown, 'Towards a NeoAristotelian Resolution of the Cosmopolitan–Communitarian Debate', in Jan-Stefan Fritz and Maria Lensu (eds), *Value Pluralism, Normative Theory and International Relations* (London, Macmillan, 1999).

30  Virginia Held (ed.), *Justice and Care: Essential Reading in Feminist Ethics* (Boulder, CO, Westview Press, 1995); Christine Sylvester, 'Empathetic Co-operation: A Feminist Method for International Relations', *Millennium: Journal of International Studies*, 23, 2 (1994).

31  David Campbell, *National Deconstruction: Violence, Identity and Justice in Bosnia* (Minneapolis, MN, University of Minnesota Press, 1998); Michael Shapiro, *Violent Cartographies: Mapping Cultures of War* (Minneapolis, University of Minnesota Press, 1997).

32  For overviews see Chris Brown, ' "Turtles all the Way Down": Antifoundationalism, Critical Theories and International Relations', *Millennium: Journal of International Studies*, 23, 3 (1994); Jim George, *Discourses of Global Politics: A Critical (Re)Introduction to Global Politics* (Boulder, CO, Lynne Reinner, 1994).

33  See the *Millennium* Special Issue, 'Ethics and International Relations', *Millennium: Journal of International Studies*, 27, 3 (1998).

34  Terms like the 'new learning' and 'late modern' theory are used in order to avoid the term 'post-modernism' which has now been drained by misuse and abuse of whatever meaning it may once have had.

35  Jürgen Habermas, *The Philosophical Discourses of Modernity* (Cambridge, Polity, 1987).

36  David Campbell, *Writing Security: US Foreign Policy and the Politics of Identity*, rev. edn (Minneapolis, MN, University of Minnesota Press, 1998); David Campbell, *Politics Without Principle: Sovereignty, Ethics, and the Narratives of the Gulf War* (Boulder, CO, Lynne Reinner, 1993), and Campbell, *National Deconstruction*.

# 10

# Signs of a New Enlightenment? *Concepts of Community and Humanity after the Cold War*

## Richard Devetak

Nothing seems to me less outdated than the classical emancipatory ideal.
Jacques Derrida[1]

## Introduction

It is scarcely surprising that momentous political change should stimulate reflection on the direction of human history. With the ending of the Cold War, an event seen by many at the time as a decisive political change, it is worth asking whether international relations has been opened up to the possibility of political thought and practice more in line with the Enlightenment project. 'Emancipatory ideals' are back on the agenda it seems, even for thinkers often, though mistakenly, associated with anti-Enlightenment views, such as Jacques Derrida and Michel Foucault.[2]

This chapter examines the ways in which recent critical international theory has speculated on the prospects for reconstructing the normative principles and political practices of modern political life in the post-Cold War era. In particular it highlights recent efforts to rethink the concept of community and its implications for international intervention based on appeals to humanity. The argument advanced is that in both the theory and the practice of post-Cold War international relations there has been a progressive willingness to employ moral discourses grounded in widespread agreement. The language of power politics, so dominant during the Cold War years, now appears unnecessarily cynical. The question raised is whether this development may be construed as a sign of humanity's continuing process of enlightenment.

Moral discourses are not new to international relations of course; indeed, they have always been integral, if marginal. The post-war era, however, has seen significant developments in this regard, largely as a result of long-term normative achievements which find their most obvious codification in the

United Nations (UN) and its humanitarian discourse. But, with the fall of the Berlin Wall, moral discourse now functions in a global context free of many Cold War constraints. If nothing else, the rise of humanitarian discourses has provided individuals, communities, states, international organizations (IOs) and non-governmental organizations (NGOs) with a growing set of rules, norms and expectations with which to assess social, political, economic and legal relations within and between peoples and states. As a consequence, it is not altogether unreasonable to wonder whether alterations in the relationship between politics and morality, evident in the occasional suspension of the principle of sovereignty, might be signs of a 'new Enlightenment'.

I begin by outlining Kant's ideas on Enlightenment and recalling his reflections on the significance of the French Revolution. The second section explains some of the reasons why it is becoming fashionable to refer to Kant in the post-Cold War era. In the third section critical international theory is examined, highlighting the crucial reworking of questions of community. Finally, the chapter addresses the concept of humanity as it is employed in both the theory and practice of international relations. The argument presented here is that signs of a new Enlightenment might be found in the recent willingness of individuals, states, NGOs and IOs to hold the principle of state sovereignty in suspension when it is used to justify massive human rights abuse. The moral, legal and political questions stemming from these developments can be broadly interpreted in terms of the Kantian attempt to rethink the normative principles upon which political life is organized.

## Kant, Enlightenment and signs of history

Kant asked, in the *Conflict of the Faculties*, whether there was an occurrence or event in his time which proved the existence of a tendency within humanity of continual moral improvement. Was there a 'historical sign', he enquired, that affirmed the human race's constant progression towards the better? Such a sign would provide a 'rough indication', according to Kant, of humanity's propensity to pass from the state of nature's 'savage and lawless freedom' to humane and civilized law-governed freedom. But it would have to be a rememorative, demonstrative and prognostic sign all at once; that is, it would need to be a sign that recalls from the past, proves in the present, and anticipates in the future, the human capacity for moral progress.[3]

Since Kant's *Conflict of the Faculties* was published in 1798, less than a decade after the French Revolution, one might have expected Kant to find such a sign right there in the momentous political upheaval that brought the *ancien régime* to an end. Interestingly, however, Kant finds such a sign not in the substantive political change of the revolution itself, but in the 'attitude of the onlookers'. Their public expression of 'universal yet disinterested sympathy for one set of protagonists' proves to Kant that humanity has a moral disposition or character. Moreover, this moral disposition is in itself testament to human improvement. What strikes Kant as significant is not so much the politico-institutional transformation the revolution wrought on the ground, but the solidarity felt in the minds of people who played no part in the revolution, but who looked on from afar with deep concern. Owing to its universality and disinterestedness, Kant believed this mode of thinking demonstrated a moral character inherent in humanity which predisposes it to hope for human improvement.[4] This invisible, but tangible, change in the hearts and minds of spectators indicates the forging of an 'imagined community' of sorts which is concerned with the self-improvement of humankind. It is a case of humankind enthusiastically supporting the cause of freedom (that is, the release from self-incurred immaturity, as Kant defined it elsewhere) in another part of the world.

Two principles, says Kant, are the source of the spectators' sympathy:

> Firstly, there is the right of every people to give itself a civil constitution of the kind that it sees fit, without interference from other powers. And secondly, once it is accepted that the only intrinsically rightful and morally good constitution which a people can have is by its very nature disposed to avoid wars of aggression . . . there is the aim, which is also a duty, of submitting to those conditions by which war, the source of all evils and moral corruption, can be prevented.[5]

These principles, the right of self-determination and the duty to eradicate war, were commonly espoused during the Enlightenment, but they were not always woven together into a coherent theory. Kant, however, systematically weaves the two together, as any reading of his other historico-political writings makes obvious.

Kant's argument in *Conflict of the Faculties* leads us back to his more famous essays on 'Perpetual Peace' and 'What is Enlightenment?' and to 'Idea for a Universal History with a Cosmopolitan Purpose'. His essay on enlightenment is essentially an argument for freedom and autonomy, since for Kant enlightenment and emancipation are intimately related, consciousness-raising being intrinsic to overcoming constraints on freedom. Enlightenment thus involves the development of humanity's capacities to think and act freely.[6] Only then will humanity emerge from the cold, dark shadows of 'self-incurred immaturity' or heteronomy into the warm light of freedom and self-legislation.

This, of course, is implicit in the first principle alluded to by Kant, the principle of self-government. Kant is here treading on the ground of one of his favourite political thinkers, Jean-Jacques Rousseau. Kant was in full agreement with Rousseau that self-enacted law was central to political freedom and that this required a civil constitution based on the rule of law and the will of all who are subject to that rule.[7] Enlightenment thinkers, from Locke through Montesquieu to Kant and Paine, insisted that political life should be governed by laws rather than 'men'. They placed human progress in close relation to constitutionalism because they saw the constitution as a medium for 'an incessant striving for improvement'.[8] Moral progress was thus intimately bound up with the co-legislation of equals under the rule of law. That much was also evident in the American and French revolutions which both sought to consolidate legal and political gains by enshrining them in a constitution. As Ulrich Preuss argues, the revolutions sought to overcome impediments to universal freedom and equality by declaring certain rights and duties as fundamental to the workings of government.[9]

For Kant the domestic make-up of a state was intrinsically related to its external disposition. Republican states, he was convinced, were more peaceable. According to Kant, republics guaranteed the rights and freedom of individuals by establishing a political order based on the separation of powers, the rule of law and representative government. This, together with a public sphere where citizens can freely deliberate and debate issues of public concern, would provide the 'internal' conditions for achieving perpetual peace.

As Kant so insistently states throughout his historico-political writings, the achievement of perpetual peace depends on more than the spread of republican states. At the same time, he also stresses that the achievement of 'domestic' political progress can only be achieved simultaneously with 'international' political progress. 'Domestic' and 'international' progress are two sides of the same coin. He first made this point as the seventh proposition in his 'Idea for a Universal History'.[10] In 'Perpetual Peace' he also emphasizes, though perhaps less explicitly, the necessary structural relation between 'domestic' and 'international' politics in the second and third 'definitive articles' which advocate a federation of free states and cosmopolitan right. As necessary as republican states might be to securing perpetual peace, they are not sufficient; two 'external' conditions must be met if perpetual peace is to be achieved.

While the second definitive article emphasizes states' rights and obligations under international law, the third definitive article, more radically, introduces a conception of cosmopolitan right. Kant here claims that the 'peoples of the earth have entered in varying degrees into a universal community, and it has developed to the point where a violation of rights in *one* part of the world is felt *everywhere*'.[11] Under these circumstances new rights and obligations are created which exceed the bonds between a state and its citizens. Obligations are not limited to fellow nationals, but extend to outsiders, even if it is only a right to be treated hospitably. As Thomas Mertens explains, this 'conception of cosmopolitan right is introduced because the requirements of republicanism and federalism are not a sufficient basis on which to define completely the just relation between human beings'.[12] They may help define justice in relations between a state and its citizens, and between one state and another, but they do not address justice in relations between states and foreigners, or between citizens and foreigners.

What is distinctive about Kant's argument therefore is that it expands the scope of the law of nations (whether conceived as the *ius gentium* or *ius inter gentes*) to include the transnational rights of individuals. To establish universal justice and perpetual peace, that is, to provide the conditions for universal human freedom, Kant believed it necessary to institutionalize a cosmopolitan law which cuts across state boundaries, enshrining the rights of world citizens (*Weltbürgerrecht*) alongside the rights of national citizens and sovereign states, thus establishing a world order based on a universal community governed by the rule of law.

The principles enunciated in 'Perpetual Peace' are not proposed as precepts of the law of nations (states' rights), but as principles of a more humanitarian law. What these principles suggest is that justice invariably cuts across different levels of social and political life and any legislation must accommodate this fact. Indeed, they suggest that the bonds between citizens and states must be renegotiated once it is recognized that the whole of humanity constitutes 'a single moral universe'.[13] As Linklater explains, under the rule of Kant's cosmopolitan law individuals would remain citizens of their respective states but they would 'expose the civic bonds within each independent state to the test of cosmopolitan citizenship'.[14] This would mean activating the categorical imperative in international relations and restructuring politics around principles of universal justice. In such a set-up, political borders would become less exclusionary as they would no longer restrict the universalization of the moral law. At the heart of Kant's argument, therefore, is a call for a radical rethinking of the normative principles upon which all politics are organized.

### A return to Kant: globalization and the post-Cold War era

With the end of the Cold War it has become possible to rethink questions of duty and obligation beyond national frontiers. Such questions have long been posed. They have, however, always run up against various practical constraints. The most significant barriers of course have been the sovereign state and its close affiliation over the last couple of centuries with capitalism and nationalism. In the twentieth century these barriers to more extended forms of ethical obligation were supplemented by Cold War politics. East–West as well as North–South relations were inevitably constrained by Cold War alliances and economic interests. The strategies of containment which shaped the Cold War seemed to reinforce a generalized politics of closure and exclusion as well as polarization.

However, the end of the Cold War seems to have coincided with another process, which also has the effect of undermining boundaries, namely globalization. This highly contested term, needless to say, cannot be properly dealt with here. But three brief remarks are in order. First, there seems to be some agreement that it is neither a singular nor a linear process, being uneven in its range and impact, and multidimensional in character. Different domains of social activity are being globalized – economic, political, technological, military, legal, cultural and environmental – combining to produce a stretching and intensification of social relations across time and space, in principle and often in practice, globally.[15] Second, these material changes mean that the fate of individual political communities can no longer be understood 'in exclusively national or territorial terms'.[16] And this is for at least two reasons. One, because globalization produces a system of complex interdependence where decisions 'here' reverberate 'there' with significant consequences. Two, because these processes are increasingly detached from states both in terms of their origins, and often in their capacity to outflank control and regulation.

This leads to a third, and perhaps the most important, point. Globalization does not mean that the state is disappearing. Globalization is not eclipsing the sovereign or national state; indeed states have been active agents in this process. Rather, globalization signifies the transformation of the state. This argument has been most fully worked out in international relations by Ian Clark, Robert Cox and John Ruggie. They have shown that globalization is best understood by jettisoning two conventional assumptions: first, that the 'domestic' and 'international' realms are separate and distinct realms in which states act; and, second, that globalization is an 'external' force acting on states and limiting their autonomy. Instead, they suggest viewing the 'domestic' realm as woven into the 'international' fabric, and vice versa, with the state viewed as the site of political accommodation or 'trade-off' between 'domestic' and 'international' pressures.

The upshot of this analysis is that the state is not at all threatened with extinction by globalization. Rather, globalization is reinterpreted as a name for the state's new accommodation of 'domestic' and 'international' pressures. More particularly, the state is increasingly 'disembedding' domestic society from the global liberal order as it pursues policies of liberalization, deregulation and deeper integration in the global economy.[17] This 'internationalization of the state', as Robert Cox calls the process, whereby the state becomes something of a 'transmission belt' between the global and national economies,[18] inevitably transforms the nature of the social bond within and between political communities.[19] It is therefore important not to think about globalization as signalling the end of sovereignty, the nation-state or territorial politics. Instead, it signals a transformation in the nature of such politics. Indeed, as Clark suggests by paraphrasing Alexander Wendt, globalization is what states have made of it.[20]

Much of the debate about the end of the Cold War has also tended to proceed on the basis of the two suppositions listed above: namely, that the 'domestic' and 'international' realms are separate and distinct realms in which states act, and that the Cold War is best understood in terms of 'international' pressures affecting state behaviour. But an alternative interpretation might see the Cold War in terms of the state's security functions. The Cold War was not simply an 'external' force acting on states; rather, it was a condition produced by the state's ongoing 'trade-offs' between 'domestic' and 'international' security pressures.[21] Domesticating and containing 'internal' threats became inseparable from confronting and containing 'external' threats. The 'domestic' and 'international' realms were thus embedded and entwined in the same global Cold War system where the definition and identification of threats became fundamental to the state's identity. The bipolarity, nuclear deterrence, militarization, mutual hostility and preparedness for war that we associate with the Cold War are not to be seen simply as 'international' forces, but forces which shaped, and were shaped by, a particular resolution of the domestic social bond in the post-war era.

The upshot of globalization and the end of the Cold War, however, is that nation-state and ideological boundaries are fading in their power, though to different degrees. For material and normative reasons, therefore, it seems the time is ripe to reconsider the normative principles upon which politics is organized. The Cold War was always an obstacle to international consensus on serious moral and political questions but, with the demise of the Cold War, consensus is not just a possibility, it has on some occasions been a reality even on questions of military intervention. This brings us to consider the relevance of Kant's political thought after the Cold War.

While it would be untrue to suggest that Kant's political thought had been ignored during the Cold War, it is certainly true to say that his thought, especially his reflections on international relations, has enjoyed an unprecedented popularity after the Cold War's end. To be sure, the revival began in the dying years of the Cold War with Michael Doyle's thesis about liberal democracies being disinclined to wage war against each other.[22] Francis Fukuyama's thesis about the end of history, announced just as Eastern Europe began dismantling the most obvious of Cold War geopolitical structures, also drew upon Kant-like suggestions about peace and democracy.[23] When the Eastern bloc disintegrated and the Soviet Union collapsed, the promise of Kantian theory as espoused by the likes of Doyle and Fukuyama seemed to be fulfilled. Kant could bathe victoriously in the optimism of the post-Cold War era without fear of being co-opted by realists, as Waltz had done back in the darkest years of the Cold War.[24]

But there is another version of Kant, or perhaps just another Kant, who has been resurrected into the bright light of the post-Cold War world. This is the more radical Kant (outlined in the previous section) who focused on the normative principles according to which modern political life should be organized. This is the Kant whose categorical imperative, whichever formulation is invoked, places human freedom at the heart of any political inquiry. It is the Kant who is the thinker of enlightenment and emancipation, rather than the publicity officer of liberalism or realism. And it is the Kant who recognized that political thought should not be split between political theory (speculation about relations between citizens and their state) and international theory (speculation about relations between states), but should also incorporate what we might call cosmopolitical theory (speculation about relations between humans irrespective of state borders). It is from this Kant that the most interesting developments in recent international theory have developed.

## Cosmopolitanism and critical international theory after the Cold War

> The globalization of commerce and communication, of economic production and finance, of the spread of technology and weapons, and above all of ecological and military risks, poses problems that can no longer be solved within the framework of nation-states or by the traditional method of agreement between sovereign states.
>
> Jürgen Habermas[25]

Before addressing critical international theory directly, it may be worth making a few points about how it relates (if at all) to the ending of the Cold War. One of the central purposes of any critical theory is to reflect on the present as a social and historical product and to analyse prospects for emancipatory change. The historical and analytical concerns of critical international theorists are therefore broader and deeper than alterations in the distribution of power among sovereign states alone. As momentous as the end of the Cold War appears to us now, at the beginning of the twenty-first century, critical international theorists would no doubt agree with Rob Walker that it is easy to overestimate its importance by interpreting it in relation to 'the entrenched expectations of a world carved up at Yalta and Bretton Woods'.[26]

This raises the interesting question of whether these alterations are in fact surface manifestations of deeper changes. For example, it may be the case that the dissolution of the superpower standoff reflects a changed attitude among the major powers to warfare;[27] or, as Phil Cerny argues, it may be indicative of the general ineffectiveness of the balance of power mechanism to regulate relations between states in an era of globalization;[28] or it may simply indicate the international agenda's new 'hierarchy of issues'. It will be suggested here, though not defended, that if there is any connection between the end of the Cold War and deeper, long-term changes it relates to the increasing difficulty of conducting politics based on strategies of containment, closure or totalization. Both the Cold War and the so-called 'Westphalian' system depend on erecting boundaries and trying to contain social, political, cultural and economic relations within them. But, as we shall see, the supposition that boundaries might contain or repel is highly problematic in a post-Cold War era of globalization.

For these reasons critical international theorists are likely to situate their arguments in relation to the broad-scale transformations associated with globalization and the unravelling of the 'Westphalian' system. Of course, neither of these contextual references is uncontroversial. What seems less controversial, though, is the intuition that social and political changes, no matter how small or large their apparent historical significance at the time, may always generate or exacerbate moral tensions and thus provoke new questions and political possibilities. At such times the crucial challenge is to understand how dominant forms of political organization are being transformed.

One of the main intentions behind critical international theory is to assess the possibility of undoing the monopoly powers of the sovereign state and promoting freer forms of community within a broader cosmopolitan structure. Mark Neufeld describes this cosmopolitan project in terms of mapping the Greek *polis* on to the globe such that the sphere of freedom and equality can be expanded to the human species.[29] Before this cosmopolitan project is explored in more detail it is necessary to recall the normative assault on the sovereign state.

This cosmopolitanism recaptures the Enlightenment belief that the sovereign state, as a 'limited moral community', promotes particularism, thus breeding greed, estrangement, injustice, insecurity and violent conflict. This type of analysis found clear expression in Kant, for whom war was undeniably related to the separation of humankind into separate, self-regarding political units, and Rousseau, who caustically remarked that in joining a particular community individual citizens necessarily made themselves enemies of the rest of humanity.[30] It was characteristic of many Enlightenment thinkers of the eighteenth century for whom war was simply an expression of the particularistic politics generated by the *ancien régime*.[31]

This critique of the sovereign state for its continued association with violence also underpins contemporary critical international theory. According to Linklater, the modern, sovereign state is the product of a 'totalizing project' to combine various monopoly powers.[32] The modern state concentrated these social, economic, legal and political functions around a single, sovereign site of governance that became the primary subject of international relations by gradually removing alternative sites of authority and allegiance. The effect was to produce a conception of politics governed by the assumption that the boundaries of sovereignty, territory, nationality and citizenship must be coterminous.[33]

This argument closely resembles, though from very different premises, the central theme in David Campbell's post-structuralist account of the Bosnian war. At the heart of Campbell's argument is the claim that a particular norm of community has governed the intense violence of the war. This norm, which he calls 'ontopology', borrowing directly from Derrida, refers to the presumed need to align territory and identity.[34] It functions to disseminate and reinforce the supposition that political community must be understood and organized as a single identity perfectly aligned with and possessing its properly allocated territory. The logic of this norm, suggests Campbell, leads to a 'desire for a bounded community'.[35] What is interesting and relevant about Campbell's argument here is that he is not simply suggesting that the outpouring of violence in Bosnia was an aberration or racist distortion of this norm, but that it was in fact an exacerbation of this very same norm. The upshot of Campbell's analysis is that the violence of 'ethnic cleansing' in pursuit of a pure, homogeneous, political identity is simply a continuation, albeit extreme, of the same political project inherent in any modern nation-state. Campbell's analysis confirms Linklater's Enlightenment argument that the modern state is a 'totalizing project' which has the effect of naturalizing exclusion and breeding injustice and violence both within and between political societies.

This analysis inevitably prompts the question: can political life be reorganized so as to avert injustice and violence and, if so, how? Alternatively stated, can modern political life reduce the 'moral deficits' created by global capitalism and the system of sovereign states so as to promote 'moral progress'? The objective of critical international theory is thus to promote the reconfiguration of political community not just by expanding social bonds beyond the frontiers of the sovereign state, but also by deepening and multiplying them within those frontiers. It is aimed at dismantling the totalizing project associated with the Westphalian system of sovereign states and rethinking the basic structures of governance which organize modern political life so as to remove all forms of injustice, including racial discrimination, material inequality and gender exclusion.

Linklater's argument promotes a cosmopolitan ethos that seeks to recognize the community of humanity at the same time as it recognizes regional, national, subnational and transnational identities. Essential to this cosmopolitan ethos is the desire to overcome the 'moral deficits' created by exclusions built into the structures of patriarchy, capitalism and the states-system. The intention here, fully in line with the Enlightenment project, is progressively to enlarge the sphere of freedom and equality by the creation of appropriate constitutional arrangements. Indeed, Linklater revives the Enlightenment notion of 'moral progress', a notion that in the twenty-first century tends to induce scepticism and cynicism.

Moral progress, for Linklater, is no longer associated with movement towards an eternal moral truth or universal conception of the good life. Instead, the key to moral progress, and here Linklater follows Habermas's lead, is the decentring of moral viewpoints.[36] It means submitting received moral values to challenge and critique whenever they beget exclusion, and this applies equally to universalistic or particularistic values. As Linklater understands it, moral progress refers to 'the widening of the circle of those who have rights to participate in dialogue and the commitment that norms cannot be regarded as universally valid unless they have, or could command, the consent of all those who stand to be affected by them'.[37] In short, it is about expanding the self-legislative capacities of all humans.

Signs of moral progress are to be found in the extent to which the nexus between sovereignty, territory, citizenship and nationalism is dismantled and replaced by freer forms of political association in which material inequality, national estrangement, gender exclusion and racial discrimination are eliminated. There are two aspects to this argument as developed in critical international theory. First, there is the Kantian argument for a cosmopolitan reconceptualization of the social bond; and, second, there is the notion that ideals of dialogue and consent must be placed at the centre of any attempt to create more cosmopolitan forms of community.

Linklater makes a case for what he calls 'thin cosmopolitanism'. Such a cosmopolitanism would need to recognize and reconcile the 'multiplicity of authorities and diversity of loyalties' identified by E. H. Carr.[38] It would thus resemble the neo-medieval image described by Hedley Bull and explored further by Phil Cerny.[39] The key to realizing this cosmopolitan vision is to sever the link between sovereignty and political association.[40] An inclusionary form of community is a post-sovereign one, according to Linklater; it would abandon the idea that power, authority, territory and loyalty should be focused around a single community. Fairer and more complex mediations of universality and difference can only be developed, argues Linklater, by transcending the 'destructive fusion' achieved by the modern state and promoting wider communities of dialogue.[41]

Linklater resorts to Habermas's notion of discourse ethics as a model for his dialogical approach. This is essentially a deliberative, consent-oriented approach to resolving political issues within a moral framework. In a sense it is an attempt to put into practice Kant's ideal of a community of co-legislators embracing the whole of humanity.[42] While we cannot provide an extensive account here of discourse ethics, we can note that it is a procedure for moral-practical reasoning that aims at establishing principles, norms or institutional arrangements that can command the assent of all relevant parties. Accordingly, any decisions resulting in exclusion must be deliberated upon and accepted by all who stand to be affected if it is to be a legitimate and just decision.[43] Linklater's vision, then, is of overlapping and intersecting dialogical communities.

Lest it be thought that Linklater is advocating the end of the state, it should be noted that he is only rejecting the sovereign form of state. Within his cosmopolitan restructuring of political life it would be necessary to retain the state, though in a much reformed configuration. One of its crucial responsibilities, as envisaged by Linklater, would be to 'enable multiple political authorities and loyalties to develop, and to endeavor to bring harmony through dialogue to the great diversity of ethical spheres which stretches from the local community to the transnational arena'.[44]

In many respects this argument follows Kant. However, there are three important differences. First, critical international theory is less persuaded by Kant's argument that nation-states should retain their separate sovereign existence. For critical international theory, state structures should be integrated into wider procedures and communities of dialogue which might, on occasion, view national differences as morally irrelevant. Second, while clearly indebted to Kant's ideal of extending legal relations to the whole of humanity, critical international theory is not necessarily buying into an idea of undifferentiated humanity. Critical international theory is here accepting feminist and post-structuralist arguments that the particularity of 'concrete others' should be recognized and respected.[45] Third, whereas Kant puts the generalizability of principles and norms to the test in an *imaginary* dialogue, discourse ethics recommends an *actual* dialogue: real speaking and listening, debating and deliberating human beings. This is, to be sure, a distinctly political, rather than epistemological, approach to deciding questions of governance.[46]

To bring this section to a close we should note that critical international theory is engaged in a reconstruction of the Enlightenment project. In common with many eighteenth-century Enlightenment thinkers it is committed to the eradication of unjust forms of exclusion and the emancipation of the species. It thus involves a serious rethinking of the normative foundations on which modern political life is organized in order better to promote the freedom and equality of humanity.

## Humanity and humanitarian intervention

> Modern universalism is built upon the experience of a new kind of crime: the crime against humanity.
>
> Michael Ignatieff[47]

The twentieth century achieved new heights in humankind's capacity to inflict inhuman levels of cruelty, violence and destruction. This has prompted critical examination of the sources of this inhumanity, including accounts such as Horkheimer and Adorno's *Dialectic of Enlightenment*, linking it to the Enlightenment project itself. This section provides a brief survey of the concepts of humanity and humanitarianism. Concurring with Ignatieff, it suggests that new articulations of humanity have arisen out of a reaction to intolerable crimes. Far from depending on an abstract conception of humanity, the revised Enlightenment project is hitched to the concrete experiences of a humanity subject to a variety of human wrongs.[48] I elucidate this first by outlining briefly the history of the concept of humanity in international relations.

Humanity, or the community of humankind, has long been invoked in legal and political theory. One can go as far back as the Greeks and Romans to see appeals made to notions of humanity in one form or another. However, it was in the early modern period with the rise of natural law and neo-Stoicism that humanity became a central moral, legal and, to a certain extent, political concept. Its centrality was no doubt heavily influenced by the 'discovery' of the New World and subsequent moral arguments over the status of the 'exotic' and 'barbaric' beings encountered in faraway places. 'Humanity' thus became a site of great contestation as moral, legal and political thinkers grappled with the status to be accorded these non-European, non-Christian beings.

By the eighteenth century strong concerns were being raised about the cruel treatment of indigenous people and the institution of slavery. Though such concerns were raised before, they were now louder and more widespread than ever.[49] Humanity thus became one of the Enlightenment's central political categories in the quest for emancipation. The objective was to liberate the whole of humankind, to bring equality and justice to *all* humans irrespective of their colour, race, sex or creed. Though all humans were born free, they were everywhere in chains, as Rousseau so eloquently summarized one of the central sentiments of the eighteenth-century Enlightenment. The increasing import-ance attached to the concept of humanity in political discourse was thus integral to what might be called the 'moral criticism of politics' associated with the Enlightenment.[50]

Two fundamental events in the modern political history of the concept of 'humanity' were of course the American Declaration of Independence and the French Declaration of the Rights of Man and Citizen. Both declared that all humans had imprescriptible, inalienable rights which formed the basis of their fundamental freedom and equality. These rights were deemed by the American Declaration to be 'self-evident' and by the French Declaration 'sacred'. As the second article of the French Declaration avows, 'The end of all political associations is the preservation of the natural and imprescriptible rights of man [sic]; and these rights are liberty, property, security, and resistance of oppression.' These rights were universally held by all humans simply by virtue of their humanity, even if they had been violated in practice by despotic forms of government. Human rights and the rights of citizens were thereby equated, since all citizens were due certain rights simply by virtue of their humanity. At one level, therefore, the Enlightenment collapsed the distinction between 'men' and 'citizens'.

By the end of the eighteenth century Kant gave further force to the moral requirement to give political expression to humanity. He argued that we have a duty to associate with all other humans as co-legislators in an imagined 'kingdom of ends'. All citizens, he believed, ought to enter into a legal rela-tionship with the rest of humanity, thus concretizing cosmopolitical law and affirming the moral dimension of politics.

The importance attached to humanity as a moral and political concept is carried on in critical international theory, as we have already seen. This work can be read as a concerted effort at bringing considerations of humanity into political decision-making processes. This critique of exclusion is premised on the idea that particularistic social orders (such as the modern system of sovereign states, the capitalist global economy and patriarchal social relations) do harm to humanity by virtue of the violence and injustice they generate and the freedom they curtail. Hence the repeated calls to work towards the emancipation of the whole human race by rethinking obligations owed beyond 'our' particularistic identifications. This brings us now to the issue of humanitarian intervention before and after the Cold War.

One of the interesting developments in the post-Cold War era is the frequent refrain of humanitarianism. Calls to act internationally on the basis of appeals to humanity and humanitarian responsibilities to alleviate suffering seem to be growing daily. Human rights, humanitarian assistance and forcible humanitarian intervention have taken on greater political significance now that the Cold War is over. We have seen several military interventions undertaken with strong humanitarian undertones, even if they do not necessarily represent the emergence of a new legal norm of intervention.[51] These include interventions in Iraq to establish a 'safe haven' for Kurds (Security Council (SC) resolution 688), in Bosnia to ensure the delivery of humanitarian supplies to Sarajevo (SC resolution 764), in Somalia to create a secure environment for the supply of humanitarian assistance (SC resolution 794), the controversial NATO intervention in Kosovo, and the deployment of the UN Intervention Force in East Timor (INTERFET).

During the Cold War humanitarian intervention was consistently curtailed by the politics of containment. Primacy was unequivocally given to the sanctity of sovereignty based on Article 2.7 of the UN Charter which was consistently interpreted to proscribe intervention in all matters deemed within the 'domestic jurisdiction' of states. As Michael Akehurst notes, appeals to humanitarian intervention were notoriously scarce during the Cold War and were generally condemned as illegal.[52] This was even the case in the 1979 Tanzanian invasion of Uganda to overthrow the genocidal regime of Idi Amin, the Vietnamese ousting of Pol Pot in Cambodia in 1978–9 and the Indian intervention in Pakistan in 1971, all cases which could also be defended on humanitarian grounds.[53] Principles of order were thus privileged over principles of justice.

After the Cold War, however, the UN Security Council passed several resolutions, as noted above, based on humanitarian rationales.[54] This suggests that there has been a change not just in international society's ability to reach agreement and to act on agreed resolutions, but also in the area of its jurisdiction. International law has conventionally worked to favour principles of nonintervention. This has meant, of course, that 'domestic' relations between a state and its citizens were off-limits to outsiders, with the primary focus being relations between states.

However, as James Mayall has perceptively noted, 'the end of the Cold War has reopened the question of how domestic and international politics should be related'.[55] Of great importance in this regard is the status accorded to the principle of sovereignty when flagrant violations of human rights are taking place within a state's domestic jurisdiction. In such cases sovereignty becomes an unjust form of exclusion and is rightly placed in suspension. In French political circles it has even been argued that there exists not simply a 'right to intervene' (*droit d'ingérence*), but a 'duty to intervene' (*devoir d'ingérence*).[56]

In general the post-Cold War atmosphere is one which permits collective action in response to the 'complex emergencies' that arise when 'failed states' return their citizens to something resembling Hobbes's state of nature. The UN has even been able to assemble (sometimes fragile) multinational military forces to undertake various humanitarian operations. The possibility of consensus among the major powers now allows for such humanitarian assistance, as exemplified by interventions in Iraq, Bosnia and Somalia. The key issue here is whether it is becoming legitimate now to make 'domestic' issues a concern of the 'international' community. Under an emerging international humanitarian law it has been argued that they become a legitimate concern when the idea of humanity itself is threatened, such as when genocidal policies are adopted, as was the case in Bosnia and Rwanda. A further condition for international society legitimately taking a concern in 'domestic' affairs is that widespread agreement be reached and that action be undertaken on a multilateral basis only.

Humanity, therefore, seems to have taken on added significance as a political concept in the post-Cold War. Whereas the Cold War legitimized an international society with minimal goals of coexistence, perhaps for good reason, the post-Cold War era is seeing a more sustained moral criticism of international politics. *Realpolitik* looks crude and barbaric in these days of nascent humanitarianism.

Recently, however, some doubt has been cast over the suitability of humanity as a political concept. David Campbell has recently argued that humanitarianism, as currently employed in international relations by theorists and practitioners, is based on a problematic conception of humanity. Critiques of humanism are not new of course. Modernity itself has a counter-discourse going back to Montaigne, Spinoza and Nietzsche for a start. But there has been something of a revival of theoretical anti-humanism in the last thirty years, evident in the thought of Louis Althusser, Roland Barthes, Luce Irigaray, Jacques Derrida and Michel Foucault, to name a few. It is this tradition of thought which Campbell appeals to when he argues that his articulation of the 'emancipatory ideal' in *National Deconstruction* differs from flawed, traditional kinds 'where the object was "the *global* emancipation of humanity" in the name of a universal subject enacting a universal history'.[57] The problem with this approach, according to Campbell, is that its promise of progressive politics is undermined by its 'depoliticizing and disenabling' aspiration to totalize all 'the many aspirations and struggles' into a single 'subject of history'.[58]

The critique here is a familiar one, namely, that appeals to humanity and emancipation all too often presuppose a universal human essence, that is, something which is everywhere and always the same, irrespective of time, place or circumstance. The effect of this supposition, therefore, is to erase the particularities of gender, class, race and ethnicity which, it is believed, ought to be recognized and 'celebrated'.

Of course it remains to be shown that the revised version of the Enlightenment project offered by critical international theory is in fact a product of such a presupposition. Humanity is not *the* subject of history, nor can it be, in Linklater's argument, since it is not an already-given community. Like any other community, its being is only constituted in the doing.[59] Moreover, humanity operates more like a regulative idea than an empirical fact in critical international theory. But more specifically, as one rather underdeveloped community among many competing, overlapping and intersecting communities, its appeals to the 'human community' do not necessarily, in all instances, trump appeals to other communities. There is no reason why they should, especially if one is committed to unconstrained dialogue among relevant participants, and if there is no *a priori* privileging of identity over difference. As Linklater argues, it is important not to assume in advance 'moral hierarchies'.[60] Moreover, 'loyalties to the sovereign state or to any other political association cannot be absolute; ... *duties to humanity do not override all other obligations*'.[61] The point is that no single community has *a priori* primacy. The key issue, then, becomes one of deciding the conditions under which loyalty to one community or cause should override another and whether these decisions give rise to unjust exclusions.[62] It should be obvious that this is not something that can be legislated for in advance. Instead, it is a political matter to be resolved by those who stand to be affected by such decisions, balancing, as they must, the competing demands of general rules and singular cases.

## Conclusion

Assessing moral progress is always a fraught exercise. If nothing else, however, it forces us to think about the present and future trajectories of the worlds we live in. For many, the present era has opened a horizon of increased violence and volatility far worse than the one it surpassed. This short-sighted view is a hangover from the Cold War, an age shot through with instability and violence where the worst-case scenario was unthinkable in its consequences for humanity. Still, it seems too optimistic to conclude that the end of the Cold War marks a clear, unambiguous advance in the ongoing process of Enlightenment. The Enlightenment, after all, is an unfinished project.[63] What Kant said about his own time, we can perhaps say of ours: we do not live in an enlightened age but we do live in an age of enlightenment.[64] Evidence for this, I would argue, is partly to be found in the universal acceptance that certain moral concepts are unavoidably a part of international relations today, despite, or perhaps because of, their contested character.

More than this, however, we might also find signs of enlightenment in the increased concern that 'outsiders' take in the human suffering caused by states in their domestic jurisdiction. The fact that 'outsiders' publicly express 'universal yet disinterested sympathy' for suffering strangers in other countries, and act on this sympathy by way of humanitarian assistance or forcible humanitarian intervention, may be a rememorative, demonstrative and prognostic sign of humanity's capacity for moral progress.

NGOs, the UN, and even individual states on occasion have heightened our awareness and sensibility to the plight of vulnerable and oppressed peoples around the world. These same actors have, under certain circumstances, acted on behalf of a notion of humanity that has led to a reappraisal of the way in which relations between domestic, international and cosmopolitan law are negotiated, especially in the more permissive conditions created by the collapse of the Cold War. Without denying the validity of the principle of non-intervention in a state's domestic affairs, post-Cold War developments have shown the willingness of international society to place the principle in suspension in circumstances of extensive human suffering. At a general level, these developments have given rise to the need to rethink the conditions under which international society should make 'domestic' issues a legitimate concern for the rest of humanity. More specifically, they have forced a reconsideration of the conditions under which non-intervention should be balanced against a duty to intervene when a state flagrantly violates the human rights of citizens or groups within its borders. Recognizing duties to humanity is integral to the Kantian project of rethinking the normative principles upon which politics and international relations are organized, and may in itself be an important sign of humanity's continuing struggle to achieve emancipation.

## NOTES

1   Jacques Derrida, 'Force of Law: the Mystical Foundations of Authority', in Drucilla Cornell, Michel Rosenfield and David Gray Carlson (eds), *Deconstruction and the Possibility of Justice* (New York, Routledge, 1992), p. 28.
2   See, for example, Jacques Derrida, *Spectres of Marx: the State of Debt, the Work of Mourning, and the New International* (London, Routledge, 1994), especially ch. 3; Derrida, 'Force of Law'; Michel Foucault, 'What is Enlightenment?', in Paul Rabinow (ed.), *The Foucault Reader* (Harmondsworth, Penguin, 1984); Michel Foucault, 'Kant on Revolution and Enlightenment', *Economy and Society*, 15, 1 (1986); Michel Foucault, 'What is Critique?', in Michel Foucault, *The Politics of Truth*, ed. Sylvere Lotringer and L. Hochroth (New York, Semiotext(e), 1997). In international relations see David Campbell, *National Deconstruction: Violence, Identity and Justice in Bosnia* (Minneapolis, MN, Minnesota University Press, 1998), p. 198. I have outlined some of the reasons for rejecting the belief that post-structuralism is anti-Enlightenment in Richard Devetak, 'The Project of Modernity and International Relations Theory', *Millennium*, 24, 1 (1995), pp. 27–51.

3 Immanuel Kant, *Kant's Political Writings* (Cambridge, Cambridge University Press, 1970), p. 181.
4 Ibid., p. 182.
5 Ibid., pp. 182–3.
6 Ibid., p. 59.
7 Ibid., pp. 44–9.
8 Ulrich K. Preuss, *Constitutional Revolution: the Link Between Constitutionalism and Revolution* (Atlantic Highlands, NJ, Humanities Press, 1995), p. 26.
9 Ibid. See also Tom Paine's comment that 'A constitution is a thing *antecedent* to government, and a government is only a creature of a constitution', in Thomas Paine, *The Rights of Man* (Harmondsworth, Penguin, 1984), p. 71.
10 Kant, *Political Writings*, p. 47.
11 Ibid., pp. 107–8.
12 Thomas Mertens, 'Cosmopolitanism and Citizenship: Kant against Habermas', *European Journal of Philosophy*, 4, 3 (1996), p. 333.
13 Andrew Linklater, *The Transformation of Political Community: Ethical Foundations of the Post-Westphalian Era* (Cambridge, Polity, 1998), p. 36.
14 Ibid., p. 37.
15 David Held, Anthony McGrew, David Goldblatt and Jonathon Perraton, *Global Transformations: Politics, Economics and Culture* (Cambridge, Polity, 1999).
16 David Held, *Democracy and the Global Order* (Cambridge, Polity, 1995).
17 John G. Ruggie, 'At Home Abroad, Abroad at Home: International Liberalisation and Domestic Stability in the New World Economy', *Millennium*, 24, 3 (1995).
18 Robert W. Cox, 'Global Restructuring: Making Sense of the Changing International Political Economy', in Richard Stubbs and Geoffrey Underhill (eds), *Political Economy and the Changing Global Order* (London, Macmillan, 1994).
19 Richard Devetak and Richard Higgott, 'Justice Unbound? Globalization, States and the Transformation of the Social Bond', *International Affairs*, 75, 3 (1999).
20 Ian Clark, *Globalization and International Relations Theory* (Oxford, Oxford University Press 1999), p. 63.
21 Ibid., p. 5.
22 Michael Doyle, 'Kant, Liberal Legacies and Foreign Affairs', *Philosophy and Public Affairs*, 12, 2 and 3 (1983).
23 Francis Fukuyama, 'The End of History?', *National Interest* (Summer 1989).
24 Kenneth N. Waltz, 'Kant, Liberalism and War', *American Political Science Review*, 56, 3 (1962).
25 Jürgen Habermas, *The Inclusion of the Other: Studies in Political Theory* (Cambridge, Polity, 1998), p. 106.
26 R. B. J. Walker, *Inside/Outside: International Relations as Political Theory* (Cambridge, Cambridge University Press, 1993), p. 2.
27 John Mueller, *Retreat from Doomsday: the Obsolescence of Major War* (New York, Basic Books, 1989).
28 Philip G. Cerny, 'Globalization, Fragmentation and the New Security Dilemma: Towards a New Medievalism in World Politics', *Journal of Civil Wars*, 1, 1 (1998).
29 Mark Neufeld, *The Restructuring of International Relations Theory* (Cambridge, Cambridge University Press, 1995), pp. 11–12.

30   Jean-Jacques Rousseau, 'The State of War', in Stanley Hoffmann and David P. Fidler (eds), *Rousseau on International Relations* (Oxford, Clarendon Press, 1991).
31   Compare this with Tom Paine's remark that 'Man is not the enemy of man, but through the medium of a false system of Government', namely, the *ancien régime*, in Paine, *Rights of Man*, p. 146.
32   The monopolies he identifies are: the right to monopolize the legitimate means of violence over the claimed territory, the exclusive right to tax, the right to demand undivided political allegiance, the sole legal authority to adjudicate disputes between citizens, and the sole right of representation in international law; see Linklater, *Transformation of Political Community*, pp. 28–9.
33   Ibid., pp. 29 and 44.
34   Campbell, *National Deconstruction*, p. 80, and Derrida, *Spectres of Marx*, p. 82.
35   Campbell, *National Deconstruction*, p. 169.
36   Linklater, *Transformation of Political Community*, p. 90.
37   Ibid., p. 96.
38   Ibid., p. 163.
39   Hedley Bull, *The Anarchical Society: A Study of Order in World Politics* (London, Macmillan, 1977), pp. 254–5; Cerny, 'Globalization, Fragmentation'.
40   Devetak, 'Project of Modernity', p. 43.
41   Linklater, *Transformation of Political Community*, pp. 60 and 74.
42   Ibid., pp. 84–9.
43   See ibid., ch. 3, and Jürgen Habermas, *Justification and Application: Remarks on Discourse Ethics* (Cambridge, Polity, 1993).
44   Linklater, *Transformation of Political Community*, p. 45.
45   See Seyla Benhabib, *Situating the Self: Gender, Community and Postmodernism in Contemporary Ethics* (Cambridge, Polity, 1994), and F. Robinson, *Globalizing Care: Ethics, Feminist Theory and International Relations* (Boulder, CO, Westview Press, 1999).
46   Contrary to David Campbell, in 'Why Fight? Humanitarianism, Principles, and Post-Structuralism', *Millennium*, 27, 3 (1998), p. 520.
47   Michael Ignatieff, *The Warrior's Honour: Ethnic War and the Modern Conscience* (London, Vintage, 1998), p. 19.
48   Ken Booth, 'Human Wrongs and International Relations', *International Affairs*, 71, 1 (1995).
49   See Shelby T. McCloy, *The Humanitarian Movement in Eighteenth Century France* (New York, Haskell House, 1972); and Dorinda Outram, *The Enlightenment* (Cambridge, Cambridge University Press, 1995).
50   Reinhart Koselleck, *Critique and Crisis: Enlightenment and the Pathogenesis of Modern Society* (Cambridge, MA, MIT Press, 1988).
51   On this point see chapter 9 in this volume, and for an extended treatment of humanitarian intervention in the twentieth century see Nicholas Wheeler, *Saving Strangers: Humanitarian Intervention in International Society* (Oxford, Oxford University Press, 2000).
52   Michael Akehurst, 'Humanitarian Intervention', in Hedley Bull (ed.), *Intervention in World Politics* (Oxford, Clarendon Press, 1984), p. 99.
53   Akehurst, 'Humanitarian Intervention', pp. 96–8.

54 Adam Roberts, 'Humanitarian War: Military Intervention and Human Rights', *International Affairs*, 69, 3 (1993).

55 James Mayall, 'Non-Intervention, Self-Determination and the New World Order', *International Affairs*, 67, 3 (1991), p. 422.

56 P. Garigne, 'Intervention-Sanction and *droit d'ingérence* in International Humanitarian Law', *International Journal*, 48 (1993).

57 Campbell, *National Deconstruction*, p. 204–5.

58 Ibid.

59 Campbell is familiar with this argument of course, since he is one of its exponents in international relations. See his earlier *Writing Security: United States Foreign Policy and the Politics of Identity* (Minneapolis, MN, University of Minnesota Press, 1992) as well as *National Deconstruction*. I have surveyed some of these ideas in Richard Devetak, 'Theories, Practices and Postmodernism in International Relations', *Cambridge Review of International Affairs*, 12, 2 (1999).

60 Linklater, *Transformation of Political Community*, p. 56.

61 Ibid. emphasis added.

62 Ibid., p. 57.

63 Jürgen Habermas, 'Modernity – An Incomplete Project', in Hal Foster (ed.), *The Anti-Aesthetic: Essays on Postmodern Culture* (Seattle, WA, Bayview Press, 1983); and Linklater, *Transformation of Political Community*, pp. 41 and 220.

64 Kant, *Political Writings*, p. 58.

# 11

# Beyond Realism and its Critics: *The Decline of Structural Neo-Realism and Opportunities for Constructive Engagement*

## Jack Donnelly

### Introduction

The Cold War was a good time for political realism in the study of international relations, especially in the United States. Hans Morgenthau's *Politics Among Nations*, published as the Iron Curtain was descending in 1948, dominated the discipline for two decades. After a flirtation with interdependence and dependency in the discipline and *détente* in the 'real' world, Kenneth Waltz's *Theory of International Politics*, published in 1979, re-established realist disciplinary hegemony during Reagan's renewed attack on the 'evil empire'. The irony is almost worthy of Thucydides. Realism, the theory and practice of power politics, is profoundly opposed to the ideological confrontation that was so central to the Cold War. None the less, its disciplinary stock, especially in the US, has remained tied to the political fate of the Cold War – with the market decidedly bearish in the decade after the fall of the Wall.

In a retrospective assessment of the realists of Morgenthau's generation, Hedley Bull perceptively noted that the laws of international politics to which some 'realists' appealed in such a knowing way appeared on closer examination to rest on tautologies or shifting definitions of terms. The massive investigations of historical cases implied in their Delphic pronouncements about the experience of the past had not always, it seemed, actually been carried out. Indeed, not even the best of the 'realist' writings could be said to have achieved a high standard of theoretical refinement: they were powerful polemical essays.[1]

In much the same way, the 1990s saw a growing recognition that Waltzian neo-realism simply was not delivering the promised goods. With the flowering of a variety of constructivist alternatives – from the self-conscious postmodernism of James Der Derian, Christine Sylvester and Cynthia Weber;[2] to slightly more modernist embraces of what David Campbell has called 'the decon-structive ethos'; to Jens Bartelson's appropriation of Foucault; to Wendt's scientific realist constructivism; to the emergence of a constructivist main-stream addressing even the 'hard cases' of security politics[3] – we seem to be moving toward something much closer to a genuinely pluralist discipline.[4] Other chapters in this book examine the rise of and need for alternative theories. My focus is on the collapse of structural realism's disciplinary hegem-ony, which both has been hastened by and has helped to create new spaces for these alternative approaches.[5]

## Abstracting from motives

Structural (neo-)realism, in Kenneth Waltz's seminal formulation, is based on a double abstraction, from the attributes of states and from their interactions. Structure, Waltz insists, must be defined entirely 'free of the attributes and the interactions of the units'.[6] The theory aims to say 'a small number of big and important things'[7] about the behaviour of states (understood as characterless 'units') knowing only that they interact in anarchy (understood as a featureless void). In this section I address the abstraction from state attributes (motives).

### Motives matter

Seeking to avoid the notorious problems of substantive theories of human nature that bedevilled 'classical' realists such as Morgenthau and Niebuhr, Waltz and his followers have tried to 'abstract from every attribute of states except their capabilities'.[8] In practice, however, this has proved impossible. 'An international-political theory does not imply or require a theory of foreign policy any more than a market theory implies or requires a theory of the firm.'[9] This does not, however, mean no theory at all. 'Market theory does not deal with characteristics of firms',[10] in the sense that these characteristics are treated as 'exogenous', assumed rather than investigated or explained. But, as Waltz notes, 'economists think of the acting unit, the famous "economic man", as a single-minded profit maximizer'.[11] 'Neoclassical economics as-sumes that men are profit maximizers.'[12]

International political theories must likewise make substantive motivational assumptions. Structure – the distribution of capabilities in anarchy[13] – impinges on all actors. Predicted responses, however, are *not* independent of the character of those actors. Faced with a particular anarchic structure, Homeric heroes seeking glory through great deeds, Nietzschean individuals driven by a will to power, and *homo economicus* may behave differently from each other – and from Hobbesian egoists driven by a fear of violent death. As Waltz admits, 'we cannot predict how [states] will react to the pressures [of structure] without knowledge of their internal dispositions'.[14] In other words, abstracting from *all* state attributes (other than capabilities) yields a theory with no predictive or explanatory power. If Waltz's theory is to do anything of interest, he needs knowledge of or assumptions about the character or motives of states.

Waltz therefore (sensibly but inconsistently) acknowledges that 'the theory is based on assumptions about states'; 'the motivation of the actors is assumed'.[15] Rather than abstract from all particulars he assumes certain ones. Rather than 'take states with whatever traditions, habits, objectives, desires, and forms of government they may have',[16] Waltz makes substantive motivational assumptions. And it is those assumptions, rather than structure, that give much of the character to his theory.

## Survival and relative gains

It would be a minor matter to allow structural realists clear and coherent motivational assumptions. And Waltz does repeatedly claim that states 'are unitary actors with a *single* motive – the wish to survive'. 'I built structural theory on the assumption that survival is *the* goal of states.' 'The survival motive is taken as *the* ground of action.' 'I assume that states seek to ensure their survival.'[17] But, as Randall Schweller – perhaps the most important new realist voice to emerge in the 1990s – has shown, a world in which all states valued only survival would be one of 'all cops and no robbers'. 'What triggers security dilemmas under anarchy is the possibility of predatory states.'[18] At least one aggressive state is needed to generate a world of inescapable conflict and fear of violent death. Furthermore, 'many large-scale wars were initiated by precisely those states that valued expansion more than their safety'.[19]

In implicit recognition of the fact that any plausible theory must assume that states seek not merely survival but gain, the pursuit of *relative* rather than absolute gains is often presented as distinguishing realists from their critics.[20] 'Realists expect nation-states to avoid gaps that favour their partners, but not necessarily to maximize gaps in their own favour. ... They are, in Joseph Grieco's terms, "defensive positionalists".'[21] However, Fareed Zakaria argues that 'the best solution to the perennial problem of the uncertainty of international life is for a state to increase its control over that environment through the persistent expansion of its political interests abroad'.[22] John Mearsheimer claims that 'states seek to survive under anarchy by maximizing their power relative to other states'.[23] Mearsheimer's realist states are 'short-term power maximizers';[24] *offensive* positionalists. And leading realists have developed theories that assume that states seek to maximize utility (absolute gains).[25]

The situation still might be acceptable if individual realists consistently assumed either offensive or defensive motivations, the pursuit of absolute or relative gains. But few if any do. For example, Grieco, who touched off the relative gains debate, argues that the 'main goal' of states is to achieve the 'greatest gains *and* smallest gap in gains favouring partners'.[26] These are two different goals, not one: absolute *and* relative gains. And – crucial for my purposes – structure is silent about when states seek which. We can make no purely structural predictions of state behaviour.

### Multiple motivational assumptions

Consider the indeterminateness of standard structural 'predictions'. 'Even the prospect of large absolute gains for both parties does not elicit their co-operation so long as each fears how the other will use its increased capabilities.'[27] But from anarchy alone we cannot know how intense that fear will be. If it is not very intense, states may rationally pursue absolute gains. Even if 'anarchy and the danger of war cause all states to be motivated in some measure by fear and distrust',[28] a lot of greed often will overpower a little fear. Allowing that 'although the level of fear varies across time and space, it can never be reduced to a trivial level',[29] we can none the less expect very different behaviours from states gripped by an overpowering fear of violent death and those under the influence of a fear just barely greater than trivial.

Such 'structural explanations' either leave open all kinds of excuses and evasions – to which realists appeal when, as often happens, states fail fearfully to pursue relative gains – or rest on additional, implicit and *ad hoc* motivational assumptions of a most problematic nature. In fact, multiple motivational assumptions, rather than an accident or error, are essential to the apparent plausibility of 'realist' theories. This is most readily illustrated by Waltz who, despite his reputation for theoretical rigour, relies on wildly divergent and entirely *ad hoc* motivational assumptions.[30]

Consider also Waltz's often quoted claim that his theory is built on the assumption that states 'at minimum, seek their own preservation and, at maximum, drive for universal domination'.[31] This is obviously inconsistent with the claim to assume *only* that states seek survival. Survival and domination are qualitatively different ends that often conflict. And the area 'between' them is neither a lot of survival nor a little domination but something else altogether – actually, many other things.

'Countries have always competed for wealth and security.' 'The force of a state is employed for the sake of its own protection and advantage.' 'States develop along certain lines and acquire certain characteristics in order to survive and flourish in the system.'[32] Wealth, advantage and flourishing, although essential to a theory that yields plausible predictions, are neither a little domination nor a lot of survival. As Waltz himself notes, 'prosperity and military power, although connected, cannot be equated'.[33] Waltz also argues that states seek to maintain their relative position, preserve their autonomy and coexist peacefully.[34] In his most recent essay, he adds concern for national honour, on a level equivalent to fear.[35]

These motives share a 'realist' emphasis on self-interest. None the less, they have not only different but often contradictory behavioural implications. Waltz, however, shifts from motive to motive entirely without theoretical justification. And he *needs* to do so because no single motive (or consistent set) yields a plausible theory with the general scope to which Waltz aspires.

## Abstracting from interaction

Waltz also claims to abstract from the *interactions* of states. This reflects the characteristic realist belief that anarchy is such a pervasive force that international norms, rules and institutions cannot significantly shape the interests or behaviour of states. But this second key move in Waltz's structuralist project has proven no more successful than the first.

Because all the terrestrial parts of the globe except Antarctica are today parcelled out to sovereign states, it may be a useful simplification to treat contemporary political orders as either hierarchic (national) or anarchic (international). This does not, however, mean accepting Waltz's further claims that anarchy and hierarchy should be viewed as a strict dichotomy[36] and that we should therefore not consider 'mixed' international orders.[37]

'The appearance of anarchic sectors within hierarchies does not alter and should not obscure the ordering principle of the larger system.'[38] But the language of sectors clearly indicates a mixture of types. And, just as we will badly misjudge structural pressures and relations within such 'anarchic sectors' if we treat the entire order as simply hierarchic, hierarchic 'sectors' may significantly alter the structural dynamics of 'fundamentally' anarchic orders.

It is not true that 'national politics is the realm of authority, of administration, and of law. International politics is the realm of power, of struggle, and of accommodation.'[39] It is an empirical, not a theoretical, matter whether in international (or national) politics 'authority quickly reduces to a particular expression of capability'.[40] Waltz is just plain wrong when he asserts that 'nationally, relations of authority are established. Internationally, only relations of strength result.'[41] For example, the European Union (EU) has meagre coercive capabilities but considerable authority – more than, say, the government of Guatemala in the early 1980s, when it was killing hundreds, sometimes thousands, of its citizens every month.

This attempt to link anarchy to power and hierarchy to authority is especially problematic given Waltz's insistence that 'a structure is defined by the arrangement of its parts'.[42] Power and authority address how an arrangement is produced or maintained, not its shape. In defining both anarchy and hierarchy, Waltz uses the language 'entitled to command' and 'required to obey'.[43] But title to rule can come from either power (e.g. conquest or military coup) or from 'legitimate authority' (e.g. election or hereditary right). Conversely, one can be 'required' to obey by either superior force or superior authority; by the highwayman or the policeman.

The differences between (and within) national and international orders are both a matter of degree and subject to extensive variation. There is no *structural theoretical* reason why national governments could not derive their authority from the control of force. And there is no structural theoretical reason why states could not stand under, for example, the suzerain or imperial authority of another state, as was often the case in much of the Near East from Alexander through to the eighteenth century.

Even Waltz abandons the anarchy–hierarchy dichotomy at several points. 'Structures may be changed... by changing the distribution of capabilities across units. Structures may also be changed by imposing requirements where previously people had to decide for themselves.'[44] In other words, obligations alter structures. But obligations, and thus elements of hierarchy, clearly exist in anarchic orders, establishing limited domains of authority and subordination.

The resulting differences, it must be emphasized, are structural. 'A structure is defined by the arrangement of its parts. Only changes of arrangement are structural changes.'[45] Obligations (re)arrange the parts. Therefore, rather than arbitrarily exclude them, as Waltz does, any plausible structural theory must make room for elements of authority and hierarchy in international society, however frequent or important they may (or may not) be in any particular international order.

Recognizing elements of authority and hierarchy in international society requires (re)introducing functional differentiation into our analysis. It simply is not true that 'anarchy entails relations of coordination among a system's units, and that implies their sameness'.[46] The division of labour between states may be 'slight in comparison with the highly articulated division of labour within them'.[47] But slight does not mean none. And the extent of differentiation is a contingent, empirical matter. As Waltz himself notes, 'within an international order, risks may be avoided or lessened by moving from a situation of co-ordinate action to one of super- and subordination, that is, by erecting agencies with effective authority and extending a system of rules'.[48] It *is* possible to create effective authority and systems of rules that *partially* replace ('anarchic') co-ordination with ('hierarchic') subordination. In fact, it would be surprising if there were not significant variation within a range of orders (anarchy) that are defined as a residual (the absence of hierarchy).

## Balancing and bandwagoning

Despite these fundamental theoretical problems, structural realism still might be able to make some important contributions. I obviously lack the space to consider the full range of Waltz's contributions. By way of illustration, I will briefly consider one of his central substantive conclusions, namely, that 'states balance power rather than maximize it'.[49]

Balancing simply does not follow from anarchy alone. In addition, we must assume that states (1) are fearful rather than competitive, and either (2) fear all other states more or less equally, or (3) value absolute gains only to the extent that they do not even marginally reduce relative position. Under less extreme assumptions, balancing need not be expected. This is the central insight behind Stephen Walt's move to 'balance of threat' theory:[50] states balance against *threatening* capabilities – which is largely a matter of perceived intentions, and thus outside the domain of structural theory as Waltz defines it. Without knowing who holds what capabilities and their intentions, as well as who we are and what we value, we cannot confidently predict whether particular external capabilities will be seen as threatening.

Balancing would seem to follow in two special cases. In the face of an emerging hegemon, great powers will balance because concentrating overwhelming capabilities in the hands of a single state starkly poses the threat of imperial domination. A similar 'defensive positionalist' logic may apply to bipolar superpowers: failing to compete poses a relatively clear and immediate threat of imperial domination that should lead each side to balance. But in multipolar orders not gripped by fear of an emerging hegemon, structural pressures to balance are regularly swamped by other forces.

'In a multipolar system, who allies with whom is structurally indeterminate . . . each state is logically eligible to be either friend or enemy of any other state.'[51] Alignment cannot be predicted from structure alone. Without knowing states' motives, we cannot even say whether multipolar allies are engaged in diffident balancing against a common threat or competitive bandwagoning to pursue joint gains against a third party. And, in practice, balancing proves not to be all that much more law-like or regular than failures to balance.[52]

## New realist research on interactions

The unfruitfulness of Waltz's central simplifying assumptions largely explain the decline of structural neo-realism. More important for my purposes, however, are promising signs of greater openness within the realist fold. The attention to motives noted above in the work of Walt and Schweller are striking examples. And at least since Snyder and Diesing's *Conflict Among Nations*, which with some justice can be called neo-realism's first major substantive study, realists who have relied on the formal methods of game theory have taken seriously variations in state interests, which define different game types, of which there are many in any given distribution of capabilities. I want to use my limited space, however, to consider not motives but recent realist work emphasizing interactions.

## System and structure

'A systems theory of international politics deals with the forces that are in play at the international, and not at the national, level.'[53] In addition to units and structure, a system includes the patterned interactions of units. These interactions take place *between* units. Therefore, despite Waltz's insistence to the contrary, they are *not* 'unit-level' phenomena – as Waltz implicitly acknowledges when he insists that a structural theory must abstract from *both* the attributes of units and their interactions. Waltzian structuralism thus does not even provide an attractive vision of system-level or 'third image' theorizing.

Not surprisingly, then, Waltz must move beyond structure to explain anything of real interest. Consider his claim that 'the longest peace yet known rested on two pillars: bipolarity and nuclear weapons'.[54] Nuclear weapons are *not* part of Waltzian structure. Their effects are produced through the character of the weapons and the quality of their effects rather than anarchy or the distribution of capabilities. In fact, if we take Waltz on nuclear weapons seriously – 'Nuclear weapons dissuade states from going to war more surely than conventional weapons do'; 'Nuclear weapons have drastically reduced the probability of [war] being fought by the states that have them'; 'The absolute quality of nuclear weapons sharply sets a nuclear world off from a conventional one'[55] – we would seem to be able to account for the Cold War 'peace' entirely independently of bipolarity.

Although the outcome is (not in)consistent with the theory, we would seem to have a case of correlation without causation. Structure does not *explain* the 'big picture' in a relatively easy case (bipolarity) dealing with the subject matter (war and peace) to which realism is best suited. And because the maximal abstraction of the structuralist project is justified only by its alleged ability to get the big picture right, this failure is of profound significance.

## Relationships and structural modifiers

Barry Buzan offers a prominent recent example of a vision of realism that carves out considerable space for systemic but non-structural features.[56] Here I want to look instead at Glenn Snyder's recent work, which is less well known (especially in Britain) and, most importantly for my purposes, explicitly situates itself within the Waltzian tradition.[57] That even Snyder's rather limited openings create substantial opportunities for fruitful conversations with institutionalists and constructivists is, I believe, an important indicator of the possibilities that now exist for a richer, more varied and more tolerant discipline. Snyder starts by noting that Waltz is guilty of 'excessive parsimony, in the sense that the explanatory gain from some further elaboration would exceed the costs in reduced generality'.[58] His remedy is to introduce three classes of 'process variables', which he calls relationships, interactions and structural modifiers.

Waltz defines structure narrowly and then relegates everything else to the 'unit level', turning it into a vast, incoherent dumping ground of explanatory variables. Snyder in effect reverses the process, specifying what counts as an attribute of the units and then defining everything else as systemic (in Waltz's sense of forces in play at the international, not national, level). The result is much more consistent with our ordinary language and intuitions. Alignment, for example, is clearly a force in play at the international, not the national (unit), level. Arms races, threats and commitments take place between, not within, nations.

Relationships, Snyder argues, provide 'the conduit through which structural effects are transmitted to behaviour'.[59] 'If, as Waltz says, system structures only "shape and shove", relationship patterns give a more decided push.'[60] For example, states rarely fear all external concentrations of power. And, even when they do, the intensity and character of their fears is likely to change with their relationships. Thus alliances, Snyder argues, are 'akin to structure' because they shape 'how resources and capabilities are aggregated in the system'.[61]

To draw the contrast with Waltz a bit crudely, it is crazy to commit oneself to a theory that predicts that a state will respond in the same way to an ally with which it shares many common interests and an enemy with which it has numerous competing interests. Such a theory may be simple and elegant. It is not very useful.[62]

Of even greater interest for my purposes, though, are what Snyder calls 'structural modifiers', system-wide influences that are structural in their inherent nature but not potent enough internationally to warrant that description. They modify the effects of the more basic structural elements on the interaction process, but they are not interaction itself. They are roughly analogous to macroeconomic influences, like interest rates or government regulation, on microeconomic relations between firms; they affect the behaviour of all actors more or less evenly, but they are different in kind from factors like the number of actors (firms) and the distribution of power among them – variables which clearly determine the structure of the system (market).[63]

Snyder's examples are military technology and norms and institutions. Even if norms and institutions 'are present only rudimentarily in international society',[64] this is a contingent empirical fact. And, once realists allow that they are in principle structural, all kinds of potentially interesting conversations become possible.

## Speaking across the institutions divide

Snyder's argument is surprisingly similar to Alexander Wendt's[65] – whatever the other (very important) differences in their work. 'Self-help', Wendt shows, is not a necessary feature of anarchy but rather a particular set of institutional strategies and relationships for handling problems posed by anarchy. Other security institutions are in principle possible, depending on the *kind* of anarchic order, its principal institutions and how obligations are established and distributed.

Even preponderant power does not always express itself in the same kinds of functional differentiations. For example, formal colonialism and informal spheres of influence divide political functions differently among superior and subordinate units. And among empires there were striking differences between the Athenian, Roman, Chinese, Ottoman and British empires – as well as between the British empires of the early nineteenth and early twentieth centuries.

Or consider sovereignty – which Waltz characteristically misunderstands. 'To call states "like units" is to say that each state is like all other states in being an autonomous political unit. It is another way of saying that states are sovereign.'[66] This is simply false. Sovereignty is a *particular kind* of political autonomy, a juridical relationship rather than a logically necessary accompaniment to anarchy (or hierarchy). And the practices of sovereignty have varied dramatically, even within the modern West.[67]

In seventeenth-century Europe, sovereignty was personal and dynastic. By the late nineteenth century, rather than viewing people and territory as an appendage of the ruler, states were seen as territorial units that included peoples and rulers. And the substance of sovereign rights has been even more variable. Something so seemingly basic to us today as the monopoly on the legitimate use of force is historically contingent. Mercenaries were a regular feature of modern Western international relations until the nineteenth century.[68] States leased rather than owned, let alone monopolized, military force.

Consider also the impact of institutions on the key realist variable of survival. States that act out of genuine and plausible fear for survival are today relatively rare exceptions. Where once it was perfectly ordinary for states to die, today it is extraordinary. And when they do, as in the case of the Soviet Union or Yugoslavia, it is largely for internal reasons. Few states today seek wealth or power to increase their odds of survival (which are already close to 100 per cent). And their survival typically owes less to their military resources or the international distribution of capabilities than to institutions such as sovereignty, self-determination, non-intervention and outlawing aggressive war. And, although force has hardly been banished from international society, its use for territorial aggrandizement has largely been eliminated (the last significant successful forcible territorial acquisition was China's incorporation of Tibet half a century ago). Military might and control over territory have in most of the world been substantially decoupled.

International society provides 'background' institutions that realists typically take for granted without acknowledging their influence.[69] There are, however, important pockets of change. Consider, for example, Randall Schweller and David Priess's argument that realists not only need to engage institutions but may have important things to teach institutionalists.[70] At the very least, conversation becomes possible and a basis is established for a certain degree of respect for diversity in the discipline. Realists and institutionalists certainly do begin at different points. Their work has different characteristic emphases. It is unlikely that they can or should be integrated into a higher-level synthesis. None the less, they should not be seen as competitors for disciplinary hegemony, as the language of neo-realism and its critics so often suggests.

## From grand theory to multiple models in a pluralistic discipline

Leading twentieth-century (American) realists sought a general theory of international politics. Morgenthau tried to uncover the 'objective laws' of politics, 'the eternal laws by which man moves in the social world'.[71] Waltz likewise sought transhistorical 'law-like regularities' that explain 'why different units behave similarly and, despite their variations, produce outcomes that fall within expected ranges'.[72] The clear implication is that the missing article in *Theory of International Politics* is definite, not indefinite.

The result, especially when linked to a falsificationist conception of social science, has been a strong tendency to see differing theories as 'competing' in largely gladiatorial terms. For example, Eric Labs presents offensive (rather than defensive) realism as 'the best realist theory available to go forward and do battle with competing approaches to international relations'.[73] Such a vision of theoretical diversity is profoundly misguided. The multiplicity and inescapable variability of state motives, and the pervasive impact of international institutions, requires that grand theoretical aspirations give way to much narrower mid-range theories.

### Realism as philosophical caution

Rather than a general theory of international politics, realism should be seen as a philosophical disposition or tradition of analysis.[74] Central to this orientation is an emphasis on what is unlikely or difficult in international relations. '"Realism" denotes the disposition to take all factors in a social and political situation, which offer resistance to established norms, into account, particularly the factors of interest and power.'[75] 'Realism depicts international affairs as a struggle for power among self-interested states and is generally pessimistic about the prospects for eliminating conflict and war.'[76] Waltz's admission that his theory yields only 'indeterminate predictions'[77] might be read in this way as well; rather than actually predict anything in particular, it excludes certain possibilities as unlikely.

But, even granting the pervasive power of the pressures toward conflict to which realists draw our attention, co-operation does regularly take place, often in highly institutionalized forms. Therefore, for understanding international relations – let alone when acting in the world – it is *not* useful to assume otherwise. Even if realists err less frequently than their competitors, that is not a strong, let alone a persuasive, reason for using realism to analyse any particular international issue. And it is no good reason at all to *be* a realist.

Realism, as Martin Wight noted, is *one* perennial tradition of international thought.[78] It persists, and recurrently rises to prominence, because the features it emphasizes regularly recur. But when it achieves disciplinary hegemony it does so more by denigrating or banishing, rather than accounting for, contradictory insights, forces and evidence. And its hegemony can be expected to be brief because some of these banished features are also important recurrent parts of international life. A commitment to realism – or any philosophy, tradition or approach – rests on contentious judgements of 'importance' and beliefs about potential theoretical fruitfulness. Although rarely unconnected with events in the world, such judgements are largely immune to empirical critique. And any support received from experience is heavily conditioned by the very commitments that are being 'confirmed'.

### Realism as a research programme

The characteristic realist emphasis on egoism and anarchy also provides a promising basis for a positive research programme that aims to develop partial, mid-level theories of international relations.[79] But 'competing' research programmes don't even try to account for the same things – or, to the extent that they do present themselves as general theories of international relations, they prove dismal failures. They are 'tuned' to different bands of the international political spectrum. They are apples and oranges rather than jousting knights or World Cup competitors. Rather than ask which research programme is 'better' – let alone 'best' – we should ask instead what uses can we find for each.

This differential tuning also takes place *within* the realist research programme. Consider Waltz's account of the realist 'hard core'. (1) States' interests provide the springs of action. (2) The necessities of policy arise from unregulated state competition. (3) Calculation based on these necessities can discover policies that best serve a state's interests. (4) Success, defined as preserving and strengthening the state, is the ultimate test of policy.[80] Both offensive and defensive realism[81] can be readily derived from this hard core through characteristically realist secondary assumptions. Rather than competitors for the mantle of 'the' 'true' realist theory, they are different realist logics that apply to different parts of international reality.

Thus John Vasquez misses the point when he complains that contemporary realists predict both bandwagoning (the offensive pursuit of absolute gain) and balancing (the defensive pursuit of survival and independence).[82] A single *theory* that systematically generates contradictory predictions violates accepted canons of 'science'. A research programme need not. Realist theories must be consistent with the hard core of the programme, not with each other. In fact, we should *expect* different secondary assumptions to generate conflicting predictions. And there is nothing wrong with this – if we treat realism as a research programme.

Colin Elman rightly observes that realism is 'a "big tent", with room for a number of different theories that make quite different predictions'.[83] And international studies is an even bigger tent, with room for various other research programmes as well. Realists thus must abandon the struggle for disciplinary hegemony, as well as talk about empirical tests confirming or supporting realism or counting against other research programmes.

'Evidence' is not irrelevant. 'Unpersuasive' programmes fail to prosper because the dissonance between theory and 'the world' strikes most analysts as too great to tolerate. Conversely, research programmes that prosper tend to have a tolerable degree of disconnect between theory and 'reality'. But what is 'tolerable' cannot be established by objective, theoretically neutral, criteria. As with philosophies or world-views, the grounds on which we accept or reject research programmes involve considerations such as interest, inclination, intuitive plausibility and expectations of fruitfulness.

Empirical tests often are not conclusive even *within* a research programme. For example, if balancing and bandwagoning exhaust aligning behaviours, as Waltz suggests they do,[84] and if good realist theories predict each (as they do), then any piece of evidence simultaneously 'confirms' and 'contradicts' 'realism'. And there is nothing wrong with this – *if* we see realism as a research programme. Offensive and defensive realism, for example, are simply different logics (tools). So long as each helps us to understand at least one 'major' case, or a 'reasonable number' of 'minor' cases – as each clearly does – there are good reasons to have them both available. And when we come across a case where, say, offensive realism better captures events in the world, it is entirely irrelevant to say (assuming that it is true) that defensive realism usually provides better explanations. In fact, to use defensive realism here would be culpable malpractice.

The task of theory thus understood is to specify clearly and precisely a particular theoretical logic. It is an empirical question whether this logic has interesting practical applications. The issue is not whether realism (or liberal internationalism, or constructivism, or whatever) 'is right', but whether insights or theories generated by a particular research programme or tradition of analysis can help us to understand things that interest us.

Realism persists because it illuminates recurrent sources and patterns of conflict rooted in anarchy, competition and diffidence. It tells us very little about co-operation, which many analysts find a no less important part of international relations. But this is not a failing – unless we happen to be interested in understanding co-operation. And that failing is largely a function of our interests and purposes. The realist research programme will continue to generate valuable theories. But the same is true of other research programmes. Rather than adversaries, let alone enemies, realists and non-realists should see each other as concerned scholars with different interests, insights and contributions.[85]

## Postscript: realism and globalization

The absence, so far, of any mention of globalization reflects the characteristic realist emphasis on the continuing centrality of inter-state military–political relations, in contrast to the globalization literature's emphasis on rapid, radical change driven by transnational economic and technological forces. As globalization is a recurrent theme in this volume – and a seemingly inescapable subject in both the discipline and the 'real' world – a few comments are warranted.

Just as a quarter-century ago, when 'interdependence' was all the rage, the realist stress on the continuing importance of the state and its interests merits careful consideration.[86] But once more the discussion seems to be falling into the 'realism and its critics' mode as we once more rehearse the tired 'debate' over the demise of the state.[87] And the standard realist 'contribution' seems to be little more than an unusually insistent reminder that states persist, and are likely to continue to persist in the coming decades.[88]

This, I would submit, is a striking example of the fundamentally negative and cautionary character of realism. *Of course* the state continues to be an important actor in international (and national) politics. Any sophisticated analysis allows this – just as all sophisticated realists allow the equally obvious and uninteresting point that states never have been and never will be the *only* actor in international politics. But repeating such platitudes and foundational assumptions deflects attention from the central question of the *character* of the state and its functions.

Waltz claims that 'the most telling refutation of the belief that state power has sharply declined is to be found in the state's capacity for transformation'.[89] This may be true. Unfortunately, structural realism in principle can have nothing to say about such transformations. And if they prove to be substantial – which is an empirical, not a theoretical, issue – the realist reminder that states persist will be of little help in understanding the development of world politics.

The standard realist emphasis on 'the state of the state' and 'the state in international politics'[90] is also unlikely to provide much illumination about the (changing and persisting) relations between states and other kinds of social actors. For example, Waltz notes that 'national *politics*, not international markets, account for many international *economic* developments'.[91] This is true but profoundly unilluminating – except in a negative sense. The question we ought to be addressing is not whether national politics has international economic impacts, but the number, kind or importance of the cases in which it does, and whether this is changing systematically over time. Once more, however, we face a question on which structural realism can in principle have nothing to say.

The structural realist emphasis on anarchy or Niebuhr's stress on the inescapable limits of human sympathy may help to account for the resilience of 'the state'. Such insights are certainly worth taking seriously – as one strand of analysis within a pluralist discipline. But because realism is tuned to other kinds of topics it is unlikely to provide much positive illumination on either 'the state' or 'globalization'. Thus, again, what we need is not *Theory of International Politics* but rather *theories* of international politics, realist and non-realist alike, that separately and collectively help us to begin to come to terms with the multiple human purposes and complex political practices that make up world politics.

## NOTES

This chapter draws heavily on Jack Donnelly, *Realism and International Relations* (Cambridge, Cambridge University Press, 2000), which develops many of the arguments sketched here in greater detail.

1   Hedley Bull, 'The Theory of International Politics: 1919–1969', in Brian Porter (ed.), *The Aberystwyth Papers: International Politics, 1919–1969* (London, Oxford University Press, 1972), p. 39. Joel Rosenthal's *Righteous Realists: Political Realism, Responsible Power, and American Culture in the Nuclear Age* (Baton Rouge, LA, Louisiana State University Press, 1991) nicely captures this dimension of twentieth-century American realism.
2   James Der Derian, *Antidiplomacy: Spies, Terror, Speed, and War* (Cambridge, MA, Blackwell, 1992); Christine Sylvester, *Feminist Theory and International Relations Theory in a Postmodern Era* (Cambridge, Cambridge University Press, 1994); Cynthia Weber, *Faking It: US Hegemony in a 'Post-Phallic' Era* (Minneapolis, MN, University of Minnesota Press, 1999).
3   R. B. J. Walker, *Inside/Outside: International Relations as Political Theory* (Cambridge, Cambridge University Press, 1993); Jens Bartelson, *A Genealogy of Sovereignty* (Cambridge, Cambridge University Press, 1995); Alexander Wendt, *Social Theory of International Politics* (Cambridge, Cambridge University Press, 1999); Peter Katzenstein (ed.), *The Culture of National Security: Norms and Identity in International Politics* (Ithaca, NY, Cornell University Press, 1996); Emanuel Adler, 'The Emergence of Co-operation: National Epistemic Communities and the International Evolution of the Idea of Nuclear Arms Control', *International Organization*, 26 (Winter 1991), pp. 101–46; Emanuel Adler and Michael Barnett, *Security Communities* (Cambridge, Cambridge University Press, 1998); Michael N. Barnett, *Dialogues in Arab Politics: Negotiations in Regional Order* (New York,

Columbia University Press, 1998); Bruce Cronin, *Community under Anarchy: Transnational Identity and the Evolution of Co-operation* (New York, Columbia University Press, 1999); and Cecilia Lynch, *Beyond Appeasement: Reinterpreting Interwar Peace Movements in World Politics* (Ithaca, NY, Cornell University Press, 1999).

4   For example, the recent survey of the field in Peter J. Katzenstein, Robert O. Keohane and Stephen D. Krasner (eds), *Exploration and Contestation in the Study of World Politics* (Cambridge, MA, MIT Press, 1999) is far more open than one might have imagined even five years earlier from the same editors.

5   To British ears this may sound like Americans *finally* abandoning their inexplicable fascination with Waltz and his odd conception of structural theory. The theoretical stupor of the American discipline is perhaps best illustrated by the fact that in the early 1990s, despite both dramatic changes in the world and Josef Lapid's often cited 'The Third Debate: On the Prospects of International Theory in a Post-Positivist Era', *International Studies Quarterly*, 33 (1989), pp. 235–54, the American disciplinary mainstream ranged from neo-realism to neo-liberalism – see, for example, David A. Baldwin (ed.), *Neorealism and Neoliberalism: The Contemporary Debate* (New York, Columbia University Press, 1993), and Charles W. Kegley, *Controversies in International Relations Theory: Realism and the Neoliberal Challenge* (New York, St Martin's Press, 1995) – which, as even many proponents of these theories now admit, are variations on a single rationalist theme.

6   Kenneth N. Waltz, *Theory of International Politics* (New York, Random House, 1979), p. 79.

7   Kenneth N. Waltz, 'Reflections on *Theory of International Politics*: A Response to My Critics', in Robert O. Keohane (ed.), *Neo-Realism and Its Critics* (New York, Columbia University Press, 1986), p. 329.

8   Waltz, *Theory of International Politics*, p. 99.

9   Ibid., p. 72.

10  Kenneth N. Waltz, 'International Politics is not Foreign Policy', *Security Studies*, 6, 1 (1996), p. 55.

11  Waltz, *Theory of International Politics*, p. 89.

12  Waltz, 'International Politics is not Foreign Policy', p. 55.

13  Waltz, *Theory of International Politics*, pp. 88–9.

14  Ibid., p. 71.

15  Waltz, 'International Politics is not Foreign Policy', p. 54; Waltz, *Theory of International Politics*, p. 91.

16  Waltz, *Theory of International Politics*, p. 99.

17  Waltz, 'International Politics is not Foreign Policy', p. 54; Kenneth N. Waltz, 'Evaluating Theories', *American Political Science Review*, 91 (1997), p. 913; Waltz, *Theory of International Politics*, pp. 134, 91 [emphasis added in all quotations].

18  Randall L. Schweller, 'Neorealism's Status-Quo Bias: What Security Dilemma?', *Security Studies*, 5, 3 (1996), p. 91.

19  Ibid., p. 106.

20  See, for example, Stephen M. Walt, 'International Relations: One World, Many Theories', *Foreign Policy*, 110, Spring (1998), p. 35; Kenneth N. Waltz, 'The Emerging Structure of International Politics', *International Security*, 18, 2

(1993), p. 60, and 'Evaluating Theories', p. 915. For clear, balanced overviews of the debate, see Michael Mastanduno, 'Do Relative Gains Matter? America's Response to Japanese Industrial Policy', *International Security*, 16 (1991), pp. 78–92, and John C. Matthews III, 'Current Gains and Future Outcomes: When Cumulative Relative Gains Matter', *International Security*, 21, 1 (1996), pp. 116–21. For the related debate *within* realism between 'offensive' and 'defensive' realists, see Eric J. Labs, 'Beyond Victory: Offensive Realism and the Expansion of War Aims', *Security Studies*, 6, 4 (1997), pp. 7–17; Sean M. Lynn-Jones, 'Offense–Defense Theory and Its Critics', *Security Studies*, 4 (1995), pp. 660–91; and Fareed Zakaria, *From Wealth to Power: The Unusual Origins of America's World Role* (Princeton, NJ, Princeton University Press, 1998), pp. 25–42.

21 Mastanduno, 'Do Relative Gains Matter?', p. 79, n. 13.

22 Zakaria, *From Wealth to Power*, p. 20.

23 John J. Mearsheimer, 'Back to the Future: Instability in Europe after the Cold War', *International Security*, 15, 1 (1990), p. 12.

24 Ibid. John J. Mearsheimer, 'A Realist Reply', *International Security*, 20, 1 (1995), p. 82.

25 See, for example, Robert Gilpin, *War and Change in World Politics* (Cambridge, Cambridge University Press, 1981); Glenn H. Snyder, *Alliance Politics* (Ithaca, NY, Cornell University Press, 1997); Glenn H. Snyder and Paul Diesing, *Conflict among Nations: Bargaining, Decision Making, and System Structure in International Crises* (Princeton, NJ, Princeton University Press, 1977).

26 Joseph M. Grieco, *Co-operation among Nations: Europe, America, and Non-tariff Barriers to Trade* (Ithaca, NY, Cornell University Press, 1990), table 2.3.

27 Waltz, *Theory of International Politics*, p. 105.

28 Joseph M. Grieco, 'Anarchy and the Limits of Co-operation: A Realist Critique of the Newest Liberal Institutionalism', *International Organization*, 42, 3 (1988), p. 498.

29 John J. Mearsheimer, 'The False Promise of International Institutions', *International Security*, 19 (1994–5), p. 11. It is perhaps worth noting in passing that this claim, like so many other sweeping realist proclamations, is obviously false: consider, for example, the United States and Canada.

30 I restrict myself to Waltz in order to avoid the charge of ransacking the realist literature to create a misleading pastiche or caricature.

31 Waltz, *Theory of International Politics*, p. 118.

32 Waltz, 'Emerging Structure', p. 64; *Theory of International Politics*, p. 112; 'Response to My Critics', p. 337.

33 Waltz, 'Emerging Structure', p. 60.

34 Waltz, *Theory of International Politics*, pp. 126, 204, 144.

35 Kenneth N. Waltz, 'Globalization and American Power', *The National Interest*, 59 (Spring 2000), p. 46.

36 Waltz, *Theory of International Politics*, pp. 114ff.

37 The following paragraphs take a slightly different route to conclusions very similar to Helen Milner, 'The Assumption of Anarchy in International Relations Theory: A Critique', *Review of International Studies*, 17 (1991), pp. 67–85; Alexander Wendt, 'Anarchy is What States Make of It: The Social Construction of

Power Politics', *International Organization*, 46, 2 (1992), pp. 391–425; and Alexander Wendt and Daniel Friedheim, 'Hierarchy under Anarchy: Informal Empire and the East German State', *International Organization*, 49, 4 (1995), pp. 689–721.

38  Waltz, *Theory of International Politics*, p. 115.
39  Ibid., p. 113.
40  Ibid., p. 88.
41  Ibid., p. 112.
42  Ibid., p. 80.
43  Ibid., p. 88.
44  Ibid., p. 108.
45  Ibid., p. 80.
46  Ibid., p. 93.
47  Ibid., p. 105.
48  Ibid., p. 111.
49  Ibid., p. 127.
50  Stephen Walt, *The Origins of Alliances* (Ithaca, NY, Cornell University Press, 1987).
51  Snyder, *Alliance Politics*, pp. 18–19; Waltz, *Theory of International Politics*, p. 170.
52  For a quantitative analysis supporting this conclusion, see Daniel M. Jones, 'Balancing and Bandwagoning in Militarized Inter-state Disputes', in Frank W. Wayman and Paul F. Diehl (eds), *Reconstructing Realpolitik* (Ann Arbor, MI, University of Michigan Press, 1994). The modern European historical record simply does not support Waltz's claim (*Theory of International Politics*, p. 57) that 'balance-of-power theory applies in all situations where two or more units coexist in a self-help system'. As Paul Schroeder puts it, Waltz gets 'the patterns and the broad outcomes of international history wrong, and predicts things of major theoretical and historical importance which on closer examination turn out not to be so'. 'Historical Reality vs. Neo-realist Theory', *International Security*, 19, 1 (1994), p. 147.
53  Waltz, *Theory of International Politics*, p. 71.
54  Waltz, 'Emerging Structure', p. 44. Compare Mearsheimer, 'Back to the Future', p. 11.
55  Kenneth N. Waltz, 'Nuclear Myths and Political Realities', *American Political Science Review*, 84, 3, (1990), pp. 743, 744, 732.
56  Barry Buzan, Charles A. Jones and Richard Little, *The Logic of Anarchy: Neorealism to Structural Realism* (New York, Columbia University Press, 1993).
57  Glenn Snyder, 'Process Variables in Neorealist Theory', *Security Studies*, 5, 3 (1996), pp. 167–92; Snyder, *Alliance Politics*.
58  Snyder, 'Process Variables', p. 167.
59  Snyder, *Alliance Politics*, p. 20.
60  Ibid., p. 22.
61  Ibid.
62  We should also note that it is an odd kind of realist theory of international politics that does not permit us to talk about alliances. But that is precisely where Waltz leaves us.

63 Snyder, 'Process Variables', p. 169.

64 Ibid., p. 169.

65 Wendt, 'Anarchy is What States Make of It'; *Social Theory*, ch. 6.

66 Waltz, *Theory of International Politics*, p. 95.

67 For recent arguments to this conclusion from close to opposite ends of the disciplinary spectrum, see Christian Reus-Smit, *The Moral Purpose of the State: Culture, Social Identity and Institutional Rationality in International Relations* (Princeton, NJ, Princeton University Press, 1999), and Stephen D. Krasner, *Sovereignty: Organized Hypocrisy* (Princeton, NJ, Princeton University Press, 1999). See also Bartelson, *Genealogy of Sovereignty*, and Thomas J. Bierstecker and Cynthia Weber, *State Sovereignty as Social Construct* (Cambridge, Cambridge University Press, 1996).

68 Janice E. Thomson, *Mercenaries, Pirates, and Sovereigns: State-Building and Extraterritorial Violence in Early Modern Europe* (Princeton, NJ, Princeton University Press, 1994).

69 This is a good example of Alexander Wendt's 'rule of thumb for idealists: when confronted by ostensibly "material" explanations, always inquire into the discursive conditions which make them work'. *Social Theory*, p. 135.

70 Randall L. Schweller and David Priess, 'A Tale of Two Realisms: Expanding the Institutions Debate', *Mershon International Studies Review*, 41, 1 (1997), pp. 1–32.

71 Hans J. Morgenthau, *Politics Among Nations: The Struggle for Power and Peace* (New York, Alfred A. Knopf, 1954), p. 4; *Scientific Man versus Power Politics* (Chicago, IL, University of Chicago Press, 1946), p. 220.

72 Waltz, *Theory of International Politics*, pp. 116, 72.

73 Labs, 'Beyond Victory', p. 48.

74 Robert G. Gilpin, 'The Richness of the Tradition of Political Realism', in Robert O. Keohane (ed.), *Realism and Its Critics* (New York, Columbia University Press, 1986), p. 304; Robert G. Gilpin, 'No One Loves a Political Realist', *Security Studies*, 5, 3 (1996), p. 6; Yale H. Ferguson and Richard W. Mansbach, *The Elusive Quest: Theory and International Politics* (Columbia, SC, University of South Carolina Press, 1988), p. 79; John C. Garnett, *Commonsense and the Theory of International Politics* (London, Macmillan, 1984), p. 111; Steven Forde, 'Classical Realism', and Jack Donnelly, 'Twentieth Century Realism', in Terry Nardin and David Mapel (eds), *Traditions of International Ethics* (Cambridge, Cambridge University Press, 1992).

75 Reinhold Niebuhr, *Christian Realism and Political Problems* (New York, Charles Scribner's Sons, 1953), p. 119.

76 Walt, 'International Relations: One World, Many Theories', p. 31.

77 Waltz, *Theory of International Politics*, pp. 124, 122, 71.

78 Martin Wight, *International Theory: The Three Traditions* (New York, Holmes & Meier, 1992).

79 Imre Lakatos, 'Falsification and the Methodology of Scientific Research Programmes', in Imre Lakatos and Alan Musgrave (eds), *Criticism and the Growth of Knowledge* (Cambridge, Cambridge University Press, 1970), pp. 132–8; Colin Elman, 'Horses for Courses: Why Not Neorealist Theories of Foreign Policy?', *Security Studies*, 6, 1 (1996), p. 18; Colin Elman and Miriam Fendius Elman, 'Lakatos and Neorealism: A Reply to Vasquez', *American Political Science Review*,

91, 4 (1997), pp. 923–6; Randall L. Schweller, 'New Realist Research on Alliances: Refining, Not Refuting, Waltz's Balancing Proposition', *American Political Science Review*, 91, 4 (1997), p. 927; William C. Wohlforth, 'Correspondence: Realism and the End of the Cold War', *International Security*, 20, 2 (1995), p. 95; and John A. Vasquez, 'The Realist Paradigm and Degenerative versus Progressive Research Programs: An Appraisal of Neotraditional Research on Waltz's Balancing Proposition', *American Political Science Review*, 91, 4 (1997), pp. 899–912.

80   Waltz, *Theory of International Politics*, p. 117.

81   See note 20 above.

82   Vasquez, 'The Realist Paradigm', pp. 908–9.

83   Elman, 'Horses for Courses', p. 26.

84   They clearly don't – see, for example, Daniel Deudney, 'The Philadelphian System: Sovereignty, Arms Control, and Balance of Power in the American States-Union, circa 1787–1861', *International Organization*, 49, 2 (1995), pp. 191–228, and Randall L. Schweller, *Deadly Imbalances: Tripolarity and Hitler's Strategy of World Conquest* (New York, Columbia University Press, 1998), ch. 3 – but the existence of more types does not significantly weaken, and may actually strengthen, my argument.

85   For a recent realist expression of a similar understanding of the discipline, see Walt, 'International Relations: One World, Many Theories'.

86   The same is true of structuralist political economy perspectives that see 'globalization' as the continuing unfolding of the development of capitalist markets. For good recent examples, see Kees van der Pijl, *Transnational Classes and International Relations* (New York, Routledge, 1998), and Christopher Chase-Dunn, Yukio Kawano and Benjamin D. Brewer, 'Trade Globalization Since 1795: Waves of Integration in the World-System', *American Sociological Review*, 65, 1 (2000), pp. 77–95.

87   For a particularly lively example of the decline literature, see Susan Strange, *The Retreat of the State: The Diffusion of Power in the World Economy* (Cambridge, Cambridge University Press, 1996). For a contrasting perspective, see Robert J. Holton, *Globalisation and the Nation-State* (Basingstoke, Macmillan, 1998). The special issue of *World Futures* ('Globalization and the Future of the Nation State'), 53, 2 (1999), provides a useful survey of perspectives.

88   This is the basic argument of Waltz, 'Globalization and American Power'. ('Globalization and Governance', *PS: Political Science and Politics*, 32, 4 (1999), pp. 693–700 is a slightly different version of this essay.)

89   Waltz, 'Globalization and American Power', p. 50.

90   These are the headings of the first two sections of 'Globalization and American Power', which make up about two-thirds of the essay.

91   Waltz, 'Globalization and American Power', p. 52.

# 12

# After the Fall
## *International Theory and the State*

## Stephanie Lawson

### Introduction

It is a commonplace assumption that theories of international political order have been predicated on the sovereign state system for over 350 years – in fact since the Peace of Westphalia in 1648. And theories of domestic political order and social structure that have developed over the same period have usually been no less state-centric in their assumptions about the form and contours of political community and the locus of legitimate political power and authority.[1] More generally, it has been argued that the evolution of social-scientific thought has itself been based largely on those principles required for the 'construction and integration of the western nation-state as the organizational form for global expansion and hegemony'.[2] The paramountcy of the sovereign, territorial state in the sphere of international theory, in particular, reflects the general identification of the Westphalian moment with the emergence of a distinctive set of legal principles and practices surrounding the structure of the state system in Europe, and its subsequent extension to the rest of the world as the primary ordering principle of international society/international relations.

Viewed in this way, the development and spread of the Westphalian state system, from its historically and geographically specific origins in western Europe in the mid-seventeenth century to almost worldwide application by the latter half of the twentieth century, is an integral part of the phenomenon of globalization. Indeed, the Westphalian sovereign state system may be seen not simply as part of this phenomenon, but as a principal force behind it. It is something of an irony, then, that globalization is now widely believed to be undermining – perhaps even precipitating the ultimate demise of – the system that helped bring it into being.

The idea that the state – and the sovereign state system – is in retreat at best, or terminal decline at worst, is hardly a new one. There have been other periods when prognostications concerning the demise of the state as the central organizing principle of political, social and economic life have been rife.[3] Equally, there have been recurring moments when the focus on the state as the most important social and political institution has been especially strong. As Weiss points out, it is not much more than a dozen years since Theda Skocpol's seminal work, *Bringing the State Back In*, announced with great confidence 'a programmatic agenda for exploring the multifarious ways in which states could be seen as important society-shaping institutions'. Just a few years on, Weiss says, 'one can only be struck by the confidence with which, in many quarters, the state is being pronounced a moribund institution'.[4]

The present time, then, is certainly one in which there has been a very strong tendency to see the state, especially in terms of its sovereign attributes, as heading rapidly towards obsolescence. This period has been characterized temporally as 'post-Cold War' and materially or technically as one of advanced 'globalization'. And there is an assumption – or at least perception – of a strong correlation between the collapse of the bipolar world order in 1989, symbolized most dramatically and televisually by the fall of the Berlin Wall, and the gathering of an irresistible momentum in globalization from around that time which is destined radically to transform the face of world order.

In reflecting on the position of the state, and the sovereign state system, in international theory, especially in light of developments over the past ten years or so, this chapter aims to assess the extent to which the phenomenon of globalization in the post-Cold War era is changing both the world of states, and the way in which we theorize about it. In doing so, and in keeping with the major themes of this collection, special attention will be paid to challenges posed by the 'new agenda' for IR – an agenda on which numerous vital issues in contemporary world politics are unquestionably transnational in character and which are therefore seen as being beyond the bounds not just of states themselves, but of the sovereign state system as a whole.

Given the prognostications about the fate of the state, a major focus must also be on the question whether globalization is indeed overwhelming the state – and with it the sovereign state system – or whether reports of its imminent demise are not simply greatly exaggerated, but whether it is in any case desirable (or not) that it should survive as the principal form of political community for the twenty-first century and beyond. I begin, however, with a review of some historical perspectives on the state as political community, its moral dimensions, and related ideas about human nature, for these aspects are central to contemporary normative understandings of the place of the state in international theory. Some background has been sketched in previous chapters, especially in relation to Enlightenment thinking, but here the span of historical thought is extended to capture a broader perspective.

## The state as political community

Although it is practically a convention of international theory to take the particular legalistic formulation of state sovereignty achieved at Westphalia as the starting point for any consideration of the state and the state system, the state as a political community, in one form or another, has obviously been around a great deal longer than that.[5] It is almost as conventional, in the history of political thought, to assume that serious and systematic thinking on the nature of political community and its normative dimensions began with the ancient Greek philosophers. This is quite unrealistic but it is hard to deny that many of the ideas formulated then resonate throughout the history of political thought – and continue to do so. Aristotle, for example, wrote of the state as a political community characterized not simply by the fact that its members – who occupy a given territory – are ruled in common, co-ordinate their economic activities, contribute to its common defence, and enjoy a measure of political independence and autonomy, but by an intrinsic moral dimension. Indeed, for Aristotle, the distinctive character and value of the state as political community lies in the fact that although it is brought into being in order better to provide for the basic economic and security needs of human existence, it goes beyond this by generating the conditions necessary for a civilized life – the good life – which is normatively attuned as well as physically secure. Aristotle also opposed the distinction – drawn by pre-Socratic philosophers (and nurtured in various influential strands of Western philosophy up to the present day) – between *physis* and *nomos*, 'nature' and 'convention'. Arguing that the moral dimensions of life derive directly from a human impulse that is just as 'natural' as the biological dimensions of existence, he came to the now well-known conclusion that humans are, by nature, sociable creatures strongly inclined to create a social and political environment to accommodate this nature, the ideal form of which was expressed in the *polis*.

Despite the universalistic aspects accorded to 'human nature', the normative ideal underpinning Aristotle's *polis* was based on a bounded, particularistic and autonomous community. In this respect Aristotle's thought is obviously compatible with key aspects of contemporary communitarianism. There was no sense in which humanity at large could conceivably be embraced within a single normative community. This was the intellectual task undertaken by post-Aristotelian philosophers, especially the Stoic school of thought in its various manifestations. The ideals of the enclosed and self-sustaining *polis* were roundly repudiated by the positing of *cosmopolis* – the universal community of humankind which embraced not just the civilized but barbarians of all kinds. This gave rise, in later Stoic thought, to strong elements of humanitarianism, tolerance and notions of equal rights to justice. And any political order which failed actively to support these failed also in its moral purpose. These ideas, of course, are strongly supported by some important contemporary critical/normative theorists as discussed by Devetak (in chapter 10 of this volume).

The rise of the Christian church brought with it transformations in the configuration of political power and authority although there were significant continuities in political thought as well. These included the universalistic elements embodied in natural law ideas which supported, among other things, the necessity for justice in the state. But the idea that the state itself was 'natural' came under challenge from St Augustine. He saw the state as a coercive and punitive apparatus made necessary only by the fall from grace, for it was only after this that humans required organized political authority and leadership. In the state of innocence, which was posited as the 'natural' state, no such authority was required. Augustine's state therefore had a very significant moral dimension but its premises clearly reflected the fallen nature of humankind.

That humans were indeed fallen creatures, capable of great evil, could never be in doubt for Christian thinkers. The pessimistic view of human nature to which this gives rise, and the idea that it must be contained and regulated by a strong political authority, resonates throughout modern political thought. It is deeply embedded in classic conservative philosophy and is central as well to realist theory in IR. But not all Christian thinkers viewed the state and its relationship to human nature in the same way. For St Thomas Aquinas, the fallen nature of humankind did not mean that the state itself was required only to contain and control human wickedness. In synthesizing Aristotelian and Christian thought, Aquinas reinvigorated the notion that the state as a political community existed prior to the fall from grace – that it was, as Aristotle had argued, in the nature of humans to live together in a political community and to be ruled in common *for* the common good. And this was so as much in the state of grace as after the Fall.

Aquinas's thought also contained the barest hints of a conceptual separation of church and state, but this was developed much more clearly by Marsilio of Padua – who also broke from the faith/reason synthesis and dispensed with the former element altogether in devising a secular theory of the state. In practical terms, the Italian city-states that formed up to the time of the Renaissance experienced considerable success in winching apart the church/state nexus. Stern reports that by the late fifteenth century – and in contrast with other parts of Europe – the Italian city-states had managed to break altogether with the global aspects of Christendom and to 'develop systems of government under rulers with unashamedly secular ambitions'.[6] Another interesting development was the elevation of material advantage over religious principle in matters of policy and the subordination of moral scruples to the pursuit of power – which gave rise to the idea of *raison d'état*. In turn, Stern suggests that, because the rulers of the Italian city-states were not constrained, or driven, by dogma, the notion of compromising or doing deals with the enemy became not only acceptable but smart practice. Moreover, by the Renaissance there had developed such a mutual acceptance of each other's existence that they developed novel techniques for dealing with each other, including a diplomatic system with embassies, formal procedures, privileges and immunities.[7]

The separation of church and state was further elaborated by Machiavelli. His work revived aspects of Roman law which tended to be grounded in a secular understanding of the political community and rule. But it is in Thomas Hobbes's theory of sovereignty that the process of subordinating the state to civil power is brought to completion.[8] In Hobbes, of course, we find some of the most significant influences on international theory and the state. He puts forward a profoundly dismal view not merely of human nature, but of the state of nature itself – which bears no resemblance at all to Eden. His thought has sometimes been adjudged 'un-Christian' (especially by some of his contemporaries), partly because of his rejection of 'original sin' as the determinant of human nature. Yet his idea that the state is not itself natural, but comes about by necessity and through human design to provide security in what is the 'real' world of fear and loathing in the state of nature, follows some of the basic premises of Christian thinking.

Hobbes, along with Jean Bodin, was of course a major figure in developing the theory of sovereignty. According to King, Bodin was the first in the modern period to develop a systematic theory of sovereignty as a cluster of rules built around the logic of a supreme power in the state. Moreover, his theory raised the question of the relationship between simply describing a social reality on the one hand, and actually recommending or approving it on the other.[9] But possibly one of the most important observations to be made about the theory of sovereignty, as it developed first in the writings of Bodin and later and more emphatically in Hobbes, is that it promoted an *ideology of order*.[10] This ideology, however, then as now, 'is intimately associated with the attempt to defend *particular orders*, not on the grounds that they are preferable to others, but on the grounds that there is an Order *in se* which trumps all other forms of moral concern'.[11] This resonates with Hinsley's notion that sovereignty is not 'a fact' but rather a concept which involves a normative claim about how political power is and should be exercised.[12]

The ideology of order may also be seen as reflecting a desire for certainty – in political terms, of knowing what the rules and boundaries are. On the theme of certainty as it pertains to sovereignty, MacCormick has drawn attention to the emergence of foundationalism in philosophical thought which developed around the same historic period as the Peace of Westphalia in the works of Descartes and Leibniz. He says that foundationalism 'seeks a starting point in something interpersonally certain and indubitable from which to carry forward the search for reliable forms of knowledge'.[13] It is quite plausible that 'a Europe weary with thirty years of religious war should be hospitable to philosophies offering some common ground of indubitable certainty, above or below the level of all religious controversies'. Furthermore, MacCormick suggests that the persuasiveness of Cartesian or Leibnitzian foundationalism was 'the outcome of that longing'.[14]

The state which emerged and developed from the mid-seventeenth century onwards is generally characterized in terms of a two-dimensional understanding of state sovereignty as possessing internal and external facets. Thus a 'sovereign state' is commonly described as: 'a territorially defined unit which has established and coherent procedures for conflict-resolution and decision-making within its borders, which is independent and neither legally subject to nor substantively bound by any other entity, external or internal to itself, and which has designated agents (rulers and civil servants, for example), to act on its behalf'.[15] The sharp division between the two dimensions – the inside and the outside – was the basis on which classical realism's well-known restriction of the application of moral principles to the domestic realm alone rested, since only a sovereign could effectively enforce the rules of moral behaviour. And, since there was no sovereign authority outside the state, the external, international sphere was indisputably anarchic and therefore lacking the essential structure within which moral rules could be enforced. To put it plainly, the classical realist approach which developed on this basis simply asserted that what went on within the boundaries of any given state was its own business, and no other state or group of states could (or should) attempt to intervene. This idea has formed a powerful basis for the doctrine of non-intervention, as discussed in several other chapters in this collection.

More generally, although sovereignty clearly has these two dimensions, the almost exclusive focus on the external dimension, which in turn leads to an almost exclusive emphasis on the relations between states in the international state system, has meant that IR theory has itself been largely one-dimensional in its view of sovereign power.[16] The same, however, can just as readily be said of much 'domestic' political and social theory which has usually taken the boundaries of the state as given and then proceeded to contain theorization within those boundaries. This is clearly demonstrated in modern democratic theory which, having developed along with the sovereign state, has been largely attuned to its contours. Indeed one can say that traditional democratic theory is itself a theory *of* and *for* the state. It is only in relatively recent democratic theorizing that attempts have been made to transcend the boundaries of the state and to formulate a cosmopolitan approach.[17]

Through democratic theory, however, sovereignty also acquires a third dimension, for the theory embodies the normative requirement that sovereignty be vested in 'the people'. The development of this idea in the modern period is closely associated with the transformation of the status of people within territorial states from subjects of a monarch to citizens of a state. This transformation reflected the inversion of the 'descending' thesis of government developed during the Middle Ages in which ultimate political power lay with God and was vested in the monarch. The 'ascending' thesis located legitimate power in 'the people' of the political community or state. This raised the question of who was to be included among 'the people' – a question subsequently addressed by the rise of nationalist ideas which defined 'the people' in terms of an entity known as the 'nation', and which subsequently gave rise to the concept of the 'nation-state'.[18]

To summarize, the particular historical achievement of Westphalia was not only to put into practice what Hobbes and others had theorized in terms of the sovereign state itself, but to set in train the development of a *system* of states. As states increasingly took the form of nation-states, people came to refer to 'international' as well as inter-state relations and so the Westphalian order became 'the international system'.[19] Put another way, states came to partition the entire globe into separate polities with 'the international' being constituted only in the relations between sovereign states – and with no empty space between them.[20]

At first the sovereign state system was confined solely to western Europe, and many there preferred to keep it that way for as long as possible. Indeed, the possession of sovereign statehood was a privilege long guarded as an almost exclusive right of the European club and it was not until the era of decolonization began in earnest in the mid-twentieth century that the sovereign state really started to become, in practical terms, a global phenomenon. When the United Nations was founded in 1945, it had fifty-one members. This increased as former colonies gained independence and applied, and were duly recognized and admitted, to the club. By 1989 membership stood at 159. With the end of the Cold War and the collapse of the Soviet empire came a further proliferation of sovereign states and by the end of the twentieth century the ranks of the United Nations had swelled to 188.[21] Now, at the beginning of the twenty-first century, when the sovereign state has reached the point of virtual ubiquity – and when, it might be added, vicious wars are still being fought in its name – we are told that the end is nigh.

## A post-sovereign world?

As noted in the introduction to this chapter, theories of 'state withering' are scarcely new, but their prominence in the post-Cold War period is undeniable, as is their close association with the process of globalization. In an earlier phase of withering theorization (that is, before the end of the Cold War), the dynamics of state decline were associated largely with the abrogation of functions to 'the market' or non-state bodies, the reining in of government revenue-raising and therefore expenditure, and the concomitant restriction of state activities and responsibilities to certain domains.[22] These dynamics remain part of contemporary withering theorizing and are clearly reflected in sociological and political critiques that have arisen in response.[23]

In IR theory, the traditional state-centric analyses reflected in the various strands of realist thought have been under attack from a range of alternative approaches including critical theory, postmodernism and feminism. The development of these latter approaches, like the intensification of globalization itself, preceded the end of the Cold War. But, in what seemed to be an enduring condition of military and ideological polarization, state-centrism consistently held centre stage. Now, as some have observed, only the most hardened of realists in the discipline could resist the temptation of asking whether a new world order really is in the offing, or whether the Westphalian system will endure as the most appropriate way of characterizing the international system.[24]

It is now commonly held that, while states may remain in one form or another, in juridical and practical terms the Westphalian state system as such is fast fading into history under the pressure of globalization. Scholte says that this view derives from an assumption that the regulatory capacity of states has ceased to meet the criteria of sovereignty as traditionally conceived. State sovereignty, he says, was premised on a territorial world in which governments exercised 'total and exclusive authority over a specified domain' which officials could keep under close surveillance: 'Yet when, with globalization, social relations acquire a host of non-territorial qualities, and borders are dissolved in a deluge of electronic and other flows, crucial pre-conditions for effective sovereignty are removed.'[25] Any number of diverse phenomena can be identified with such flows: migration, trans-boundary pollution, nationalist and fundamentalist movements, missiles, military movements, surveillance by global governance agencies, communication technologies, merchandise trade and electronic money transfers – indeed, many of the phenomena now associated with the 'new agenda' for IR. Beyond this, globalization has also prised loose some important 'cultural and psychological underpinnings of sovereignty' including new loyalties that may supplement and in some instances outweigh national ones. These may be reflected in associational activities or simply sentiments of solidarity ranging from the women's movement to an amorphous transnational managerial class.[26]

Kenichi Ohmae has made a name for himself as a leading 'globalist' by such bold announcements as:

> The Nation-State has become an unnatural, even dysfunctional, unit for organizing human activity and managing economic endeavour in a borderless world. It represents no genuine, shared community of economic interests; it defines no meaningful flows of economic activity. In fact, it overlooks the true linkages and synergies that exist among often disparate populations by combining important measures of human activity at the wrong level of analysis.... On the global economic map the lines that now matter are those defining what may be called 'region states'. The boundaries... are not imposed by political fiat. They are drawn by the deft but invisible hand of the global market for goods and service. They follow, rather than precede, real flows of human activity, creating nothing new but ratifying existing patterns manifest in countless individual decisions.[27]

Even more generally, Ohmae and others speak of the 'global mind' made possible for the first time in history by the advent of a borderless cyberspace.[28] However, as Higgott, in his discussion of international political economy, has pointed out, there is nothing especially new in ideas about the increasing irrelevance of the state as an economic unit and one can cite similar opinions dating back at least thirty years. But contemporary globalist thought – whether it is celebratory or not – does embody an assumption that there are significant *fin-de-siècle* transformations under way, symbolized by the fall of the Berlin Wall, which have picked up where the Cold War left off.[29] Thus globalists of all varieties have picked up on the language and imagery of a post-Cold War 'new world order' that is allegedly in the making and which owes much to the release of synergies made possible by the end of geopolitical and ideological polarization. The contours of any new world order being shaped by the forces of globalization, however, are scarcely confined to economic and financial matters, as several contributors have earlier made clear. We should also consider the growth of global forms of governance in the post-Cold War era as well, and their impact on the state and its sovereign attributes.

The institutions of global governance are both formal and informal and extend well beyond the United Nations and its various agencies. They can include anything from bodies like the World Trade Organization, the World Bank and the International Monetary Fund to the myriad of NGOs both large and small, regional networks, provincial and regional authorities, professional associations, clubs, labour organizations, international courts, religious denominations and social movements as well as business enterprises and private agencies of all kinds. If global governance really does embrace all these actors and the dynamics that attend them, then it can only be conceived, as Rosenau has elsewhere pointed out, in the very broadest of terms; as encompassing the activities of governments as well as innumerable other channels (such as those set out above) through which authoritative 'commands' flow in the form of 'goals framed, directives issued and policies pursued'.[30] At another level, many discussions of global governance have a strong normative overtone in that there are assumptions about *good* global governance embedded in them.[31]

Earlier in the 1990s, Groom and Powell had observed that, while the growth of issues of global governance was characteristic of the times, global governance had an amorphous quality and lacked conceptualization as a whole: 'In short, global governance is a theme in need of a focus.'[32] Any such focus, they said, should bring into the purview of world order studies the whole gamut of human needs issues including development, the environment, feminism, human rights and identity together with an analytic framework which would also include sovereignty and security. And the remedy? Nothing short of a new period of heroic conceptualization.[33]

The most heroic of conceptions might, on some accounts, be one which demands not merely the reassessment of global governance and world order in terms of the diminishing importance or relevance of the state and its sovereign claims *vis-à-vis* other actors and forces, but its relegation to past history as an anachronism in the twenty-first century. Here is where some postmodern critics of traditional state-centrism in international theory find common ground – if not common cause – with globalists such as Ohmae.

While the proliferation of networks of global governance may at least be bypassing the state, developments in international law and the growing legitimacy of collective action in the form of 'humanitarian intervention', as discussed by a number of contributors to this volume, seem to have challenged its sovereign attributes more directly. An important impetus for this came early in the post-Cold War period, and from what can only be described as the 'peak organization' of the sovereign state system – the United Nations. I mentioned in the Introduction that in 1991 the then UN Secretary-General, Boutros Boutros-Ghali, was asked by the Security Council to prepare a report canvassing various strategies that the UN might pursue in terms of peace-making, peacekeeping and preventative diplomacy. This was in the wake of the Gulf War – an action seen then (and still by many now) as a shining example of an effective collective security operation against a rogue state. Boutros-Ghali's *Agenda for Peace* provided a broad outline of possibilities for future collective action by the UN.[34] The pursuit of the *Agenda*'s recommendations was to be in accordance with the traditional organizing principle of international relations – namely, the fundamental integrity of the sovereign state. But this was softened, if not contradicted, in a further passage which emphasized that the principle of sovereignty had to be reassessed and balanced by equally important ethical considerations concerning activities within state borders, including those impacting on human rights and good governance.[35]

I shall not spend much time on the subject of humanitarian intervention, as it has been dealt with quite extensively already by other contributors to this collection. But, in terms of its apparent undermining of state sovereignty, David Campbell has made an interesting and relevant point. He points out that, although many concerns about security in the post-Cold War period relate to the way in which sovereignty is being brought into question in the context of intervention in intra-state disputes, the way of thinking which seeks to address these concerns remains firmly statist. In looking specifically at UN intervention (although the same would apply to NATO intervention), Campbell points out that the trajectory of thinking here 'moves up the scale of sovereignty from the state to the inter-state, from the problem of commitment on behalf of states to the strategies for supra-state (that is, UN) resolution'. As a consequence, the issue of intervention becomes another way in which sovereignty is simply revitalized. Here he cites Cynthia Weber's notion of the 'alibi function' that intervention serves: 'for intervention to be a meaningful concept, sovereignty must exist because intervention implies a violation of sovereignty'.[36] This also implies that intervention is an extraordinary action taken only when the 'normality' of the legitimacy of state sovereignty comes under serious question. In short, the sovereign state, attending to its own 'internal' affairs without outside interference – in fact without the *necessity* of any external interference – remains the norm, while intervention is clearly an aberration.

Even so, it is clear from some of the earlier discussion that thinking about intervention and collective action in respect of such issues as human rights, however tentative and contradictory in some respects, has also helped in shifting the discourse of security in international theory from an almost exclusive emphasis on the military security of the sovereign state to a much more wide-ranging concern with 'human security' as part of the new, less statist-oriented agenda for global security in the post-Cold War era. Paul Stares notes that a communiqué issuing these days from a summit meeting of political leaders will invariably reveal that one or more 'new security challenges' has been on the agenda for discussion. These challenges could constitute anything from 'civil or ethnic conflict, environmental degradation, resource scarcity, and uncontrolled migration to organized crime, drug trafficking, and trans-national terrorism'.[37] This, too, is seen as a welcome development from various globalist perspectives: those, for example, who invoke 'notions of a planetary ecosphere, a global economy, or the collective humanity now threatened by global processes and technologies of mass destruction'.[38] Fierke and other critical commentators on security have pointed out, however, that what security really means in any of these contexts remains unclear. As Walker says, while the more familiar conception invoked in the context of national security may be inadequate, 'so, too, are most attempts to reframe what any other kind of security might be like'.[39]

In this section I have so far touched on a selection of issues that are commonly seen as deeply implicated in globalization and impacting significantly on the ability of the state to retain its sovereign attributes and integrity with respect to a range of traditional state activities: control of a national economy, of national security, of national welfare, the care of the environment, and so on. Whether one 'approves' or 'disapproves' of the phenomenon of globalization is to some extent irrelevant. The question is whether one accepts it as a more or less accomplished 'fact'. This raises the issue, then, of how much substance there is to the 'fact' of globalization and therefore to its impact on the sovereign state and the state system. This is a theme which, while not as prominent in the literature, none the less resonates throughout the more reflective approaches to contemporary international theory.

A number of commentators have noted that one problem with arguments promoting the idea that state sovereignty is under threat from the forces of globalization is the corollary presumption that, once upon a time, things were very different. Robert Holton argues that this kind of presumption usually reflects a belief in 'a golden age when states possessed some kind of absolute control over their territory and the movement of resources, people, and cultural influences across their borders'. This, he says, is very much a myth – sovereignty has always been much more conditional than absolute.[40]

Another, similar, myth is noted by Weiss. In a detailed account of contemporary aspects of the global economy and state activity, she concludes that 'the myth of the powerless state' that seems to have such a powerful hold on general perceptions in the contemporary world is based on some very questionable assumptions. One of these is that the new constraints on state power discerned in the present era often tend to be viewed in an absolute sense rather than in a more nuanced relative perspective. The latter perspective allows one to discern a longer-term process of state adaptation to both internal and external challenges, while the former standpoint represents a short-sighted and simplistic 'end of state history' thesis. The tendency to err on the 'endist' side is due to three factors influencing analysis: first (*qua* Holton), an exaggeration by globalists of the extent of state powers in past eras which serves to emphasize alleged feebleness in the present; second, an overstatement of the uniformity of state responses which assumes that a new logic of global capitalism is effectively forcing convergence, among other things, of national fiscal policy models; and, third, an exercise in the 'construction of helplessness' in the face of global trends, engaged in very largely by political leaders, especially – although not exclusively – in the English-speaking world.[41] In short, these modes of analysis have led almost to an 'end of politics' standpoint.

Alan Scott's sociological analysis takes up similar critical themes. To the extent that ideological politics still exists, he points out that critical responses to some of the presumptions about the impact of globalization on state capacity in the UK have come from both the left and the right. He cites both John Gray, who has been a prominent spokesperson for new right ideas, and Will Hutton, a leading left-of-centre commentator, as evincing significant concern about market forces undermining community and social solidarity in domestic society. Both are critical of the idea, as Scott puts it, that 'globalization is an unstoppable historical force in the face of which politics is helpless'.[42] Furthermore, both call for a regeneration of a political project to defend society against market forces. It may seem ironic that, in making virtually the same call, Gray and Hutton draw respectively on the ideologies of conservativism and social democracy which have always seemed so at odds with each other.[43] However, this convergence of conservative and social democratic ideas reflects the inherent communitarianism of both ideologies which, in response to the perceived threats of globalization, calls implicitly for a strengthening of state institutions and capacity – in fact of state sovereignty – in resistance to global market (and other) forces.

Cognate themes are discussed by Chris Brown (in an essay of 1999) who, while acknowledging that the present period has obviously seen significant changes in the context in which state power is exercised, emphasizes not only that states remain important entities in global politics but that political power has scarcely been abolished, much less politics itself. For these reasons, it would be quite foolish to discount all elements of realist theory. He continues:

> One of the striking features of so many of the models for a new world order is the extent to which they are apolitical – they assume that the forces they identify will work themselves out in the world without reference to political power. It is

(hardly) necessary to be a realist of any kind to regard this as implausible.... More generally, the future of globalization will be a product of political practice rather than of cultural or economic theory...[and] the contingencies of political power may have the last word.[44]

## Concluding remarks

In this chapter I have sought to provide a broad overview of the historical development of the state and the sovereign state system as well as some of the more prominent contemporary perspectives and prognoses on the fate of the state in the post-Cold War era of globalization. By way of conclusion, I shall examine some theoretical positions regarding the sovereign state system and its components that address the contingent and contested nature of these structures, and which are at the centre of many contemporary normative debates.

First, recalling the earlier discussion of the 'ideology of order', it is clear that, in conventional international theory, sovereignty has often been treated as virtually synonymous with order – and Order has, at least since Hobbes, been defended as necessary for keeping its antinomy, Chaos, at bay. Thinking along these lines therefore has a long history – as long as the modern period itself. But, more than this, it has also been the dominant mode of thinking in both domestic and international political theory since at least the seventeenth century. This led prominent international society theorists such as Hedley Bull to privilege, over and above all other considerations, the notion of order in world politics. He not only saw it as trumping moral concerns about justice and human rights, but actually being a necessary, if not sufficient, condition for those more complex, moral goals. But in the final analysis the system of states functions to preserve order and that is all that it can be expected to do at this stage.[45] As King points out, however, this is a very limited view of order. Sovereignty, after all, gives us only one particular construction of order – there are many other possibilities and it is therefore only one among many possible avenues to peace[46] (although, it must be added, it scarcely guarantees peace and can also work to undermine it).

The insight that sovereignty is simply a particular, albeit dominant, construction of order rather than the only possible order also emerges from Jack Donnelly's analysis (in chapter 11 of this volume). He argues that neo-realists like Waltz characteristically misunderstand the nature of sovereignty as a logically necessary accompaniment to anarchy rather than a *particular kind* of political autonomy. Similar points are also well illustrated in studies in historical sociology from which IR clearly has much to learn. In describing his orienting principles, for example, Michael Mann says that comparative and historical sociology, in focusing on societies through time and space, produces an acute awareness of the diverse and curious ways in which humans have ordered their affairs:

We tend to relativize, not reify social institutions. Thus we treat states as only one possible form of political and military organization. For most of history, central-ised states had little salience for most social actors. States might be essentially the possession of certain lineages or classes, oligarchies or ruling classes. Questions of war and peace might be largely their private concerns, having little to do with 'whole societies' . . . . All political institutions, including states, have their particu-larities . . . . To understand them we must study their variable relations with other social institutions.

Mann goes on to suggest that IR specialists have been inclined to reify modern states, 'crediting them with a solidity, cohesion, autonomy and power in society that they rarely have'. In order to explain more and to analyse better the multiple social pressures operating on international relations – whether or not these influences go through states – traditional assumptions of state sovereignty need to be loosened.[47]

Historical and comparative sociology, then, examines how states and other institutions have come into being and developed over time and place. Given the basic task that historical sociologists have set themselves, they cannot logically take any institution for granted. In this respect, and as another recent contri-bution from a historical sociology perspective points out, the approach of the historical and comparative sociologists has strong resonances with critical theory.[48] Critical IR theory takes no social formation for granted – indeed its purpose is to call any such formation into question – especially (although by no means exclusively) the modern sovereign state and the state system. This obviously contrasts with the generally taken-for-granted status awarded to these entities in traditional IR theory (including, of course, neo-realism). Other writers, such as Youngs, have also critically analysed the 'embedded state-centrism' of both realist and neo-realist thought and the profound influ-ence it has had on shaping the discipline as well as the way in which the political world is understood.[49] And Andrew Linklater says that a common contention among neo-realists is that the 'anarchical international system will be reproduced indefinitely and that competition and conflict will remain endemic in the relations between sovereign states'. This approach, he argues, fails to recognize that the international system is capable of transformation. Linklater's particular interest is in how this may be done by reconstituting political communities.[50] More generally, following a now fairly common criticism of traditional theory, it has been pointed out that to award sovereignty the status of a transhistoric concept and to posit the bordered, territorial state as a naturally occurring entity is to commit the simple but important error of masking their actual 'historical and geographic specifi-city'.[51]

This brings me to some final observations on a number of important con-temporary debates about international theory and the state. I referred, in chapter 1, to the development and spread of the Westphalian state system, from its 'historically and geographically specific origins' in western Europe in 1648 to its ubiquitous presence today. In doing so, I obviously used the language of contextualism.[52] The major purpose of emphasizing the historical and/or geographical particularity of any social structure, institution, idea or practice such as 'sovereignty' or 'the state' or 'democracy' is to defeat grand universalist perspectives that construct any of these things as either natural or eternal – or both. Traditional international theory has tended to do precisely that and in doing so, according to critical theorists of virtually all stripes, it has been very much mistaken. It has invested in an ideology not only of order, but of a *particular* order that is assumed to be a more or less natural and enduring feature of the geopolitical landscape of world politics. The dynamics of the present period, which include at the very broadest level the collapse of a much more predictable and stable structure of Cold War polarization followed by the apparent intensification of this thing called globalization, have revealed quite clearly what many more critical observers had long been suggesting. And that is that the state, its sovereign attributes, and the international system which had been constructed on this basis could conceivably collapse under the weight of these dynamics.

But the demonstration through historical study, critical theorizing and globalist observations and prognoses that this is *possible* is one matter. Whether it is actually going to happen (or is happening) is another matter altogether. Although the contributors to this volume are generally oriented around a critical perspective on state sovereignty and the extent to which sovereignty as a *'fact'*, as well as a principle, has permeated traditional IR theory, none has adopted a 'hyperglobalist' stance in relation to the state. As we have seen, James Rosenau has strongly criticized the 'states-are-for-ever' habit and the limitations it has long placed on how we even begin to think about problems and issues. But he stresses that he is not anticipating the demise of the state as a political entity. Rather, he has suggested that there are other 'spheres of authority' that have become crucially important in the post-Cold War era and that these should move to a prime position on the IR agenda.[53] And Richard Higgott, in agreeing with Susan Strange that attention to interdependence and the power of markets is crucial if IR is to challenge the dominance of economics in the analysis of globalization, says that she none the less went too far in deciding that the state was redundant as a meaningful unit of analysis in IR. Nor does Richard Devetak's critique of the normative shortcomings of the sovereign state as a political community conclude by advocating the end of the state.

What these and other critiques do portend is a transformation in world politics. The state will no doubt remain, but it will not be the sovereign state of traditional IR theory. As Rosenau, Donnelly and others have pointed out, this means that IR theory must also transform and adapt. State sovereignty as an 'ideology of order' may still be defended in many parts of the world, but not only does it fail to match many contemporary realities, it clearly lacks the moral resonance that it may once have had. In addition, it is now more clearly recognized not simply as an impediment to the resolution of any number of injustices, but a primary cause of at least some of them. For these reasons, among others, the normative issues that now dominate the agenda for IR also require a transformation in habitual modes of thinking that have taken the state as perennial and essentially unchanging. All social institutions change and adapt and the state is clearly no different. Exactly how it does so in the twenty-first century obviously remains to be seen, but it is this process, as much as anything else, that is likely to remain a core concern for the discipline of IR for a long time to come.

## NOTES

1  This is so even when the concept of the state has been through periods of neglect in political and social theorizing, as it did in the 1960s and 1970s. For, even then, the state was the implicit basis of most forms of theorizing.
2  Stephen Castles, 'Studying Social Transformation', *International Political Science Review*, 22, 1 (2001), p. 14.
3  See Cornelia Navari, 'On the Withering Away of the State', in Cornelia Navari (ed.), *The Condition of States* (Milton Keynes, Open University Press, 1991), pp. 143–66.
4  Linda Weiss, *The Myth of the Powerless State: Governing the Economy in a Global Era* (Cambridge, Polity, 1998), p. 1.
5  See, for example, Charles Tilly (ed.), *The Formation of States in Western Europe* (Princeton, NJ, Princeton University Press, 1975); Michael Mann, *The Sources of Social Power*, 2 vols (Cambridge, Cambridge University Press, 1986); John A. Hall (ed.), *States in History* (Oxford, Basil Blackwell, 1986).
6  Geoffrey Stern, *The Structure of International Society: An Introduction to the Study of International Relations*, 2nd edn (London, Pinter, 2000), p. 72. For a comparative discussion of city-states from ancient to more recent times, which ranges beyond European examples, see Peter Burke, 'City-States', in Hall, *States in History*, pp. 137–53. Burke also points out that his non-European examples stand as a warning against regarding the city-state as a uniquely Western phenomenon. He notes also the ethnocentric tendency to regard Western political arrangements generally 'as the norm from which deviations may be measured' (p. 149).
7  Stern, *Structure of International Society*, pp. 72–3. Here Stern is citing G. Mattingley, *Renaissance Diplomacy* (London, Cape, 1955).
8  See George H. Sabine, *A History of Political Theory* (London, George G. Harrap & Co., 1948), p. 401.
9  Preston King, *The Ideology of Order: A Comparative Analysis of Jean Bodin and Thomas Hobbes*, 2nd edn (London, Frank Cass, 1999), p. 74.
10  See ibid.
11  Ibid., pp. xv–xvi. Emphasis added.
12  Cited in Joseph A. Camilleri and Jim Falk, *The End of Sovereignty? The Politics of a Shrinking and Fragmenting World* (Aldershot, Edward Elgar, 1992), p. 11.

13 Neil MacCormick, *Questioning Sovereignty: Law, State and Nation in the European Commonwealth* (Oxford, Oxford University Press, 1999), p. 123.

14 Ibid.

15 King, *Ideology of Order*, p. xvi.

16 Robert J. Holton, *Globalization and the Nation-State* (London, Macmillan, 1998), p. 102.

17 See especially David Held, *Democracy and the Global Order: From the Modern State to Cosmopolitan Governance* (Cambridge, Polity, 1995), and the more recent collection by Daniele Archibugi, David Held and Martin Köhler (eds), *Reimagining Political Community* (Cambridge, Polity, 1998).

18 For more detail see Stephanie Lawson, 'Dogmas of Difference: Culture and Nationalism in Theories of International Politics', *Critical Review of International Social and Political Theory*, 1, 4 (1998), pp. 73–4. Another point to note here is that the concept of 'the nation' as possessing a certain character has been a crucial factor in the formation of state identity *vis-à-vis* other states. Since identity is usually relational, and often involves viewing others negatively, there is a great deal of scope for state identity to be constructed in such a way that it leads to exclusion and repression (for example, against minorities). This view of state identity construction is explained by Hobson as deriving from a radical constructivist view which is distinguishable from the more benign approach adopted by the 'international society-variant' of constructivism. See John Hobson, *The State and International Relations* (Cambridge, Cambridge University Press, 2000), p. 157.

19 Jan Aart Scholte, 'The Globalization of World Politics', in John Baylis and Steve Smith (eds), *The Globalization of World Politics: An Introduction to International Relations* (Oxford, Oxford University Press, 1997).

20 Anthony P. Jarvis and Albert J. Paolini, 'Locating the State', in Joseph A. Camilleri, Anthony P. Jarvis and Albert J. Paolini (eds), *The State in Transition: Reimagining Political Space* (Boulder, CO, Lynne Rienner, 1995), p. 4.

21 Extracted from http://www.un.org/Overview/unmember.html.

22 Navari, 'Withering Away', p. 146.

23 See, for example, Alan Scott, 'Introduction: Globalization: Social Process or Political Rhetoric', in Alan Scott (ed.), *The Limits of Globalization: Cases and Arguments* (London, Routledge, 1997), pp. 1–22.

24 Barry Buzan and Richard Little, 'Beyond Westphalia? Capitalism After the "Fall"', *Review of International Studies*, 25, special issue (1999), p. 90.

25 Scholte, 'Globalization of World Politics', p. 21.

26 Ibid.

27 Kenichi Ohmae, 'The Rise of the Region State', *Foreign Affairs*, 72 (1993), p. 78. The position represented by Ohmae is sometimes called a 'hyperglobalist thesis' which has been described generally as 'privileging an economic logic and, in its neo-liberal variant, celebrates the emergence of a single global market and the principle of global competition as the harbingers of human progress'. See David Held, Anthony McGrew, David Goldblatt and Jonathan Perraton, *Global Transformations: Politics, Economics and Culture* (Cambridge, Polity, 1999), p. 3. Cf. Richard Higgott, chapter 6 in this volume.

28 See the various contributions on 'The Global Mind' in *New Perspectives Quarterly*, 17, 1 (2000), pp. 4–27.

29   Linda Weiss, 'Globalization and National Governance: Antimony or Interdependence', *Review of International Studies*, 25, special issue (1999), p. 59.

30   James N. Rosenau, 'Governance and Democracy in a Globalizing World', in Archibugi, Held and Köhler, *Reimagining Political Community*, p. 29.

31   See Gary Smith and Michael Muetzelfeldt, 'Global Governance and Strategies for Civil Society', *Pacifica Review*, 12, 3 (2000), p. 266.

32   A. J. R. Groom and Dominic Powell, 'From World Politics to Global Governance', in A. J. R. Groom and Margot Light (eds), *Contemporary International Relations Theory* (London, Pinter, 1994), p. 81.

33   Ibid., p. 84.

34   Boutros Boutros-Ghali, *An Agenda for Peace: Preventive Diplomacy, Peacemaking and Peacekeeping*, Report of the Secretary-General pursuant to the statement adopted by the Summit Meeting of the Security Council on 31 January 1992 (New York, United Nations, 1992).

35   Ibid., p. 9. For a more detailed discussion see Stephanie Lawson, 'Introduction: Activating the Agenda', in Stephanie Lawson (ed.), *The New Agenda for Global Security: Cooperating for Peace and Beyond* (St Leonards, Allen & Unwin, 1995), p. 5.

36   David Campbell, 'The "New Mind-set of International Relations"? Security, Sovereignty and Responsibility in *Cooperating for Peace*', in Lawson, *New Agenda for Global Security*, p. 71.

37   Paul Stares (ed.), *The New Security Agenda: A Global Survey* (Tokyo, Japan Centre for International Exchange, 1998), p. 11.

38   R. B. J. Walker, 'From International Relations to World Politics', in Camilleri, Jarvis and Paolini, *State in Transition*, p. 32.

39   Ibid.

40   Robert J. Holton, *Globalization and the Nation-State* (London, Macmillan, 1998), p. 83. Cf. Boutros-Ghali's comments in *An Agenda for Peace*, p. 9.

41   Weiss, *Myth of the Powerless State*, pp. 189–94.

42   Scott, 'Introduction: Globalization: Social Process or Political Rhetoric', pp. 1–2.

43   Ibid., p. 2.

44   Chris Brown, 'History Ends, Worlds Collide', *Review of International Studies*, 25, special issue (1999), p. 57. Note that there is also a significant body of literature that has simply ignored the whole debate and continues to analyse states without reference to the issues discussed in this section. A recent example is Daniel Drezner, 'State Structure, Technological Leadership and the Maintenance of Hegemony', *Review of International Studies*, 27, 1 (2001), pp. 3–25.

45   Mervyn Frost, 'What Ought to be Done about the Condition of States?', in Navari, *Condition of States*, p. 186. Note though that Bull believed that issues of morality, and calls to actually do something about them, often turned out to be merely the disguised interests of the great powers. The NATO action against Serbia in 1999, officially an act of humanitarian intervention and therefore a 'just war' in the words of Tony Blair, could be read in this light.

46   King, *Ideology of Order*, pp. xii, xvi.

47   Michael Mann, 'Authoritarian and Liberal Militarism', in Steve Smith, Ken Booth and Marysia Zalewski (eds), *International Theory: Positivism and Beyond* (Cambridge, Cambridge University Press, 1996), pp. 222–3.

48 Stephen Hobden, 'Can Historical Sociology Be Critical?', *Alternatives*, 24 (1999), pp. 393–406.

49 See Gillian Youngs, *International Relations in a Global Age: A Conceptual Challenge* (Cambridge, Polity, 1999), pp. 17ff.

50 Andrew Linklater, *The Transformation of Political Community* (Cambridge, Polity, 1998), p. 14.

51 Hobden, 'Can Historical Sociology Be Critical?', p. 393.

52 This language, incidentally, now seems *de rigueur* for anyone engaged in critical studies of international theory. While there is insufficient space to say much more about the use of this language here, I want to point out briefly that although I agree that the language of contextualism has some important analytical uses – such as those illustrated above – it also has its problems, especially when deployed in arguments in support of cultural and ethical relativism. Jill Steans (in chapter 4 of this volume) touches on this where she notes that critics of human rights deploy a notion of the 'historically and culturally bounded' character of these rights, as if they had no broader resonance. This is similar to Fred Halliday's very pertinent point about the 'fallacy of origin' (chapter 3 in this volume).

53 Cf. the 'crisis of authority' discussed briefly in the introductory overview presented by Yale H. Ferguson and Richard W. Mansbach, to 'What is the Polity? A Roundtable', *International Studies Review*, 2, 1 (2000), pp. 3–6. The other essays in the Roundtable deal with a number of the issues discussed above, especially the fate of the Westphalian state.

# Index